D0041639

364.163 Wade
W119g   Great hoaxes and famous
         impostors

CHRISTIAN HERITAGE COLLEGE
2100 Greenfield Dr.
El Cajon, CA 92021

Great Hoaxes
and Famous
Impostors

Great Hoaxes and Famous Impostors

by

CARLSON WADE

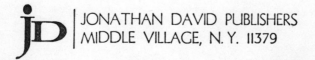

JONATHAN DAVID PUBLISHERS
MIDDLE VILLAGE, N.Y. 11379

GREAT HOAXES AND FAMOUS
IMPOSTORS
by
Carlson Wade
Copyright © 1976
by
JONATHAN DAVID PUBLISHERS

No part of this book may be reproduced in any manner
without written permission from the publishers. Address
all inquiries to:

Jonathan David Publishers
68-22 Eliot Avenue
Middle Village, New York 11379

Library of Congress Cataloging in Publication Data
Wade, Carlson.
      Great hoaxes and famous impostors.
      1.   Swindlers and swindling—Biography.
2.   Impostors and imposture—Biography.   I.   Title
HV6245.W33   364.1'63'0922 [B]   75-14072
ISBN 0-8246-0200-5

Printed in the United States of America

DEDICATED TO
LENA

29196

TABLE OF CONTENTS

CONTENTS (continued)

INTRODUCTION

The first recorded hoax in history appears in the Old Testament. Jacob, prompted by his mother, dressed himself in kidskin, and pretended to be his hairy brother, Esau. Since that time, countless incidents of hoaxing, imposture and deception have been perpetrated in every corner of the world.

This book recounts the stories of many of the most famous connivers of all times—their exploits more thrilling than fiction. Hoaxers and impostors are a special breed of people, a breed that lives by their wits, their cunning and their common sense. There is no limit to the ingenuity of the con artist, no end to the cleverness of crooks; and there is no dearth of meek sheep eager and ripe for fleecing.

In *Great Hoaxes and Famous Impostors,* you will be introduced to the man who swindled millions by selling shares in a nonexistent Panamanian oil well; the "medium" who communicated with the dead—for a price; the master counterfeiter who nearly bankrupted the world's financial institutions; the clever jewel thief who masqueraded as a member of high society; and the brilliant swindler who almost won his claim as the rightful owner of the state of Arizona. You will become acquainted with the brilliant art forger who duplicated masterpieces; with a clever female hoaxer who practically toppled a government; with the 70,000 "heirs" of Sir Francis Drake; and with the man who wrote the "authorized" biography of Howard Hughes.

As you read about some of the most ingenious swindlers of all times, you will find that they all had one thing in common: a passionate desire to achieve great fame and recognition in their lifetime. They all succeeded in achieving their goals— which in turn became the Waterloo of each of them.

CARLSON WADE

New York, N. Y.
February, 1976

1

CASSIE CHADWICK

The Beauty Who Posed as Carnegie's Mistress

CONSTANCE CASSANDRA CHADWICK had three exceptional gifts: brains, beauty and boldness. She knew how to use these gifts with an adeptness that millionaires use when making financial investments and she used them to great personal advantage.

Constance Cassandra Chadwick was red-haired, green-eyed, and beautiful; but she was not known by her distinguished appellation. In early life, she was just plain Cassie Chadwick. Born in 1845, she came from a poor background (a hardworking family in Toronto, Canada), and received very little education.

Like most impostors, she was self-taught. Early in life, she realized that she would be able to put her beauty to good use if she became "socially acceptable." This meant observing the rules of etiquette, and conversing with dignity and lucidity. If she could only sprinkle her conversation with references to literature, music and art, she knew that she would easily be able to captivate whatever man she desired.

Originally, Cassie Chadwick had no intention of perpetrating a hoax that would earn her a reputation as the greatest female impostor of the decade. Her original intention was merely to surround herself with an aura of culture which would enable her to break out of the poverty into which she was born.

Cassie read voraciously. In the course of her readings, she learned that New York society revolved around Andrew Carnegie, the owner of massive steel corporations. She noted how impoverished he had once been, and how he had had to stuff newspapers and wrappings into his shoes to enable him to

11

walk the 15 miles to a local grocery store where he clerked, his salary being a few loaves of bread and some discarded vegetables.

In the many stories she read about Carnegie, one line in particular attracted Cassie Chadwick's attention. It read: "Just the mention of the name Andrew Carnegie is sufficient to prompt any banker in the world to open his vaults!"

True, this was pure "newspaperese," but it did spark an idea in Cassie's mind, an idea which led to a fabulous hoax, the likes of which New York had never seen.

Cassie Chadwick planned everything to the last detail. Since the name Andrew Carnegie could open vaults, she would take advantage of the two secret words, and employ them to unlock the treasure she was anxious to acquire. She set as her first goal a visit to every Toronto library, to read and discover as much as she could about Carnegie. For nearly seven months, she virtually lived, breathed, ate and slept with Andrew Carnegie. She later confessed, "I put my real identity out of my mind. I wanted to forget my poor Toronto family, my very poor upbringing. All I wanted to know was that I was a favorite of Andrew Carnegie, had lived in his Fifth Avenue mansion in New York as his house guest, travelled with him, dined and entertained with him and, in fact, performed all the duties of a . . . very familiar friend.

"I had to know every little detail about Carnegie's life," she continued, "from his early childhood, right up to the present. I studied up on the types of clothes he wore, his favorite colors, his desired tastes in foods, his business schemes, his political likes and dislikes, his mannerisms and personality pointers.

"Oh, I wouldn't go directly to him. Nothing like that. But I would use my knowledge and his name to convince others that I was his . . . familiar lady friend . . . and their vaults would open. Indeed, that was exactly what happened. My investment was very profitable."

In 1866 Cassie made a casual visit to a very exclusive restaurant in a good section of downtown Cleveland, Ohio, near a much cherished Civil War monument in Public Square. She went there for a light lunch and a look at the ticker tape that was conveniently placed for the use of the patrons who invested in Wall Street.

Cassie was attractively dressed in green and red velvet, with a beautiful necklace and matching earrings. Her red hair was brushed into an upsweep and was topped with appealing ringlets. Her face radiated youth, vigor and charm. It was smooth and white and flawless—like a Dresden doll. Like her green necklace, her brilliant green eyes sparkled mischievously.

Cassie had come to the restaurant with more in mind than simply to charm the waiters or the men who hugged the bar in the adjoining room. Her intention was to meet a well-known Cleveland attorney who, according to newspaper accounts, lunched there almost daily. He had a reputation for carrying large amounts of money, which he needed to make stock purchases.

Phineas T. Barber wore a cutaway coat over his white starched shirt. His hair was well groomed; his mutton chop whiskers were meticulously shaped. He was the epitome of wealth and security, and was to be the first victim of Cassie Chadwick's hoax.

Discreetly, she cast a quick glance at the distinguished investment attorney. Luckily, he was seated just a few tables away. Off to a side was the ticker tape installed by Western Union. After sipping her tea and nibbling on some honey muffins that she had spread with a bit of jam, Cassie decided to make her first move.

Gathering up her skirts, she walked over to the glass-domed ticker machine, looked at the tape, and clucked her tongue. She repeated this several times. Out of the corner of her eye, she noted that the investment attorney, Phineas T. Barber, was observing her.

In a muffled voice, just loud enough for him to barely distinguish her words, Cassie said, "Mr. Carnegie is going to be very happy with this rise in stock. Good thing I told him."

She turned slightly, and saw Mr. Barber raise his eyebrows.

"Oh, I beg your pardon," she said, a gloved finger going to her colored lips. "I did not mean to disturb you, sir. It's just that Mr. Carnegie took my advice, bought this stock, and it is rising. He's sure to be grateful." A discreet smile spread over her face, and then she started to move back to her table.

The investment attorney rose politely. "Oh, that's good news. Would you care to divulge the stock? Any investment that is good for Mr. Carnegie is good for my clients. Permit me to introduce myself, if I may?"

They exchanged names, and then he said, "Perhaps you would do me the honor of joining me for a bit of tea."

She glanced at her wrist watch. "Oh. I'm so sorry," she said with what sounded like genuine regret. "I have an appointment this very afternoon. The man does not like to be kept waiting. He's very punctual."

"He is most fortunate to have you for company. Who is he, if I may dare ask?"

"Do you know Mr. Andrew Carnegie?" she asked.

"Why, I've never had the good luck to meet him."

She smiled. "Well, since I cannot accept your invitation to join you for tea and crumpets, perhaps you will accept my invitation to introduce you to Mr. Carnegie, and join him for tea this afternoon. He always has tea at this hour."

"That's very kind of you," Mr. Barber said, anxious to meet the millionaire. "Yes, I know it's a punctual habit of Mr. Carnegie's to have tea and . . ."

". . . Crumpets with a bit of jam . . ." she added.

"Yes, exactly. It's well known in Cleveland that Mr. Carnegie so indulges. May I?" He extended his arm and she took it.

As she did so, the lovely Cassie blushed. "Thank you."

Outside, they hailed a hack and Cassie ordered the driver to take them to the prestigious Cleveland home of Andrew Carnegie.

They chatted idly while the horses clapped their hooves on the cobblestone pavements which led to the Carnegie home. The lawyer was visibly impressed by her acquaintance with the great millionaire, and by the fact that he shared his investment plans with her. He hoped that he could draw close to this "familiar friend" of Andrew Carnegie, and that she would drop hints of worthwhile investments that might be passed on to clients. It was rare that Andrew Carnegie made a poor or losing investment, and if Barber could know in advance of the magnate's intentions, what an advantage that would be.

As the carriage pulled up to the mansion and drew to a halt, the lawyer was about to step down. But, softly, she placed her hand on his arm. "Perhaps it would be wiser if I spoke to Andrew . . . I mean, Mr. Carnegie," she blushed at the exposed intimacy, "and told him that a luncheon acquaintance of mine wanted to discuss a few matters with him. That would be so much better. Would you mind remaining here? It willl take only a few moments. As you know, Mr. Carnegie does not waste time in talk."

"Yes, everybody knows that, Miss Chadwick. I shall be happy to wait here."

She smiled, then quickly left the hack. She made her way through the iron gates, and up the pathway to the door of the mansion. Surprisingly Cassie Chadwick felt little fear as she took the first step in her fabulous career as an impostor. She had so trained herself for the hoax that she was about to engage in that she actually believed that she was a personal friend of the world famous millionaire.

She straightened her dress, adjusted her floral hat, then very quickly opened the door and entered the house as if it was her own home. She knew the lawyer was watching.

Once inside, she approached a housemaid. "I telephoned to speak to the housekeeper this morning. May I speak to her, please?"

The housemaid bowed and said in a hushed tone, "Please follow me, ma'am."

Moments later, she was in the domestics' parlor, speaking to the housekeeper. She came right to the point.

"I am about to hire a maid. Her name is Annette Dupre. She is a new arrival from Paris. When I asked her for references, she said that as soon as she came here, she worked for Mr. Carnegie, and then decided to leave for a better opportunity. Would you be able to advise me as to her capabilities?"

The housekeeper arched her eyebrows. "I'm very sorry, ma'am. I know of no Annette Dupre. She must be using the name of Mr. Carnegie under false pretenses. She certainly did not work here."

Cassie showed no surprise. "But she even gave me a note or a letter of reference from Mr. Carnegie."

"May I see the letter, ma'am?"

It was a ruse to gain time. For the better part of half an hour, she pretended to look through a variety of different papers and letters in her bag. She displayed typical womanly confusion as she handled, over and over again, the many trinkets and objects, papers and letters that filled her bag.

Finally, she sighed with exasperation, "How stupid of me. I must have left it in my other bag. Oh well, if you say that Annette Dupre never worked here, then it is obvious she is an impostor."

Cassie relished the role. "I am sorry for having taken up your time. Do accept my apologies for the inconvenience."

"Quite all right," the housekeeper smiled. "I am delighted to have been of service to you. Mr. Carnegie would not have wanted it otherwise."

After a parting word, she quietly exited from the house.

Back in the hack, Cassie said, "How can I ever apologize to you, sir? Mr. Carnegie is not feeling well. He is always sensitive to the chill air, as you know, and foolishly left without his favorite Scotch plaid muffler." This, too, was a habit of the great millionaire, and she wanted to impress him with her intimate knowledge. "Now he has a bit of a cold and feels unable to converse with you. Please do forgive me."

Mr. Barber concealed his disappointment. "Quite all right. His health does come first."

Just as the hack cab started up, a pronounced jerk caused Cassie Chadwick's bag to fall to the floor. Out slipped many documents and papers.

"Oh, how careless of me," she said.

The investment attorney bent down. "Do let me help you." He tried to gather everything up. But he could not help seeing that there was a note made out to Constance Cassandra Chadwick, signed by none other than Andrew Carnegie. In a florid handwriting, the amount—$500,000—was clearly visible.

As he handed other notes and papers to her, the investment attorney could not help but notice the huge sums recorded in some of the documents and securities that had spilled onto the floor. Mr. Barber quickly returned the papers to the nervous and embarrassed "friend" of Carnegie.

For a while, they rode in silence. But just before reaching

her hotel, she finally said, "Mr. Barber, you did see the contents, didn't you?"

"Yes, I must be honest. I just could not help it. I did not look with deliberate intent. It was unavoidable."

Cassie appeared crestfallen. "You impress me as being a man of great personal honor."

"I thrive on personal integrity, ma'am."

"May I . . ." she paused and lowered her voice, ". . . beg you, sir, not to reveal . . . never, but never, divulge what it is I must tell you. I would not reveal these secrets, but since you have seen the notes, it behooves me to share a sacred confidence with you."

"I promise to share your secret only with you, ma'am."

Now she would make use of her year of research and investigative studying. Cassie Chadwick broke out in tears as she confessed a secret. She told him that Andrew Carnegie had been so devoted to his mother, he would not marry while she was with him. She told how she had met Carnegie while he and his mother were on a brief holiday in Skibo Castle, in Scotland. Then she told how she and Carnegie had fallen in love, but there was no possibility of marriage as long as his mother remained by his side.

She then said, "Mr. Carnegie and I were . . . were . . . intimate . . . and . . . there is a child . . . but, please, I beg you, not to tell anyone about the child or the whereabouts. . . ."

Phineas Barber was amazed. All the details were accurate. There could be no disputing the truth of this lovely lady. "Then you were . . . unable to ever marry?"

She shook her head. "I'm afraid not. But Mr. Carnegie was and is a gentleman. He wanted to provide for me and our child. He told me, just now, that he wants me to have an attorney—not any of his, since this is very secretive—draw up an agreement to protect investments he has given to me." She pointed to the envelopes. "These are lists of my investments . . . drawn up in Mr. Carnegie's own handwriting."

"Are you familiar with investments, ma'am?"

"Not very. But I follow his advice. Still, I cannot keep coming to see him like this. I must follow his best advice. He suggests I deposit some seven million dollars of my securities" —she did not bat an eyelash at the way the investment lawyer gawked at hearing the amount—"with a good bank for safe-keeping. Now, I do have some $12 million worth of securities, in total, and some should be used for trading, to be sure. I dare ask, sir, if you could give me some advice."

The lawyer felt that he had struck it rich. To represent an account of $12 million meant that legal fees and commissions would soon make him wealthy in his own right. Quickly, he said, "Yes, I shall be happy to recommend you to a good bank and also to an excellent banker."

The banker Barber recommended was Daniel N. McIntosh, a man reputed to possess a Scotman's reverence for thrift and secrecy. He was known to be a banker's banker, the very soul of integrity. He would protect her investments, and he would guard her secret with his very life.

"Then I shall be glad to be one of your clients, Mr. Barber."

With that, she handed him a sealed envelope in which, she said, was a list of her securities. Then she said, "This other envelope has the seven million dollars in securities, municipal bonds and other investments. Please take good care of them."

Cassie Chadwick had put her plan in motion. She managed to get a receipt from Phineas T. Barber for the contents of the sealed envelope. She read him a list of the contents which he scribbled on a letterhead. He then signed the receipt and handed it to her. It never occurred to Barber to open the sealed envelopes to verify their contents. As soon as he went to the bank, he had the envelopes placed in a vault . . . unopened.

Cassie Chadwick could now begin to profit from her scheme. She had a letter signed by an attorney, and soon after received a verifying letter from Daniel N. McIntosh.

On the strength of these two letters, Cassie went to the bank and was able to borrow money. She began with a modest $75,000. She promptly paid the interest and, when due, repaid the loans. She was anxious to establish her credit.

To make up for all her years of deprivation, Cassie bought jewelry and dresses. She travelled throughout the country in the best of style. And she was able to do all this simply by using various letters she received from leading members of the financial community.

Everyone knew that Andrew Carnegie could be irascible. He had such power that if he were in the least displeased, he could bring disaster upon the most prestigious financial institution. No one dared cross him. If Cassie Chadwick was the whispered unwed wife and mother of his child, then she had best be treated properly. To do otherwise would surely be stepping on the toes of the magnate.

She would now often enjoy the luxury of reflecting upon her past, and would chuckle over the petty hoaxes she had once perpetrated. They were trifles compared to her current undertaking.

Cassie revealed some of these earlier activities and feelings when, some time later she wrote:

"In 1859, before coming to the States, I assumed the identity of a well-known clairvoyant. The poor lady had left for Europe and was never heard from again. So I pretended to be the clairvoyant. I dressed well and made it known that I was available for séances and meetings. I managed to hoax some very wealthy investors into transferring their holdings to me by saying that, if they didn't, they would be brutally murdered in the dead of night.

"When they would sign over their properties to me, then no one would want to rob them . . . since they had nothing. It never occurred to them that a thief wouldn't know that they had no more investments. As soon as everything was in my name, I quickly converted it to cash and then disappeared . . . in the manner of the real clairvoyant.

"But I netted a few hundred thousand that way . . . very paltry compared to the millions that I netted as the unwed wife of Andrew Carnegie and the unwed mother of his child."

Cassie threw caution to the wind and soon started taking loan after loan, from one bank after another, up and down the coast. Having agreed to pay a very high interest rate, she had little difficulty in getting the money.

Some of her heavy borrowing had also been for the purpose of investing in stocks which she felt would increase in value. She figured that she would use the profits for repayment of the loans . . . and retain a good portion of it for herself. And so, trading on the name of Andrew Carnegie, and with notes signed by Phineas T. Barber and banker Daniel N. McIntosh, Cassie continued to operate.

But Cassie could not foresee the stock market crash that the turn of the century brought with it. Her stocks not only plummeted, they became completely worthless. She was again a pauper.

When bankers started asking for repayment of her loans, they were met with cold stares. "Do you doubt my integrity? Do you doubt the financial stature of Andrew Carnegie?"

Both Barber and McIntosh now went to the vault and opened the envelopes purportedly containing some $12 million. The horrified investment experts discovered sheets of newspapers, many of which, ironically, bore pictures of Andrew Carnegie.

They were enraged! They had been fooled by this cunning woman. And, as it soon became evident, Cassie Chadwick had borrowed more than $40 million from banks all along the East Coast, and brought many of them to financial ruin.

In 1870, Constance Cassandra Chadwick was brought to justice. A note from Andrew Carnegie's attorney confirmed the fact that he had never met the "lady" and had nothing to do with her at any time in his life.

During the court trial, it was calculated that the lovely red-haired, green-eyed beauty had cost the country's banking institutions at least $100 million—none of it ever to be recovered.

Cassie said little in her defense except that "Pretending to be the mistress of Andrew Carnegie was so . . . so grand . . . it was a dream come true. I wish the dream had never ended. If I had the opportunity, I would live that dream again. It was so wonderful!"

Cassie was found guilty on nine counts and sentenced to eight years in the Ohio State Penitentiary.

Prison life did not agree with her. She became ill. Within two years, her good looks began to fade; she had aged 20 years!

One evening, still garbed in her dreary prison uniform and creaky shoes, she stretched out on the hard cot in her cell and turned toward the cold wall. She fell asleep and never again awoke.

2

OSCAR MERRIL HARTZELL

And the 70,000 Heirs of Sir Francis Drake

OSCAR MERRILL HARTZELL, a farmer in Madison County, Iowa, was totally committed to his life's work—at least, that was the impression he often gave. As many as 70,000 people were so impressed with his modesty and sincerity that they willingly parted with over $2,000,000. Oscar's pockets swelled sufficiently to make him one of the wealthiest men of his day.

The swindle began in 1913 when the plow-jockey decided to leave the earthly environment and venture forth to Des Moines. There he met a group of people who were the victims of Mrs. S. B. Whiteaker, a rather attractive widow who had claimed to own shares in the estate of Sir Francis Drake and was making them available to a select group of people. By the time she was exposed, many unsuspecting investors had been relieved of $100,000.

The innocent Iowa farm boy was fascinated by the activities of Mrs. Whiteaker. He studied the scheme and became convinced that there lay opportunity. In the true spirit of a hoaxer, he decided that if he wanted a plan of his own to succeed, it would be necessary to do extensive research.

Oscar Merrill Hartzell went to the Sioux City library and started reading all the material he could find about the British buccaneer, Sir. Francis Drake. In his imagination, he lived the life of Drake and steeped himself in the lore of the Spanish Main, the somewhat legal plundering of Spanish ships that carried the approval of Queen Elizabeth. He also studied and learned all he could about the Virgin Queen.

He probed so deeply that he felt at one with the famous freebooter, up to Drake's death on a ship off Portobello, Panama on January 28, 1596. When Hartzell was satisfied that he was sufficiently familiar with Drake's life and times, he studied the wealthy pirate's estate carefully.

When Hartzell had assembled all the facts, his conclusions were rather simple: Drake's entire estate had been confiscated by the British government. His will was so complicated that it never went to probate. Some suggested that Queen Elizabeth and Sir Francis Drake had something more than just a friendly relationship and that the government wanted to suppress the will to keep the scandal covered up. For this reason, the disposition of the will was still pending in 1913. A fortune awaited anyone who could help the legitimate heirs force the British courts to act on the will.

And so began what was to become the greatest scandal of the era.

Hartzell saved as much money as he could, and started to travel. He learned of the many who had given all their savings —large and small—to impostors who promised them a large share of the profits of the Drake estate, if they would help pay for legal expenses.

This was all Hartzell needed to know. Soon, he formed the Sir Francis Drake Association, its function being to force the British Crown to release the illegally impounded estate of the deceased freebooter. Hartzell planned to contact every person with the name of Drake. He would begin by telling them that his research had led him to meet one Ernest Drake, a Missouri farmer and the sole surviving heir to the Drake fortune. But money, he explained, would be needed to fight the powerful British Crown. If all Drake descendants would help pay the legal expenses, they could share in the profits.

Hartzell mailed letters to many people with the surname of Drake. He said that the true heir, who he represented, might receive about 22 *billion* dollars. This fortune would be divided among those who helped finance the legal battle, each receiving a share commensurate with the amount invested. Therefore, the more one would invest, the more he would receive.

The hoaxer claimed that the offer was being made largely to those who were heirs of Sir Francis Drake, and since the name Drake had once been so common, Hartzell had no difficulty in preparing a mailing list of some 20,000 Americans with that name.

Aside from those selected individuals, thousands who knew they were not related to Drake eagerly requested to be included; they, too, would invest in the plan so as to reap a large reward. Some people mortgaged their homes; some sent their life's savings. Hartzell appointed special agents throughout the country. These agents were promised percentages if they would help collect money. Responses came by mail, cablegram and even by American Express.

Whenever a person sent money, Hartzell insisted that a pledge of "secrecy, silence and non-disturbance" be signed. Should anyone make idle boasts or reveal the secret, he would almost certainly forfeit his investment; the money invested was not refundable. (It is believed that very few, if any, did reveal the secret. So absolutely sure were they that they would receive a share of the massive fortune!)

Hartzell then prepared reproductions of the purported birth certificate of Drake and sent these to his investors. In addition, Hartzell sent them reproductions of documents which he claimed to have used to force the ever-powerful British Crown to bring Drake's will to probate and eventual settlement. He also distributed copies of an alleged tear sheet from a leading magazine in which a noted reporter had stated that money would be forthcoming, and that there was no disputing the valid claim of Oscar Merril Hartzell.

Through Hartzell's directives, small groups were formed. They were encouraged to discuss the impending lawsuit, and to offer suggestions of all kinds, including means of raising more money. All suggestions and monies raised were mailed to a central office in Sioux City. This was later found out to be nothing more than a mailing address. Only Hartzell picked up the mail; only Hartzell collected, counted and kept the money.

In the regular mailings to his clients, Hartzell would include "published" reports stating that Sir Francis Drake's estate was now worth some $400 billion, and that the reason for England's reluctance to release that large sum was only too obvious: it might bankrupt their financial institutions! Throughout Iowa, many ministers (themselves sucked in by the hoax) took to their pulpits and denounced England for withholding money that was rightfully that of the heirs of Sir Francis Drake.

In 1914, Hartzell thought it wise to make his way to England where he might press his claim in person. Once in England, he sent regular dispatches to his faithful followers in the United States. He explained that he was filing depositions in the courts so that legal proceedings could begin.

Hartzell had a wonderful time in England. He met a lovely girl and courted her. She soon bore his child. Hartzell had told his girl about his activity, and she told her father. For a while, Hartzell feared that he might be in serious trouble. But, being quick-witted, he told the father that he would be glad to make a "settlement," and offered him a goodly share of the Sir Francis Drake estate for the modest sum of $25,000. The irate father was calmed, and he paid the $25,000 for the "privilege" of being involved in the deal. Hartzell was relieved of any further obligation to the girl and their child—and he was that much richer for his efforts.

Hartzell's American investors were quite impressed by his prolonged stay in England. They assumed that he had undertaken a long and difficult legal battle, and they continued to support him by making more and more mailings to the Iowa address. When Hartzell returned from England and opened the post office box, he was amazed by the number of letters it contained—and their contents. Close to one million dollars had been sent in. He promptly banked the money and enjoyed both the principal and interest.

The fervor of the Drake Association members kept growing —so much so that even Hartzell was amazed. They were absolutely confident, despite the fact that in all this time Hartzell had never seen or spoken to any of them. All communications were carried out through the mails.

In some cities, as many as 3,000 believers would rent a hall and hold a meeting. Many prominent members of the clergy, government officials, leaders of industry, politicians, and others, happily paid large sums so they could be rewarded with the promised $5,000 for each $1.00 invested.

Because nobody complained or sought to question, no suspicions were aroused. Hartzell was very careful to keep up pretenses. He repeatedly voyaged to England, ostensibly to involve himself in the court battle. In actuality, his trip abroad were for his own pleasure. And each time that Hartzell returned, his mailing address yielded him sacks and sacks of money.

When in need of more money, he would send an additional few thousand form letters to the "Drake heirs." He explained that the British Crown was employing its top legal experts in the court battle, and more money was needed to carry on the fight.

And more money poured in.

But before long, a few of the "heirs" began to grumble. Too much time was passing, they said. They doubted the legitimacy of Hartzell's claim.

Some of the doubters undertook an action that marked the beginning of the end: they filed complaints with the post office. This in itself, however, was not immediately helpful. For one thing, the postal inspectors could discover no wrongdoing. There was no misrepresentation. It *was* true that there was a Drake estate, and that someone, somewhere could be the heir. There could even be 70,000 heirs! Oscar Merril Hartzell had claimed he needed money to fight for the heirs in the courts. Hence, he could not be accused of misrepresentation. At this point, no one thought to verify whether or not Hartzell was, indeed, fighting the case in England. Also, many of those who had vowed to keep their association with Hartzell secret, refused to talk. So the post office met resistance from the victims, too.

In 1913, just when Hartzell thought that the hoax was progressing perfectly, several of his associates (who had helped in collecting money) were brought before the authorities. They were charged with fraud, but they protested that they, too, had been duped. Even more significant, not one of the associates had ever received a dime from Hartzell, so how could they be held responsible. Only when they were accused of being co-conspirators did they agree to sign a stipulation stating that they would discontinue their activities.

Hartzell was not prepared for this eventuality. Now that his associates had openly admitted that they had been duped, word would soon spread. The so-called heirs would probably cease sending money and, worse, they might demand refunds. Bit by bit, the hoax would surely be exposed.

American investors went to great trouble to obtain a copy of the actual will of Sir Francis Drake. The original had been written on parchment. It was filed on August 13, 1595 in the Historical Documents Room at Somerset House in London. In addition, British officials provided many copies of court proceedings of the probate.

One British solicitor testified that there had been a court battle between Drake's widow and his brother regarding the property listed in the will. But the conflict had been resolved.

It was 1933, 337 years since Drake's passing. The English statute of limitations for probate was 30 years. The statute, in Drake's case, had long expired.

A British scholar translated Drake's will from Elizabethan English into modern language. He confirmed the authenticity of the records in the Prerogative Court where the will *had been* probated. It was obvious that Hartzell was a fraud. He was charged with being a hoaxer and an impostor and was forthwith deported from England, brought back to Iowa, and arrested. Throughout his trial, he insisted that he was going to settle the estate.

Another problem arose. How could the government charge or even convict the hoaxer? There were no witnesses.

Those who had paid money, but received nothing, had never seen him—and this presented a legal problem.

Furthermore, some new facts were now exposed. It was revealed that Sir Francis Drake had left his entire estate to his widow and his brother. Neither he nor his brother had any children. Therefore, Drake had *no* heirs! There was talk that he had fathered several illegitimate children, but no proof was available, so no claim could be filed.

The government began to prepare a better case against Hartzell. While it was true that none of Hartzell's victims ever saw him, it was charged that he caused them to be defrauded by means other than in-person contact. Postal fraud became the main charge and Hartzell was soon brought to trial and convicted of using the mails to defraud.

But Oscar Merril Hartzell would not give up that easily. He claimed that his conviction was part of an international conspiracy, that the British Crown wanted to keep the money, and that it placed political pressure on the American government to have him jailed.

Surprisingly, Hartzell's many thousands of followers believed him. They rallied to his side. They even raised money to finance his legal battle, and he assured them that he would be exonerated. Hartzell's lawyers filed appeal after appeal. All were denied.

Little by little, disgruntled followers sheepishly suggested that perhaps they *had* been duped. Slowly, it looked as if Hartzell's fall was near.

In 1934, after being examined by psychiatrists who adjudged him mentally incompetent, Hartzell was convicted in Federal Court in St. Louis. He was sent to the Medical Center for Federal Prisoners at Springfield, Missouri. He remained there until his death on August 27, 1943.

What happened to the more than two million dollars that had been bilked from 70,000 victims? Inspectors were able to seize some of Hartzell's bankbooks, and a sum of money was retrieved. But it was difficult to figure out how much was donated by whom. As it turned out, Hartzell never kept records of the amount each individual had donated. It became more apparent than ever that he had never intended to pay them anything.

The courts managed to refund some monies to those who could produce receipts. But it is believed that nearly two million dollars was never accounted for, and never retrieved.

Oscar Merril Hartzell had enjoyed success for a time. He had fooled many highly respected people from all walks of life. In many ways he was as much a pirate as Sir Francis Drake.

3

LEO KORETZ

The Million Dollar Panama Swindler

HE WAS A PLAIN MAN who appeared to be content and secure. Happily married and the father of a daughter, Chicago stockbroker Leo Koretz exuded warmth and charm. His friendly attitude infused confidence in his many customers, and they would buy or sell whatever stocks or bonds he recommended.

The early 1900s were years of financial stability for the stock market: more money could be made than lost. But Leo Koretz was dissatisfied with the quiet, sedate, unexciting life of a broker. He earned regular commissions, took home a good salary, and lived a comfortable life—but he was not happy.

Leo Koretz's life was all *too* comfortable. He conceded as much when he was later apprehended as a master impostor: "Everything worked out *too* well. It was all *too* self-satisfying. I always knew that I would be earning a good amount of money. I wanted something better. I wanted to use my influence to gain me millions of dollars in a short time. I saw all of these trusting souls come in and out of my office, and I had this insatiable urge to fleece them. I would take them for everything . . . and then some. I would create a hoax that would be the laughing stock of the stock market. That would show them that I was more than just an 'always faithful, always secure' type of nonperson."

To look at Leo Koretz induced immediate sympathy. He was of diminutive size, with an expanding paunch. He wore thick glasses through which his baggy eyes peered in bored contemplation, and invariably he sported a conventional blue serge suit with dark necktie. There was no charisma about

Leo and he was destined to remain a "secure" broker unless he undertook an exciting venture.

After poring over volumes of stock market books and records, he came upon a small item which caught his attention. It stated that there was strong evidence that oil could be found in the banana republic of Panama. Furthermore, stated the item, speculation existed that the 4,000,000 acres of good timberland on the Bayana River could be bought, and then chopped down for wood pulp.

It was just an idea, and under ordinary circumstances Leo Koretz would not permit any of his clients to touch such an investment. He would never even mention it to any clients. But he was determined to break out of his safe and secure life and this was his chance.

Within a few days, Koretz's Chicago office was visited by some of his most trusting, influential and wealthy clients. Each one was told of the possibility of offshore oil reserves existing along the Bayana River in the Central American Republic of Panama. Koretz explained that the rich timberland could be a literal goldmine for those who invested *immediately*. The government of Panama, he continued, was anxious to receive revenue to meet internal needs and would be more than willing to permit exploration for a small sum of money and a percentage of the profits; the world would be needing more timber and oil, especially since there was much talk of impending war. It was 1916, and Europe was embroiled in World War I (as it would later be called). If America *did* go "over there," Koretz advised, there would be a *great* need for such raw materials as timber and oil.

Leo Koretz told client after client that he, himself, was investing in the Bayana River Oil Company and that he was planning a trip to this Central American land to purchase as much of the vast property as was available.

The clients were enthusiastic. They offered to finance Leo's trip. They offered to give him money right on the spot so as to buy into this fantastic investment. But Koretz cleverly turned them down. No, he said, he was going to Bayana River country on his own. He would check it out completely before allowing any of his clients to invest their money. "Far better for me to lose my money than for you to lose yours," was his persuasive talk.

After a month of expressing such "concern" for his investors, Koretz announced to his clients that he was going to Panama for two weeks. He would pay his own way.

Leo Koretz did not go to Panama. Instead, he boarded a train for New York. There, he went wild, indulging himself in a two-week spree on the town. It was all part of his new personality. He was preparing to be a millionaire.

Settled in a plush Manhattan Hotel, Koretz began to make the rounds of New York's bright spots, moving on from one night club to the next. He developed a liking for alcohol; prohibition whetted his thirst for the best gin or whiskey available at the speakeasies. At one speak-easy, he picked up a long-legged blonde show girl, and she became his constant companion. Together they hurried to and fro, from noon until dawn, day after day. When his two-week fling had reached an end, Koretz returned to Chicago. All appearances indicated that he had endured an exhausting jaunt in the wilds of Panama.

When he once again met with his clients, Leo Koretz was ecstatic. He fought to control his enthusiasm about the rich oil and beautiful timber that he had discovered along the Bayana River. He left the distinct impression that he already had been deluged with offers from leading tool manufacturers anxious to have him use their devices for his exploration. With these funds, he said, he had been able to furnish a suite of new Chicago offices with thick, ankle-deep carpeting, soft sofas, and beautiful modern furniture and had hired several secretaries capable of handling the long distance calls to Panama.

Koretz actually received and made telephone calls to Panama. But they were not *business* calls. Silly as it sounds, the calls were to and from theater booking agents, hotels and the like. Leo's secretaries were unsuspecting of the "staged" calls. They made the connections and buzzed Mr. Koretz when the long distance operators announced that a party in a Central American country was on the line. Koretz always spoke in the privacy of his office; his conversations were never overheard. It was a simple deception, but it worked.

Koretz continued to refuse any investments from his now

overanxious clients. He was baiting the fish and he was not yet going to let them bite. The more anxious they became, he reasoned, the more they would invest. Instead, he kept drawing on his own savings from a bank in suburban Evanston, Illinois, where he was not known.

When the time was ripe, Koretz decided to meet with potential investors in his plush suite of offices. He took them to lunch in his costly Rolls Royce, dining in the best restaurants along Michigan Boulevard. He entertained his guests in the most luxurious of surroundings. Waiters and waitresses vied for his attentions, hoping to be rewarded with crisp $50 bills. Often, Leo Koretz would offer a $100 tip to a chef if a meal was specially prepared. He gradually became known as a man who was involved in a project that would be lucrative beyond anyone's wildest dreams. It was the legendary pot of gold at the end of the rainbow.

Before long, the many clients, who knew one another, implored Leo Koretz to permit them to invest in the Bayana River treasure. Again, he refused. He preferred to be cautious, to be extremely careful, he said. He admitted to having invested some of his small savings in the project, but wanted to protect his clients from even the slightest degree of speculation.

A knowledgeable lawyer—one who represented some of the wealthiest families in Chicago—proved to be Leo's ace-in-the-hole. The lawyer, Chauncey Sanders, appeared in the office of the "wealthy" broker one day, and pressed for more information.

"My clients keep telling me that they want to invest in whatever projects you have invested your money. There should be room for more investors. You're on to something and owe all of us—your long-time trusted friends and clients—an opportunity to invest. You know that my clients trust you, Leo. All you have to do is approve an investment, and I sign the checks. Your word is as solid as your selected investments. Now, you've got to tell us more about your secret project. My clients see how well your little investment has done for yourself. Are you going to keep it a secret and alienate all of us?"

Shifting his very long, very black, very expensive Cuban cigar from one side of his mouth to the other, Leo Koretz gazed at the eager Chauncey Sanders. In a flash, he saw that he was about to snatch the juiciest plum of all. Yes, he was going to hoodwink his prestigious attorney. He would use him as part of his cleverly calculated scheme to defraud the wealthiest and most honored names of Chicago society. Indeed, he resolved, he would bankrupt the members of the Social Register.

"Very well, Chauncey. As you know, I would rather risk my own money than a single cent of our clients'. But by now, I feel confident that a good investment is possible. I was in Panama, as you probably know. Down there, I surveyed a region that borders the Bayana River. It's very primitive. The natives don't know the unlimited millions of dollars they have right beneath their feet, right in their own backyards."

"What is it?" he asked anxiously. "Come on, Leo, don't keep me in suspense. Tell me what it is."

"Two treasures. Oil . . . and mahogany. That's right. The area is literally soaked with oil, and there are thousands of acres of trees that can be turned into mahogany. Furthermore, those Panama natives will work dirt cheap. Just give them 18¢ a day, a few bottles of tequila, maybe some women, and they'll bring out the oil, chop down the trees and even load them on boats for shipment here to the States. I calculate that if we have 300 natives working around the clock, we can import about $100,000 worth of oil and timber per week! We can sign an exclusive contract with the government of Panama so that, in effect, we will own all of the territory. A few bribes here and there should do it. Furthermore, Chauncey, we are now on the brink of a war. This means that the prices of oil and mahogany will skyrocket. We can make ourselves millions upon millions of dollars in a short time."

Chauncey Sanders was goggle-eyed. While he represented some of the wealthiest families in Chicago, he had not yet come across any investment that would bring such a fortune in so short a time. But he continued to be cautious.

"How can you be sure of all this?"

Leo Koretz opened his expensive desk drawer, brought out a cablegram. He pushed it to Chauncey. "I already have a resident manager in Panama. We're setting up a corporation. Boatloads of oil and mahogany are on their way. So far, Chauncey, I've invested only my own money." He looked serious. "My life savings. With a wife and children, it was quite an investment. But I have no regrets. I took a chance and it has paid off."

Chauncey read the cablegram:

MORE SHIPMENTS OF PRIME MAHOGANY AND OIL CAN BE MADE ONLY AFTER ADDITIONAL CAPITAL IS RECEIVED. MORE MANPOWER AND EQUIPMENT ARE REQUIRED. GUAR-ANTEED RETURN OF TWELVE TO ONE.

Leo Koretz dangled his discovery much like a carrot before a rabbit. He smiled. "As you can see, this is a gold mine. But I don't want this to turn into a Sutter's gold rush where everyone rushes in and spoils it for *us*." He carefully included the lawyer in the intimate arrangement. "Now, I already own the property. All I need is some additional capital. If you have a few clients . . . remember, I said a *few* clients, with a small amount of money, I will consider it."

Chauncey Sanders sputtered. "Leo! How can you do this to me? You know that I have at least 15 clients who own almost all of the wealth in Illinois, not to mention much in New York and San Francisco. I have to give all of them a chance to invest in this treasure. I can't discriminate in favor of just a few."

Leo Koretz smiled to himself. The rabbit had bitten the bait. He got up and put a friendly arm around the lawyer's shoulder. "Chauncey, I will let you work that out."

In no time at all, word of the Sanders/Koretz discussion spread. Wealthy Chicagoans learned that Leo Koretz owned vast properties in the lush oil and mahogany regions of the Bayana River. All he needed was more money and the return would be *twelve to one*. If a Chicago socialite invested $100,000, she would receive $1,200,000 in return. Who could resist such an opportunity? Especially because it was being offered by Leo Koretz, whose reputation was as good as the gold in their jewelry! They *had* to participate.

Bowing under pressure, Leo announced that he would accept only limited investments ranging from $10,000 to $100,000 in the newly formed Bayana Oil and Timber Corporation. He did not want to press his luck too far. Koretz now began to act swiftly. There was the slightest, just the very slightest chance, that one of the many traveling socialites would venture down to Panama to view the coveted treasures.

The mastermind used precise legal machinations for forming his corporation. Shares of stock were then issued; they were sold at $1,000 per share—but only to "special investors." This created a quiet uproar.

One wealthy Chicagoan demanded, "What do you mean by *special?* You have been handling my investments for over two decades. My family and your family are like one. You just *can't* leave me out of this!"

Leo Koretz sighed and repeated what he had said to other disgruntled callers: "Very well, since we have known each other for so long, I will allow you to invest. But I must be fair to the other people I handle. I can only sell you a minimum of 10 shares!"

I want to have 50 shares!"

"B-but. . . ."

"Leo, send me the bill for 50 shares and you'll get your check for $50,000 in the morning!"

Leo Koretz nodded. His plan was working perfectly. Now, he used another ploy. He moved out of his already luxurious offices, to a suite in the newly appointed Sir Francis Drake Hotel, just far enough from the Loop to create an aura of privacy and distance. It was beautifully furnished. Over the wood-burning fireplace hung a guilt-edged framed photograph displaying half-naked natives loading timber planks aboard a freighter. In the distance could be seen oil barrels and oil drilling rigs. It was a carefully pasted-up photograph, but placed beneath a glass cover and kept at a distance; it looked authentic.

In order to gain entrance to Leo Koretz's office, an investor had to announce himself to several secretaries and pass through endless locked doors. When a visitor reached Koretz's office, he found that he was separated by a twelve-foot mahogany desk, embellished with a brass plate upon which was glitteringly engraved:

HAND-CRAFTED FROM THE FIRST LOG CUT
AT BAYANA, FEBRUARY 12, 1917.

Most investors were summarily honored with a round mahogany paperweight which bore the imprint, *Bayana,* in gold-leaf letters. These paperweights had actually been bought for two cents each from a South Carolina lumber manufacturer. They looked so impressive, however, that it dawned on no one to test the paperweights to determine their authenticity.

Before long, Leo Koretz had accumulated a cool half-million dollars. But he was not yet satisfied. Neither was he ready to pull up stakes and vanish. He wanted to fleece the lambs even more.

To accomplish this, Koretz would have to maintain his image. So, he escorted his wife and daughters, garbed in the most expensive furs, all over town. Frequently, he could be seen in the best jewelry shops along Drexel Boulevard purchasing sparkling gems for his family. He moved from his nondescript apartment into one that was close to the North Side of town, and spared no expense in decorations and lavish furnishings. The chosen few who came to his apartment were highly impressed. They concluded that Koretz had discovered more than just a gold mine; it must be a veritable *treasure*. He was called the man with the touch of Midas.

No one, not even his trusting wife and two daughters, knew that when Leo made his regular trips, his destination was New York, not Panama. Little did they know that he was spending his ill-gotten money in the burlesque houses of New York.

Leo Koretz would send telegrams to his Chicago office (he instructed his staff to open all mail in his absence) that appeared to be coming from leading furniture and railroad corporations. These telegrams pleaded with him to allow them to buy into the mahogany and oil treasures. They offered unlimited capital to pay for labor and shipping costs. Each time Koretz returned to Chicago, the leading financial tycoons were clamoring to get in on the deal. As the broker had hoped, his talkative secretaries had revealed the contents of the telegrams. Competition soared. Soon, the price of a single share of Bayana Oil and Timber Corporation stock was selling for $3,000.

To further complete the ruse, Leo arranged to pay a 5% dividend. He very casually suggested that the stockholders might do better to reinvest their dividends (a privilege accorded only to the lucky investors) and perhaps invest an additional $50,000. All transactions were made quickly and with careful attention to detail. Everyone was impressed. Investors saw that Bayana had made Leo a millionaire . . . and they wanted to share in the fortune.

Leo purchased two Rolls-Royces, a Pierce Arrow and a 70-foot yacht with full crew. At lunch and dinner, his fortunate guests were treated to costly caviar, imported champagne and venison served by a fleet of liveried servants. As soon as he was seated with his guests, Koretz proudly announced, "Enjoy yourselves. It is my pleasure to entertain you."

Koretz began to develop a love for the pleasure that life had to offer. Lovely ladies awaited him in hotels in New York, Miami and even in nearby Evanston where he remained unrecognized. On his frequent trips to these three cities, ostensibly on business, he enjoyed those luxuries of the flesh for which he had always yearned. A lifestyle about which he had always dreamed was now his.

Leo was now ready to launch the next part of his plan. One morning, he telephoned his largest investor-source, Chauncey Sanders. At the Drake Hotel, they dined on a lunch of breast of guinea hen, bubbling champagne, artichokes, and Hawaiian fruit compote especially brought in for special guests.

"Chauncey," said Leo Koretz blithely, "most of our profits are coming in from the timberland. You know, we've been digging for. . . ." He lowered his voice. "Oil."

"Yes, but didn't you say that there may not be too much oil for a long time?"

"Yes, I said so only to halt the stampede. As you know, that Bayana area is like a Garden of Eden. I had to delude the investors or else I would have a million of them trying to buy in. So, I said there was only a small amount of oil. But, read this. . . ." He offered him a cablegram; the date line read Panama City.

Sanders read aloud:

AT THIS WRITING, SIX GUSHERS HAVE BEEN STRUCK. COMPANY GEOLOGISTS CONFIRM A MINIMUM OF 500,000 BBL DAILY MINIMUM. FLOW IS MORE THAN ANTICIPATED. NEED MORE EQUIPMENT, PIPELINES, TANK CARS, LABOR. FUNDS REQUIRED IMMEDIATELY.

—JOSE SANCHEZ

"Oil! You mean at least 500,000 barrels . . . daily . . . at a minimum?"

"Yes," Leo Koretz nodded. He looked around, then said, "Please keep your voice down. It could create a panic. Now, we're making out very well with mahogany, but this oil will be 10,000 times more profitable. It's already bringing in profits. All that we need is to hire equipment and men."

Chauncey Sanders was astonished. His excitement was manifest. His clients would forever be indebted to him for his help. He was determined to buy into this discovery; he had to get the lion's share.

"Yes, you'll have the money," promised Chauncey.

But Leo Koretz was not going to let it look so easy. He told Chauncey to be at his office next week. When the appointed time came, Leo was not in the office. His secretaries announced that he had gone to Panama to take care of some business. For over ten anxious days, 100 eager investors were kept in suspense. All this time, Leo Koretz was in New York, enjoying nights out on the town, romantic affairs with show girls, secretly laughing at the way the elite of Chicago were playing right into the palms of his hands.

Upon his return, Leo found his office swamped with offers from buyers eager to acquire stock. Before the day was over, he had accumulated an additional $300,000 in funds invested in Bayana Oil and Timber Corporation stock. To maintain the illusion of independence and selectivity, he refused offers from some customers, and even rejected bundles of cash, saying he had to be fair and could only sell stock to a few select people.

His most fantastic coup occurred a few weeks later when he was entertaining some customers aboard his yacht. They were cruising along Lake Michigan, enjoying good food and expensive liquors when a cablegram was handed to him. He read it aloud:

STANDARD OIL WILLING TO PURCHASE CONTROLLING IN-
TEREST IN BAYANA. WILL MAKE AN OFFER OF $25 MIL-
LION. REPLY SOON.

His guests were aghast. One whispered: "Leo, are you going to sell out to Standard Oil? After all . . . $25 million!!!"

"Certainly not! If they offer $25 million, then Bayana is

worth ten times that much. Besides, the company belongs to all of us and I am not going to sell it." He crumpled the cablegram in his palm, and tossed it into Lake Michigan. Everyone cheered his decision. "Let's have some more drinks," he then said casually.

Koretz's deliberate action served to fill his coffers many times over. The wealth of Bayana was much, much greater than the investors had anticipated. Leo Koretz had spurned Standard Oil. Nobody, but nobody, spurns $25 million. It stood to reason that Bayana Oil and Timber Corporation was worth at least $100 million. And they were ecstatically grateful to Leo Koretz for having included them in such a once-in-a-lifetime deal.

Koretz was now dubbed the "Miracle Man of the Loop," the "Oil Baron," or the "New Rockefeller." To live up to his new image, he bought expensive pieces of art, maintained a luxury penthouse in New York, and acquired a small resort in Colorado Springs where he could enjoy a brief vacation with several lovely women. Of course, he used assumed names for his various escapades, and never took his wife along with him on these "business" trips.

But Leo Koretz was not this easily satisfied. He was so inwardly excited over the success of his scheme that he developed illusions of grandeur. If he could dupe a high member of the judiciary, he thought, he would have it made. His decision came at a time when his lavish taste for life was depleting his income. He needed more money to maintain his standard of fine living.

To accomplish this end, Leo Koretz displayed his financial wizardry by forming a new corporation. It was called Bayana Redevelopment Corporation. Its purpose was to further exploit the "resources" of the Central American land that had yielded great profits thus far. Now he was going to harvest cocoa, sugar, coffee and bananas. He predicted that Bayana enterprises would soon be so valuable that the corporation would own all of Panama, and might, one day, control the coveted Panama Canal.

This announcement reached the ears of Judge Edward B. Tyler. He was a highly respected jurist, civic leader, honored member of the community and influential attorney for Cook

County Court. Judge Tyler, through his financial advisors, was now ready to purchase any available stock in the Bayana enterprises.

Judge Tyler was invited to Koretz's luxurious home. After being feted and served by maids and servants, the judge and Leo retreated to the library. In the mahogany panelled room, Leo said quite gently, "It is unfair that you have to subsist on a $9,000 a year salary. I pay more than that for a Rolls Royce. A man with your legal background should certainly be paid much more. The laborer is worthy of his hire.

Now, I need a good legal advisor to handle my negotiations with the various oil companies. I want the very best. So I will pay you $50,000 a year as a salary. Furthermore, I shall award you a large block of Bayana stock—let us say, $100,000 worth— to handle all legal details. Later on, there will be increases. Judge Tyler, you deserve much more, and I want to give it to you."

Judge Tyler was amazed. While he may have earned a modest salary, he was not yet ready to toss it overboard without some investigation. He was greatly tempted by the offer, and did not want to close the door on what could be the opportunity of a lifetime, but as an astute judge, he could not act hastily.

"Give me a little time to think it over, Leo. I want to discuss it with my wife, too."

"Good, good, Judge Tyler. Let me know whenever you're ready."

Soon after the meeting, Judge Tyler managed to acquire a list of some of the bigger Bayana investors. He approached them, and casually asked about the Panama treasures. Each investor spoke glowingly . . . of Leo Koretz. It was "Mr. Koretz says," or "Leo knows what he's doing," or "If Leo says so, it's right."

Had anyone ever been to Panama?

Not even the leading member of the social set—the man who had handed over $300,000—had ever seen the Bayana territories. The same could be said for the others. True, they had been given mahogany paperweights; they had seen and/or heard cablegrams being read; they had looked at the photographs in Leo Koretz's office. But not a single investor had been to Panama to examine the Bayana region and verify its treasures.

Judge Edward B. Tyler's legal mind began to work. He decided that there were some flaws in the financial empire set up by Leo Koretz. Everything had been predicated upon the words and guarantees of Koretz himself. Thus far, no one, to the judge's knowledge, had even seen the Bayana territories. He conceded that it might all be authentic, but there was also the possibility that all was not as Leo Koretz claimed it to be.

Judge Tyler, one week later, lunched with Leo and over cocktails, he said, "I like your proposition, but before I could accept being the legal overseer of the Bayana territories and enterprises, I should see them. Suppose that some stockholders go down there to look them over and report to both of us? That would make it more ethical for me to become the legal representative, don't you think so?"

Without a moment's hesitation, Leo Koretz agreed. "Certainly! You have a fine legal mind, Judge Tyler. That's precisely why I want you for the firm. Yes, we'll make those arrangements very soon."

But that was the last time Judge Tyler lunched or dined or even conferred with the Koretz "wonder boy." Thereafter, Koretz was unavailable to the judge.

This convinced Judge Edward B. Tyler even more that something was amiss in the Bayana setup. It appeared that everything was being done for Leo Koretz. Little, if anything, was being done for the stockholders who were doing the paying but receiving nothing more than small dividends which were reinvested. Now, he resolved to investigate further.

Leo Koretz had made the mistake of thinking he could deceive a very astute judge. His paper empire started to disintegrate.

It was early spring of 1923. One of Leo's Chicago lady friends kept demanding jewelry and small tokens of friendship. She proved to be so annoying that Leo sent her on a world cruise and promised to meet her in Paris. No sooner did he see her off—after having paid all the bills in advance—than he started to feel excessive thirst, and other frightening reactions. He consulted a physician who told him he was developing diabetes, and had to be put on a newly discovered medication called insulin. This meant no alcoholic drinking of any kind! He was also to go on a strict diet. He could no longer treat himself to the lavish and luxurious foods he so delighted in.

As this was happening, he learned that a committee of 10 stockholders, representing the most prestigious names and families of Chicago, had gathered for the purpose of making a trip to Panama. It would be a pleasure trip as well as a business voyage. They invited Leo Koretz to join them.

The hoaxer decided to use his influence to dissuade them from making such an enervating and costly trip. Instead, he prepared a special evening of entertainment, dinner at an exclusive club (even though he himself, because of his diabetic condition, could no longer partake of the feast), and to top it all, he showed them a special display of the Bayana enterprises.

This consisted of a papier-mache creation—a scale model— of the extensive holdings. These included oil derricks, mahogany forests, the Bayana River, men, mules, machines, all involved in manufacturing their wealth. The "New Rockefeller" gave a glowing and convincing speech of how all of them were part of a "family." They were not just investors; they were part of a great and growing future.

But no amount of persuasion could discourage them from making the trip, so he wished them good luck.

Leo Koretz was neither frightened nor worried. Instead, he saw them off on their ship and quickly made his way to New York. There, he continued his hoax by establishing a New York office for the expansion of Bayana enterprises and investments. He appointed a well-known banker who had resigned from a lucrative position to become financial head of the New York division.

When the *Santa Luisa*, bearing the 10 stockholders, docked at Balboa, they started to search for Jose Sanchez, president of the Panama Investment Trust Company, who was also the local representative of Bayana Oil and Timber Corporation. But Jose Sanchez, who was supposed to meet them at the dock, was nowhere to be found. Neither was the Panama Investment Trust Company. Neither was any part or parcel of the Bayana Oil and Timber Corporation. All that the 10 stockholders could find were little shacks, sleepy natives, a jungle-infested region in a hot and humid climate, and an atmosphere of general malaise."

One stockholder remembered seeing many cablegrams date-lined Koretz Panama. But, querying the local cable office, they were informed that no such cable address existed. The stockholders then approached an American geologist who had lived in Panama for several decades—someone who knew every inch of swampy ground. They showed him blueprints, maps and documents purporting to be the Bayana region that was a rich source of mahogany, oil and other treasures.

The American scoffed. "I know that ground. Sure, it's right here in Balboa. But all it has are swamps, alligators, snakes and head-hunting Indians. If you set one foot in that area and don't get sucked into mud or eaten by wild animals, your head will end up on top of a totem pole while the rest of you will be given to the cannibals. Gentlemen, you've all been taken—by a head-hunting American." He laughed heartily as he observed the looks of horror and consternation on their faces. "You've been devoured, too!"

Immediately, the outraged stockholders took action. They hurried to the local cable office and wired the State Attorney in Chicago. They explained that there was no Bayana property at all. Leo Koretz was totally unknown.

Quickly, State Attorney George Layton set the legal wheels in motion. Other Chicago investors had been notified and, in a group, they swarmed into the luxurious offices owned by Leo Koretz. He was nowhere to be found. There was a large supply of expensive liquor and a vault filled with stock certificates of the Bayana Oil and Timber Corporation, as well as those of other divisions. They had been thoroughly duped; even his secretary said she had invested in the enterprise.

State Attorney George Layton looked over the books of the corporation. Yes, dividends had been paid, but they were actually small fractions of the original investment. Banking authorities were notified. A close scrutiny was made and it was found that Leo Koretz had had at least 13 different bank accounts throughout Chicago, as well as many safe-deposit vaults. All had been closed.

Leo Koretz had vanished . . . along with a reported one million dollars.

By now, the investors learned that Koretz had had many women ensconced in various hotels. The women were closely questioned. None knew where he was. Few had anything to show for their "cooperation" other than a few trinkets. What they had assumed were articles of value, turned out to be costume jewelry. One girl friend said she had been given as much as $5,000 in cash by Leo Koretz.

Where was the money?

"I invested it in his corporation! . . . He talked me into it!"

No matter how the police searched, they could find neither hide nor hair of this upstart hoaxer.

But one jealous ladylove provided the obvious and simple clue to his whereabouts. She was an attractive, perfumed blonde.

She was bitter as she spoke to police: "Sure, you can find him. I hope you do, that little rat! Know what he promised me? That he'd divorce his wife and marry me. Said he'd take me to Panama, and I could live on a plantation with hundreds of servants. He showered me with gems. But they're all fakes! Gave me money, but talked me into investing it in that company of his. Now I'm down to nothing.

"Know what he did the last time we met? Took my last twenty dollars, saying he left the house without cash. Said he had to pay a doctor for that . . . that new diabetes drug . . . insulin. That's it. So, if you want to find him, find out where he's getting his insulin."

The one mistake Leo Koretz had made was to let anyone know of his diabetic condition. Because insulin was a new drug, few physicians had it. The police queried the only insulin manufacturer in existence and obtained a list of those physicians who had purchased the drug. Each one was questioned. But Leo Koretz was unknown to them. The police persisted.

Since insulin, at that time, had to be injected solely by a physician, it meant that Koretz had to appear in an office for the treatment. The police kept querying the limited number of physicians who dispensed diabetic drugs. Their search led them to a small suburb outside of Toronto, Canada. A doctor there said that a man with the name of Arthur Gibson had been in his office for an insulin injection.

Where was this Arthur Gibson? The doctor said he was going to Vancouver, British Columbia because he liked the climate. Could he get an insulin injection in that city? Yes, there was one doctor who had insulin, and the Toronto doctor had recommended Gibson to him.

The search narrowed. In Vancouver, they queried the doctor who said that a man answering Koretz's description, but with the name of Arthur Gibson, had come in for an injection. He would come in again within three days. The police waited in an outer office.

Leo Koretz, under the name of Arthur Gibson, made his appearance. He was promptly arrested, and without resistance was returned to Chicago.

An outraged financial committee demanded that Koretz be executed. The biggest names in society and banking had been hoaxed. Approximately one million dollars had been given to the Bayana Oil and Timber Corporation. Where was it? *All of it had been spent.*

On December 13, 1924, after a 30-day trial, Leo Koretz was convicted on the charge of robbing the public of one million dollars. He was sentenced to 10 years in Joliet Prison. As he left court, he was overheard saying to an attorney who represented him, "I won't survive more than a month in prison."

True to his word, he spent less than three weeks in prison. He managed to get hold of a large box of chocolate covered cherries which he devoured in one sitting. The three pounds of deadly sugary confection were like poison to a diabetic. Koretz died in his sleep in a bare cell, all alone and penniless.

Even after his funeral, some doubted that the real Leo Koretz had been buried. One former investor said: "I know for a fact that he was seen in Toronto just the other week. He must have bribed someone to escape. You know how tricky he was. Maybe he managed to escape and had another body replaced for his own. I still maintain that the real Leo Koretz is still alive."

The Joliet prison physician had an irrefutable reply: "I took his fingerprints just before burial. They match the fingerprints on file. The real Leo Koretz is dead."

4

MADAME THERESE HUMBERT

The Lady Who Hoaxed the Financiers of Europe

FRIENDS OF THE STRAWBERRY blonde referred to her as "petite," as most of the famous, dainty Parisian girls were called. But she was small—and not at all attractive, yet she managed to attract many men. Her sparkling blue eyes, sensuous smile, and gentle tone of voice made most men anxious to give her whatever she desired. And, often, her desires were insatiable.

Very early in life, Thérèse Daurignac Humbert started to socialize with France's most celebrated and wealthy personalities. She was able to convince them that she was a most important figure. The world's leading political figures, she claimed, were at her beck and call.

She possessed a feeling of great power. And often she would blithely remark, "It is so satisfying to know that with a few words or a few deeds, I am able to topple a government."

Thérèse was born in June, 1902, the eldest of twelve children, to a poor, rural couple. The couple managed to eke out a living outside of Toulouse, either by farming or by selling the few vegetables that were left over after the family had provided for their sparse meals. Little is known about Thérèse's early life except that she suffered much privation and endured many hardships. But, what *is* known is that by the time she had entered her twenties, she had left her family and had moved to a small suburb of Paris where she occasionally clerked in a small shop for a meager salary.

At that point in her life, she suddenly announced to her neighbors: "I have just inherited a tidy sum. It will make me very comfortable. It is about $20 million, minus the expenses to the lawyers, of course."

Her astonished neighbors pressed her for more details. It was a shocking surprise, to say the least. Here was a plain girl, who never had much money, suddenly announcing that she had inherited $20 million. They were curious to learn the details. And employing her imaginative mind to the fullest, Thérèse concocted the following story:

"It began when I was away on a trip to the United States. I was in a railway train, and saw an American who was looking ill. I offered to help him. No doubt, he must have eaten some food that made him sick. I always carried with me a selection of little herbs for healing. I mixed several of them together in a glass of wine, and gave it to him as a potion. He immediately recovered. He was so grateful, he insisted upon rewarding me, but I politely refused, saying that I would not accept payment for having helped a man become well.

"Somehow, he managed to get my name and address and told me that he would like to write me a letter of thanks. I forgot all about it. I recall hearing from him a year ago, with his thanks, but that was all.

"But yesterday I received a letter and a will. It was the last will and testament, signed by the late Robert Henry Crawford. He was the man I had helped. The letter, from his attorney, stated that Mr. Crawford was so grateful for my having saved his life that he had instructed that I be the heiress to his $20 million. Isn't that marvelous?"

So began the hoax.

Thérèse Daurignac's fame spread fast, along with the message that she was about to inherit so many millions as soon as the various legal requirements could be complied with.

One man who heard of her fortune was Frédéric Humbert. His father had been Minister of Justice. Later, he had been named vice-president of the Senate.

Frédéric was an attorney and offered his services to Thérèse in 1924. She managed to decline politely, but did accept his offer for dinner. And before long, he became her constant escort. All of Paris was gossiping about Frédérick Humbert and his protégée. Since both were independently wealthy, or so it seemed, there was no suggestion that each sought the other's money.

Thérèse was accepted by high society with no questions

asked. And, it did not take long before Frédéric proposed marriage and the new "heiress" demurely accepted.

So it was that Thérèse Daurignac became Thérèse Daurignac Humbert. The former peasant girl who had until recently
been penniless, and who, everyone thought, stood to inherit a
fortune from the wealthy American, had actually become the
sole heir of her husband's wealth. This was *real* money—and
what could be more exciting to Thérèse!

Thérèse soon showed an uncanny type of genius. She, like
her fellow compatriots in the art of duplicity, unconsciously
began to expand upon her original hoax. She made it so involved and complicated that no one dared ever to question its
validity.

Shortly after her marriage, while the will of the alleged
Crawford was being probated in America, she and her husband
moved into a lovely French mansion on the stylish Avenue de
la Grande Armée. They also acquired a country estate—all
with Humbert's money.

Then she announced that there was a second will discovered
by the American millionaire, Robert Henry Crawford. In this
second will, the $20 million was not left exclusively to her.
Rather, it stipulated that the money was to be divided into
three parts: Equal portions were to be given to Marie Daurignac (her youngest sister), and to Crawford's nephews, Henry
and Robert Crawford who now lived in America.

The will further stipulated that Robert Henry Crawford
was so grateful for the help offered by the French girl, that he
wanted to reward both her and her country. Therefore, his
two nephews were directed to invest enough of their inheritance in French companies, to assure Thérèse Daurignac an
annual pension of some $25,000.

But there was still another clause that surprised everyone.
The will suggested that one of Crawford's nephews *marry* a
Daurignac. Until such a marriage took place, the estate would
not be settled or divided.

In the meantime, Madame Humbert received a signed,
notarized, and seemingly legal document which stated that all
properties of the Crawford estate were sequestered and placed
in full charge of the heiress and her husband until all the
terms were met. Simply stated, this meant that one of her sis-

ters would have to marry Crawford's nephew. Not until then would Thérèse be able to claim any of the money.

In 1927, a large package was shipped to a Paris bank. It was sealed and notarized, and bore many special signatures and statements. It contained the money, the securities and the various negotiable papers that would be held in escrow by the bank until the terms of the will were fulfilled. The package, containing a purported $20 million in cash and securities, was secured in a vault, and would be safeguarded by the bank until such time as the will was legally probated and met all the requirements of French law. Yes, Madame Humbert was indeed an heiress!

Various legal battles ensued. Madame Humbert had first claimed to be sole owner of all the money, according to the original will. But Crawford's nephews insisted that the money was rightfully theirs because of technical errors in the will, and they engaged excellent lawyers whose plan it was to malign her character to prove their point.

Madame Humbert fought back with excellent French lawyers who countered with statements to the effect that the will had been legally prepared and executed and that their client was entitled to her full inheritance.

But, Madame Humbert had achieved her goal—at least partially. There was no doubt, insofar as the French saw it, that she stood an excellent chance of inheriting at least $20 million. The money would appreciate in value, and, according to all indications, by the time she took possession of it, it would double in value, and she might very well become the wealthiest woman in France, or even Europe.

Madame Humbert grew impatient. She said she needed more financing, and banks were only too eager to advance her huge loans at agreed-upon interest rates. After all, she had $20 million in a Paris bank, and there could be no question about the security of these loans. Before long, various banks had advanced her sums ranging from $25,000 to $100,000. All the banks required was her signature on promissory notes which stated: "Payable upon the consummation of my actions in the courts for the impending inheritance."

Using the funds she borrowed, Thérèse soon acquired a collection of rare and costly jewelry, and a fine portfolio of the best stocks and bonds available. Within a few years, it was estimated, she had accumulated about $13 million in cash, securities, jewelry and expensive antiques.

Not only did her reputation spread as the wealthy heiress-to-be of the Crawford estate, but as the wife of the wealthy Frédéric Humbert as well. No banker ever thought twice about advancing money to Madame Humbert. She was considered a very good risk in the banking profession.

It was this type of advance financing that enabled Madame Humbert and her husband to enjoy life in a grand and luxurious style. He knew nothing of her hoax. He was deluded into believing she was wealthy by legal inheritance. By now, they were the owners of four luxurious country estates, furnished with some of the most costly antiques in Europe. Each was adorned with rare and exquisite paintings and with the most elegant silverware, all purchased from the more elegant European shops—with promissory notes, of course.

The Humberts also owned several yachts, a private railway car and a fleet of automobiles. Trained servants served them around the clock, and waited on them hand and foot.

In an effort to emphasize her affluence and position of promise in the world of high society, Madame offered a bid for the special opera seat that had formerly been held by a baron. Bids for the seat were entered by several crown heads of Europe, and by several shipping magnates as well.

Madame Humbert's bid won and she was tendered the box.

In her mansion, Thérèse held open court. Here, the élite of Europe came at her invitation. Included were noteworthy authors, artists, performers, political leaders, judges, and nearly all members of the French Academy.

Though she was poorly educated and had little knowledge of the arts, Thérèse's immense wealth made her more than "acceptable." It was considered an honor to be invited to her salon. And to be invited to join Madame Humbert for *dinner* marked one with a badge of distinction. She was accorded the respect usually reserved for royalty.

By 1929, Madame Humbert was taking out loans from the leading banks of France, Britain, Switzerland and Italy. Together with her husband, she invested this money in real estate, and purchased more and more antiques, rare objects of art, and rare paintings. In particular, she loved houses and she acquired many. The report had it that she owned 30 different buildings in and around Paris, and she collected handsome rentals from all. All of this was acquired with borrowed money on promissory notes.

And so it went. The magic words were "the inheritance." Madame would sign a note for money or property. If she received money, she agreed to repay it with interest *when her inheritance came due.* If she wanted property, she would sign a note with the promise to pay *when her inheritance came due.* Everything was predicated on the inheritance.

The newspapers continually reported on Madame Humbert's activities. She was practically the reigning Social Queen of Paris and Europe in the fabulous 1920s. She was news, and the newspapers were eager for more and more copy about her. This, too, helped to condition the leading bankers of Europe to believe that an inheritance awaited her, and that it was only a matter of time before the money became hers.

Madame Humbert kept growing in stature in the eyes of the finance moguls. Bankers adored her. She never quibbled about interest rates, and she was eagerly advanced large sums at high interest rates. It was the greed of the bankers, who charged these exorbitant rates, that led to the eventual catastrophe. Had they taken the time to carefully investigate *the inheritance,* and had they been less greedy, they might not have been instrumental in toppling so many staid European banking establishments.

Madame Humbert invested her borrowed money in real estate. This real estate was then used as security for making more and more loans. On one occasion, she requested that her attorney prepare a list of all her assets, exclusive of the $20 million in the Paris bank. These were assets obtained through borrowing at high rates. The list was approximately twelve pages long.

The bottom line stated that Thérèse had some $35 million worth of investments and real estate. But more important, the attorney noted that all of her properties were "free and clear" of mortgage obligations. This made them even more valuable.

In 1930, the nephews, Robert and Henry Crawford, had instituted litigation. More and more decisions were handed down, and there were endless appeals. In nearly every contest, Madame Humbert emerged victorious. But no sooner did she win a round, when the Crawfords came up with a technicality that challenged her claim to the estate.

All the while, Madame Humbert presented various documents and papers in court. These were romantic letters wherein the nephews indicated that they wanted to meet the Daurignac sisters. (Incidentally, none of the sisters were ever located or contacted.) And it began to appear that it was only a matter of time now; the estate would soon be settled in her favor.

There were times when creditors would gently remind Thérèse of her obligations, whereupon she would quickly produce a letter from an attorney. They were kept satisfied that the matter was in the process of final settlement. One of the important requirements of the will still left to be fulfilled was for one of the Crawfords to marry a sister of Thérèse. Should this happen, the terms of the will would have been met and it could then be probated.

The creditors were content: they agreed to wait a little longer. Needless to say, because of the high interest rates she was paying, the longer they waited the greater their profits would be.

Gossip items began to appear in various French newspapers. Rumor had it that the American nephews had come to Paris, had met Thérèse's sister, Marie Daurignac, and that there was a possibility of an engagement. Because they so treasured their privacy, the Crawfords would not consent to being interviewed. Newspapers also reported about various visits to restaurants and exclusive shops by the Crawford nephews, both of whom had come to win the hand of Marie Daurignac.

No one actually saw the Crawford nephews, but their presence in France seemed very real. Press releases and reports emanating from publicity people who had been engaged for the purpose confirmed that the nephews had appeared and dined, wined and romanced Marie Daurignac, and then departed.

Madame Humbert succeeded in perpetuating her hoax, and her financial standing was never questioned—nor did it weaken.

But several bankers had made such huge, outstanding loans

that they were becoming concerned. They began to insist at least upon a partial repayment of the loans. But whenever talk of foreclosure became strong, Madame Humbert was said to be ill and unable to talk with the banker who had come to discuss his loan. He was politely asked to leave.

Rumors of Madame Humbert's ill-health started to spread. Creditors became even more fearful and jittery. If she died, they would lose everything. But her charming manner was assurance enough to assuage even the most intrepid of creditors.

For nearly ten years, the hoax continued. Thérèse was able to continue to collect money by saying that she needed it to pay her attorneys. If she did not pay them, she warned, court litigation might result, and all would be lost. If nothing else, she could always count on obtaining additional loans in order to pay her legal fees.

The deception could have continued forever, but Madame's large number of transactions, and the growing number of creditors who pestered her, seemed to draw her into a corner. It became increasingly difficult for her to escape the annoyances and to enjoy a life of affluence.

Thérèse engaged excellent lawyers. There was the chance that they would "win" against the fictitious nephews—and she could not allow that to happen. For, if it did happen, the lawyears could then claim the inheritance. They would have the legal right to open the vault and withdraw the cash and securities which had allegedly been placed within.

Madame Humbert's lawyers knew nothing of her scheme. They made every effort to win the case for their client, and she had to continue playing the game. So, while she was cooperative, she remained somewhat aloof whenever her lawyers appeared to be close to bringing the case to a head.

This aroused the suspicions of one very well-known jurist, and also the Premier of France, the distinguished Waldeck-Rousseau. He took time out from his many duties to examine the case.

The premier embarrassed his colleagues with some very simple and obvious questions. Crisply, he asked, "Who has seen the Crawfords in America?"

No one had.

"Do they exist?"

Nobody had thought to verify that fact. They had depended solely upon letters received by Madame Humbert . . . or rather, letters she claimed to have received from American attorneys representing the Crawford nephews.

Now, a thorough investigation was undertaken. It proved quite embarrassing to the French attorneys who had represented Madame Humbert. The elementary action of establishing the existence of the other parties to the case had been totally disregarded. But could they be held responsible?

Who would ever have thought to doubt Madame Humbert? She was married to a man of modest wealth. There was no reason for anyone to suspect the grand style in which she was living. No one except Premier Waldeck-Rousseau.

The premier ordered a thorough and intensive investigation. The result: authorities on both sidts of the Atlantic discovered that the Crawford nephews did *not* exist, and that there was no record of a Robert Henry Crawford; nor was there proof that Madame Humbert had ever visited America!

In February of 1933, the courts ordered the vault to be opened and the true nature and magnitude of the hoax that was perpetrated became known. They discovered a small amount of cash, and yellowed, worthless, old papers stuffed into envelopes to give the appearance of containing a great many securities and documents of value.

By now, it was apparent that the scandal involved about $50 million. The banks of Europe had been bilked. How could they have lent out such large sums of money without investigating the person who was receiving the loan! There followed a run on many of the banks. A few collapsed; others went into bankruptcy. The world markets were almost on the brink of disaster.

When the hoax was discovered, Madame Humbert reportedly said, "You just cannot believe everything you see and hear."

It now emerged that in order to carry out her hoax, Madame Humbert had conspired with an American whom she had once met while he was on a trip to Paris, to send letters on the stationery of a fake law firm.

Madame Humbert was trapped. She could find no further excuses, and was accused of being an impostor, a hoaxer—a woman who had almost bankrupted some of the finest financial institutions in all of Europe.

In March, 1934, Thérèse stood trial in Paris. She was quickly convicted and sentenced to a term in a Paris prison. Outraged by the hoax she had perpetrated even on him, her husband immediately divorced her.

After her release ten years later, Thérèse Daurignac Humbert slipped out of France, and vanished somewhere in Europe, or perhaps America. She left behind the smoldering ruins of a grandiose hoax that was to be an embarrassment to the financiers of Europe for many years.

5

ORSON WELLES

The Man Behind the Invasion of Earth

IT WAS INTENDED TO BE a simple radio drama, but by the time it was over, the program had created world-wide panic. Tens of thousands of listeners believed that what they had heard on radio was not a work of fiction, but an event that was actually taking place.

RADIO WAR TERRORIZES U.S.—so screamed the headline of the *New York Daily News,* on October 31, 1938.

Originally, the purpose of the program, according to its creator, was to highlight the possibility of an invasion of our world by enemy forces from Mars, the legendary warlike planet. But listeners had apparently let their imaginations run away, and before the show was over, millions of Americans had run into the streets, shrieking, weeping and raving that the world's end had come, that Martians were threatening to invade Earth.

Ironically, listeners were terrified of the men from Mars— rather than the Nazis and Japanese, who were very real threats to world peace at the time.

How did it all happen? As we dip into history, we discover H. G. Wells' *War of the Worlds,* which explains in amazing scientific detail how a Martian invasion could take place. It took the efforts of several brilliant, modern writers and performers to convert this classic into a radio show. Heading the team was Orson Welles, host of the radio show and members of the Mercury Theatre, the program's stars.

The real beginning of this hoax (it was a hoax, although it *began* as an authentic radio drama) occurred when several producers, directors and performers conferred with Orson Welles. They wanted to create a truly powerful experience for the public. The suggestion was made to take the scientific fantasy by H. G. Wells and put it on radio.

One producer shrugged it off. "That's impossible. Who is going to believe such a silly story about Martians invading the earth? I'll agree that H. G. Wells is a classic writer, but when you dramatize some of his books on radio, you lose the real impact. It'll probably be a big flop. Let's not even do it."

It was generally agreed that *reading* about an invasion did not have the same impact as *hearing* about one on a radio program that gives the illusion of being a news show. It would, therefore, have to be constructed so as to give the impression of being a news show.

The members of the Mercury Theatre felt that such a show would work if done properly.

The Mercury Theatre was working against a deadline. It needed to have a show prepared for CBS by the following Friday afternoon, for broadcasting Sunday evening. The members wanted something full of life and action, something vigorous, something that would earn them good ratings.

But they were up against very stiff competition. The nation overwhelmingly tuned in the very popular *Edgar Bergen and Charlie McCarthy Show* at this hour each Sunday night. Nothing short of a miracle could pull listeners away from Bergen and McCarthy. So the producers came up with an idea to create their own little miracle. They planned it so that the public would not realize that the entire matter was inauthentic and fabricated. They would shock their listeners, in the hope of earning better ratings for the Mercury Theatre.

With all this in mind, the producers started to rewrite *War of the Worlds*. They reworked the dialogue so as to give the listening audience a feeling of being eyewitnesses to mob scenes in which people shrieked and moaned over the sight of spaceships approaching earth.

As they reworked the *War of the Worlds*, preparing a script that was scientifically sound, a few changes had to be made. To avoid legal problems, they did not use the actual name of any existing hotels or buildings. Instead, for example, of saying the "Hotel Biltmore," they said "Park Plaza" which did not exist at that time. Instead of the Columbia Broadcasting Building, they referred to the Broadcasting Building. Other minor changes were made to protect them from legal repercussions.

Great effort went into the preparation of sound effects. These included the usual shouts of crowd scenes, the roar of cannons booming in the Watchung Hills of New Jersey, the sounds of New York harbor as anxious hordes of New Yorkers struggled to leave before the invasion of the Martians.

After the sound effects had been prepared, the script was polished, and several rehearsals were held. Reportedly, Orson Welles did not attend any of them, leaving it all under the control of the able staff of the Mercury Theatre. A gifted performer, the producers were confident that Mr. Welles would be able to read his part with no advance preparation.

Promptly at 8:00, E.S.T., on Sunday, October 30, 1938, Orson Welles entered a CBS studio. He took his seat before the microphone. Sound engineers in the control booth went through the testing ritual. Welles relaxed for a moment, sipped some fruit juice, then put on his earphones and signalled to the engineer.

At that moment, the Mercury theme was sounded: the "Tchaikowsky Piano Concerto in B-Flat Minor #1." The music built to a crescendo, then segued into a few routine announcements. Next came the formal introduction of the program: a dramatization of *War of the Worlds,* a classic written by the renowned H. G. Wells. Little emphasis, if any, was placed on the fact that the program was a dramatization (a fact that the broadcasters were later to deny).

At 8:01 Orson's mellifluous voice was heard by millions of listeners:

> WELLES: We know that in the early years of the twentieth century, this world was being watched closely by intelligences greater than man's, and yet as mortal as his own. We know now that as human beings busied themselves about their various concerns they were scrutinized and studied, perhaps almost as narrowly as a man with a microscope might scrutinize the transient creatures that swarm and multiply in a drop of water. With infinite complacence people went to and fro over the earth about their

little affairs, serene in the assurance of their dominion over this small spinning fragment of solar driftwood which by chance or design man has inherited out of the dark mystery of Time and Space. Yet, across an immense ethereal gulf, minds that are to our minds as ours are to the beasts in the jungle, intellects vast and unsympathetic regarded this earth with envious eyes, and slowly and surely drew their plans against us. In the thirty-ninth year of the twentieth century, came the great disillusionment. . .

So spoke Orson Welles over network radio on October 30, 1938. On this particular evening, the Crossley service estimated that thirty-two million people were listening to their radios. Then, without any noticeable pause, an announcer's voice broke in with the following bulletin:

ANNOUNCER: For the next twenty-four hours, not much change in temperature. A slight atmospheric disturbance of undetermined origin is reported over Nova Scotia, causing a low pressure area to move down rather rapidly over the northeastern states, bringing a forecast of rain, accompanied by winds of light gale force. Maximum temperature 66°; minimum 48°. This weather report comes to to from the Government Weather Bureau. . . . We now take you to the Meridian Room in the Hotel Park Plaza in the heart of New York, where you will be entertained by the music of Ramon Raquello and his orchestra.

This was the cue. The engineers now turned on a record of "La Cumparsita," a familiar South American tune. Although it was not planned as a hoax, the entire event might never have gripped the American radio public had the show on the opposite network been a good one that night. The Mercury Theatre was popular, but its rating was far lower than the highly popular Edgar Bergen-Charlie McCarthy team. An audience measuring service estimated that Edgar Bergen usually got about 34.7 per cent of the listening audience, the Mercury Theatre far less.

But radio ratings had always failed to take into account one important factor: listeners would often tune in one show, and then switch to another—especially if a string of commercials or an unpopular performer was introduced. And it so happened that on this evening, at 8:12, E.S.T., the *Edgar Bergen and Charlie McCarthy Show* featured a new singer. The abrupt change in format, from comedy to the unexciting singing of an unknown, inspired a large number of listeners to turn their dials. This large number of people did not hear the announcement made at the opening of the Mercury Theatre program in which credit was given to the classic *War of the Worlds.* To all who tuned in late, the announcements they heard about a real Martian invasion sounded real. These new listeners, spellbound and alarmed, stayed with the show. The Mercury Theatre now had a very large listening audience. Even many of the original listeners forgot that the program was a mere dramatization. They, too, began to believe that an invasion had actually taken place.

When Orson Welles described how strange meteorites had come crashing down in Grovers Mill, New Jersey, the residents of the town took it seriously. Panic erupted in the little town. Grovers Mill residents were frightened at the thought of horrible-looking "little green men" overtaking their streets. The situation started to get out of hand.

When CBS alerted the Mercury Players that listeners were reacting to the program as fact rather than fiction and that New Jersey state troopers were already speeding to the scene to repel the invaders, the Mercury Players announcer pleaded for order.

The panic was spreading; many were fleeing. "Do not tie up the telephone lines!" the announcer pleaded. "Do not make unnecessary calls." Ambulances and police cars were dispatched. The military was being called in. If everyone would organize and obey orders, the Martians might be driven off.

But these words did little to alleviate the situation. The word had spread and hundreds of thousands of new listeners tuned in and heard about the so-called invasion, hundreds of families left their homes and raced out into the streets. In Trenton, New Jersey it was reported that solid blocks of houses were vacated by screaming, alarmed people. Many held damp cloths over their faces, fearing the poisonous gases or strange vapors that the Martians might be bringing with them.

One man later said, "I was terrified. All I wanted to do was take my wife and children and hide somewhere. We got into our car. But where could we go? If the Martians were invading, they would probably cover the entire earth. The only hope was to escape to another planet. But how could we get there? We were terrified. Everybody was running in the streets!"

New York City streets were filled with frightened people. New Yorkers got into their automobiles and listened to car radios, turned up to full volume.

The Mercury Theatre continued its broadcast. The announcer continued to describe the invasion by strange creatures from outer space.

Many people raced to bus terminals, willing to pay whatever was demanded in order to get them out of the city. Churches filled up with those who wanted to make peace with God now that the "end of the world" was near.

An "eyewitness" told this story: "I held both hands together in prayer. All the time, I looked through my window and thought I saw some falling meteors. I could just about see strange ships and shadows on the dark waves of the Hudson River. They were coming to New York. The Martians would soon be swarming all over Riverside Drive. I wanted to race up to my rooftop. I wanted to get a closer look at them. But I had to stay next to my radio. Also, I was afraid of going out into the open. What if they would grab me?"

Mass hysteria soon took hold of the entire eastern seaboard. Every available vehicle was being used to carry frantic people away. But where to? No one knew where to go to find safety.

"My feeling was that this would be the end of the human race," a radio listener declared after the event. "We were all doomed to perish. All that we had built up, all that we had struggled to develop now would perish as the Martians would devour our planet. It was hopeless!"

The switchboards of the leading eastern newspapers were flooded. Callers inquired as to the seriousness of the invasion. Some even urged the city's utilities to turn off the lights. If the city was protected with a blanket of darkness—a blackout—it might be made safe from the invaders. But many argued that this would not help; if the Martians had supernatural powers, they would certainly be able to see in the dark. Others claimed that the Martians had futuristic types of light. With just one flicker of a flashlight, the entire earth could be bathed in artificial sunlight. There was virtually no escape.

One Bostonian hurried home after hearing about the broadcast. He found his wife on the bathroom floor, clutching some poison. "I want to die this way!" she screamed. "I don't want a Martian to kill me."

Soon, the panic had spread to Chicago where a woman ran screaming into a public building: "New York is destroyed! The Martians have devoured everyone. We're next! We're going to die! Oooooo, God have mercy on all of us!!!"

Not much later, Los Angeles became overcome by panic as well. The population was convinced that the Martians would soon reach them, too.

Because it was network radio, the entire country was exposed to this hoax, creating repercussions from coast to coast.

Word had spread to the south, too. In some southern colleges, students and teachers huddled together praying that a miracle might save them. After all, they had been God-fearing people all their lives.

Orson Welles continued to broadcast, quietly pausing so the announcer could break in, pleading for order, begging the listeners not to panic, explaining that military help was on the way to repel the invasion. As soon as the announcer ended his plea, Orson Welles continued to relate the details of the Martian invasion. It was so convincing, even the engineers in the radio studio were becoming alarmed.

Just how was it possible for a single radio broadcast to have such overwhelming ramifications?

There are several logical explanations.

First, there was historical timing. The broadcast was made at the time Adolph Hitler was demanding conquest of the world. Americans knew that there was the impending threat of a Nazi war. Their ears were constantly glued to radios. They wanted "instant" news; only the radio could fulfill this need. And living in an atmosphere of world crisis, the news of an invasion was not difficult to believe.

Second, radio broadcasters did more than just report news

or read it from a press sheet or wire service. Broadcasters had developed techniques whereby they would use interviews, dramatic backgrounds and various other methods to make news programs more interesting, dramatic and vital. The Mercury Theatre used these new techniques effectively, and made full use of eye-witness reports, interviews, and break-in announcements. Their dramatic script became a believable news broadcast.

Furthermore, this was the 1930s, long before television had yet been invented. It was an age of radio listening and radio dramas were most popular. There were few, if any, quiz shows or game shows on the air; soap operas ruled supreme. The public identified closely with radio dramas; they were eager to suspend their disbelief and did so readily. So, when it came to a dramatization of a Martian invasion it was not difficult for the listening audience to accept it as fact.

Actually, the public had been witness to a similar real-life situation on May 6, 1937 when the dirigible, Hindenburg, exploded and burned at a mooring in Lakehurst, New Jersey, with a loss of 38 lives. First, the explosion. Then, the news reporter (at the real-life explosion of the Hindenburg) took a moment to register shock. Then, the reaction of the public. Split-second descriptions through sputtering words. Confusion between what is seen and what must be described. Then, the awful horror of the explosion was described: human figures falling, engulfed in flames, from the huge white wreckage.

The announcer had to stop; fight back his tears. He then continued to describe what was happening at the site of the Hindenburg explosion.

This technique was followed by the broadcasters and writers of the Mercury Theatre. It was good drama, true. But it was so realistic that the broadcasters were charged with being impostors and Orson Welles was labelled a "hoaxer." Welles argued that if his drama was so vivid that it was accepted as real, then he should be considered a good theatrical *innovator*, not a hoaxer. This was, he claimed, an unfair accusation.

The script devised by the Mercury Players had very closely followed the style used by newsmen who reported the disaster of the Hindenburg.

It described how a spaceship had fallen, how meteorites

had come crashing down in a field at Grovers Mill. Announcers then explained how the strange cylindrical spaceship was opening. Out came the horrifying, green-faced, scale-covered creatures.

"The Martians have landed."

There were various fumbles, a few pauses, to maximize the shock effect.

"They . . . they are going . . . Oh, God have mercy . . . the Martians are here . . . in the United States!!!"

Another pause. A deadly silence.

A new voice was now heard over the microphone. The shocked and unprepared voice: "The announcer has been killed! He is the first victim to fall beneath the ray guns of the Martians."

Silence that seemed infinite followed. Then, from somewhere, the network's emergency fill-in was heard over the airwaves. It was agonizing suspense. A piano was playing "Clair de Lune," a soft and gentle tune in contrast to the shock of the cataclysmic horror of the Martian invation.

Moments later, the audience heard the voice of Brigadier General Montgomery Smith, Commander of the New Jersey State Militia. He spoke from Trenton, New Jersey. He announced that "the counties of Mercer and Middlesex as far west as Princeton and East to Jamesburg" were being placed under martial law.

If there were ever any doubts about the authenticity of the program, it was now dissipated. It seemed more official than ever: Mars was threatening the entire country, and a war of the worlds was inevitable.

Eyewitness accounts of various battles followed. And then, as the country walked a tightrope, the music came on again. This was known as a "theatrical retard"—that is, stretching suspense by delaying the full story. Orson Welles was a master of this technique. And thusly, the program continued. It was no wonder that the country was in an uproar.

At 8:31, when the crisis in the country had reached its height, and as the program continued, another fictitious Welles character (this time the Secretary of the Interior) was heard on the radio.

SECRETARY: Citizens of the nation: I shall not try to conceal the gravity of the situation that confronts our country, nor the concern of your Government in protecting the lives and property of its people. However, I wish to impress upon you—private citizens and public officials, all of you—the urgent need of calm and resourceful action. Fortunately, this formidable enemy is still confined to a comparatively small area, and we may place our faith in the military forces to keep them there. In the meantime, placing our trust in God, we must continue the performance of our duties, each and every one of us, so that we may confront this destructive adversary with a nation united, courageous, and consecrated to the preservation of human supremacy on this earth. I thank you.

By now, the switchboard of CBS was flooded with calls from listeners who reported having seen the Martians. They were described to be as huge as skyscrapers, partially invisible, even totally invisible.

The end was said to be near.

Shortly thereafter, the announcer came on:

ANNOUNCER: You are listening to the CBS presentation of Orson Welles and the Mercury Theatre in an original dramatization of *War of the Worlds* by H. G. Wells. The performance will continue after a brief intermission.

After a pause, Orson Welles went on to describe the gradual defeat of the Martian invaders. "After all man's defenses had failed, the humblest thing that God in his wisdom had put upon this earth had turned the trick—bacteria. Bacteriological action had ended the Martian threat and earthlings could now survive."

Orson then changed his tone. He chuckled as he said that it was his hope that the listening audience had enjoyed this dramatization of *War of the Worlds*—and how very appropriate it was to the Halloween season. The program was over.

But by now, the hoax had so aroused the nation that many sought vengeance. While authorities started to alert the public, many demanded that Orson Welles be punished in the manner of a criminal. Hordes of angry people descended upon the CBS building. Quickly, the entire staff of the Mercury Theatre was escorted down a rear staircase, out of the building and into a waiting limousine. By midnight, all of the country's radios and major newspapers were exposing the hoax. One tabloid paper showed a picture of Orson Welles. Beneath it, a caption read: "I Didn't Know What I Was Doing."

It took several weeks before the excitement subsided. Hearings were held before the Federal Communications Commission. Columbia Broadcasting System offered a public apology.

Orson Welles always maintained that he had presented a good drama; he denied being an impostor. And because his show had so aroused the public, reviewers praised him as a theatrical genius.

The Mercury Theatre zoomed upwards in the ratings, winning a larger listening audience than the popular *Edgar Bergen and Charlie McCarthy Show*. Many charges continued against Orson Welles; none were substantiated. In the end, Orson welles was hailed as a brilliant performer.

6

DANIEL DUNGLAS HOME

The Man Who Talked to the Dead

ON A CRISP, WINTERY LONDON NIGHT, at the height
of the Victorian Age, a group of men and women assembled
in the imposing town house of a member of the nobility. They
spoke in whispers, charging the air with anticipation. An event
was going to take place that evening, an extraordinary event
that would erase the barriers of time and space—of life and
death. The participants could scarcely control their anxiety as
they talked of what would occur in just a few moments.

The living room doorbell rang, and a uniformed servant
announced: "Ladies and gentlemen, the arrival of Mr. Daniel
Dunglas Home."

A nobleman, master of the elegant town house, hurried to
greet the new arrival. He shook his hand warmly, then introduced him to each of the eager guests.

Mr. Daniel Dunglas Home kissed the hands of the ladies,
and shook the hands of the gentlemen, studying each one
intensely as he moved down the line.

While everyone attempted to behave casually and naturally,
a strange, invisible wall separated them from the newcomer.
Daniel Home was *different.*

Home paused as he approached a younger member of the
assemblage who had enjoyed several audiences with members of
royalty at Buckingham Palace. Home stared at him. His jet
black eyes penetrated the young man. In a hollow voice, with
just the slightest tinge of a Scottish burr, he said, "You have
been grossly disappointed. The young lady did not want to
marry out of her class. You feel that everything is hopeless.
But you should not despair. You will soon reap huge rewards
from your efforts. You shall very shortly be involved in an
arrangement that will bring meritorious consequences."

The young man colored slightly.

"Yes, sir."

This was all the young man could whisper, his voice barely audible. He had just suffered the loss of the woman he loved. A British princess with whom he was in love had been forbidden to marry him. But it had all been kept secret! How did this man know of the romance?

Those who doubted the powers of Home began to feel otherwise. His demeanor and words inspired confidence. He moved with regal bearing, seemingly aware of all that was transpiring around him. Soon, he would attempt to prove what everyone had come to witness: that he could make contact with the *World Beyond*.

"We shall now begin," he announced.

The eight guests gathered around a hand-carved, oak table. Home drew up his armchair. Everyone sat watching Daniel Dunglas Home, one of the most celebrated London mediums. His reputation for communicating with the dead, and talking with the spirits was well known. It was said that he used secret powers to pierce the Fourth Dimension, the dimension of time. For his miraculous powers, he was admired and adored.

"Lord Henry," he called toward the royalist who owned the house as the séance was ready to begin, "please lead us in prayer."

In soft, muffled tones, as if speaking loudly would disturb someone, Lord Henry said, "Let us pray for clear hearts, knowing truth, great courage and a tireless journey into the great beyond, as we are permitted to do so, by the grace of God. Amen."

The others mumbled, "Amen."

Then there was a hushed silence, and everyone, as if on cue, placed their hands on the table, palms down. Little fingers connected one person to the next.

Then there were sounds . . .

Rap! Rap! Rap! Rap!

Daniel Dunglas Home announced: "The spirits wish to hear the alphabet. Sir, please begin . . . letter by letter."

Slowly, one member of the group started to recite the alphabet.

"A—B—C—D—E—."

There was another loud rap.

Home announced: "The message calls for less illumination. Am I correct?"

Rap! Rap!

He got up and extinguished one of the candles. The room was now bathed in a soft, gentle light from the fireplace. The cracking of the logs lent a cozy, intimate feeling. The outside world had been shut out. Only the invisible world, the world in this room, was in existence.

The room began echoing with the sound of strange noises. The table tilted. Hushed gasps. The table gyrated. The entourage tried to push the table down but to no avail. Home remained tranquil. He shut his eyes. His thin lips moved.

The voice was not that of his own. It was a high-pitched, squeaky . . . child's voice.

"Hi, everyone. My name is Billy Crawford. Your Lordship . . . if it please you, m'Lord . . ."

Lord Henry moved forward. His beady eyes were glazed with intent. "Yes, my boy?"

"Tell Mum and Popsy that I'm very happy. It is so nice here. I have a nice little cat, so much like little Sissie that we used to play with at home in Liverpool. It is so nice here."

There was a pause. Then, as Home continued to move his lips, other voices came forth: voices from soldiers who had perished in the wars of India, Afghanistan, and deep Africa; voices from departed wives, from departed husbands; even voices from departed members of royalty. All spoke through Home, who appeared to be in a trance. The voices spoke of their contentment and happiness. The "other world," they said, was satisfactory. Soon, they forecast, all men would be united.

Daniel Dunglas Home was finished. He fell back in his chair, and opened his eyes. He looked at Lord Henry. "May we have the trumpet?"

As quickly as the order left his lips, it was carried out.

Home put the trumpet to his lips. A soft, gentle melody issued forth from the instrument. The room resounded with the familiar Scottish tune.

The faint flames of the fireplace gave off the only light in the room. The participants had to strain, but they could see what was happening.

The trumpet moved from Home's lips and from his hand . . . and started to float in mid-air. More miraculously, *the trumpet continued to play the Scottish melody even as it floated in the air.*

But there was a slight off-note.

Home quickly declared, "A discordant note. Someone here is inharmonious. You must all concentrate. You must all believe in unity!"

Soon, the trumpet was playing in tune.

A girl's voice was now heard. All listened in disbelief. "Oh, there is something . . . something *alive* under the tablecloth."

The velvet tablecloth was moving, something was emerging from beneath it. In the ghostly light, it became clear. *It was a hand!* There were moans and strange gasps from the group. The hand started to float across the table.

The pale, ghostly fingers picked up a pencil. Written words were beginning to appear on a piece of paper. The paper was folded and tossed before one of the men.

"I cannot believe it . . . but I must believe it. That paper is a note from my late grandmother . . ."

A second participant broke in. "She is not 'late' but very much alive . . . in the spirit world. You have just been given proof of that."

The hand kept moving. It floated until it reached the medium. The hand patted his cheek. It moved to Home's shoulder . . . and very slowly, it started to fade away . . . until it was gone, leaving behind only a receding luminous cloud.

By now, Home was showing signs of exhaustion. He stood up, went to the fire . . . and, with thumb and forefinger, picked a hot coal from its midst. Holding the blazing coal, he carried it to Lord Henry. His voice, cold, as if from beyond the grave, asked, "My Lord, have you faith?"

Lord Henry fumbled for the right words. He was confused. In a way, he had accepted the phenomenon of communication with the beyond, and yet, he had his doubts. At the moment, he was unable to respond to the question.

Home then moved to another guest. "Do you believe, madame?"

"I . . . I . . ."

He put the red, hot coal in her outstretched palm. "What do you feel?"

"Just warmth!"

He retrieved the burning coal. "It is all in the power of faith. Believe and ye shall be saved. Believe and ye shall be given the powers reserved only for a chosen few. It is all in faith and belief."

He returned the coal to the fireplace.

Then followed new happenings.

He moved and took a seat near the curtains that framed the window. The voice of a very young lad was heard coming from Home's lips.

"I . . . I am going upward . . . take me . . . take me up . . . cradle me in your arms as a mother holds her sleeping babe . . . I will go with you . . . up . . . up . . . higher and higher . . ."

Someone whispered, "Look! He is going upward! Lord have mercy upon us. Mr. Home is floating upward!"

The medium *was* floating upward. Then he appeared to be horizontal, soon vertical, soon upside down, and then his body appeared to be going around in a circle. Very slowly, then, his feet came down and he stood on the carpeted floor.

Daniel Dunglas Home now moved toward them. "I have returned amongst those who live on this level." Very slowly, he came toward the table. He cried out—a chortled cry—as if someone had blocked his windpipe.

Everyone gasped, fearing danger.

Home collapsed in his armchair. Someone lit a few candles. Another person whispered, "He is as pale as death itself!"

Lord Henry signalled for a glass of sherry for the distinguished medium who had gone to the Great Beyond, walked and talked with the spirits, and then floated back down to this world.

This episode took place in London in the late 1860s. Daniel Dunglas Home, one of the most popular mediums of the day —and one of the most gifted hoaxers—was said by some of his contemporaries to have been born with the extraordinary gift of being able to unravel the mysteries of death so that he could talk with those who had departed this world. He had displayed his talents to monarchs throughout Europe. He was even hailed as one who possessed divine powers.

These years of the mid-nineteenth century were times of psychic exploration. Only a short time earlier, Darwin had promulgated his theory of the origin of the species. There was a great outcry for realism and free thinking. The shackles of fundamentalism were being shattered. At the same time, hell-fire preachers were now on the defensive. Even the Bible was being questioned. This was part of a cycle: a period of religious fervor, followed by doubts, and culminating in a return to religious fervor.

In the midst of this religious revolution, spiritualism was gaining a foothold. More and more were beginning to believe that there was a power which, if understood, enabled man to walk and talk with the departed. Organized religion said it was the work of the Devil, to attempt to pierce the Beyond. But with so many mediums appearing on the scene, each conducting séances and delivering messages from the departed, the belief was growing that this was the will of God. If God did not want such practices to exist why did he permit them to? And so, it was not unusual to find tens of thousands becoming involved and believing in spiritualism.

Of all the mediums, it was Daniel Dunglas Home who had a reputation that appeared to be beyond reproach. He was born in the spring of 1833 in the small hamlet of Currie, in Scotland, a short distance from Edinburgh.

Daniel was one of a family of several children. Little is known about his mother, but it is known that his father was a barroom brawler who met his equal at an Irish waterfront pub and was never heard from again. The children were split up. Young Daniel was taken in by an aunt who did her best to raise the sickly, ailing boy. It is believed that he had tuberculosis. As a result, he was confined to the house and spent most of his time alone, reading. When he expressed a desire to play with youngsters his own age, he was invariably told that he was "too sick" or "too young" or "too little."

Because he was compelled to avoid physical activity, his thoughts turned inward. He would daydream and fantasize. He developed a high degree of sensitivity, perception, and imagination. Often, he would close his eyes while in bed, and spend hours in a romantic world of his own. The seeds of his future as a medium were planted during those solitary periods.

By the time he entered his teens, he felt that he could effectively communicate with the departed. He fortified himself in this belief when he became aware that on his mother's side (the McNeills) he was descended from Highlanders. It was known that the Highlanders, historically and traditionally, did have the gift of "second sight." This was his heritage and Daniel was determined to make the most of it.

He became a self-styled expert in spirit raps. He would tell his aunt, Mrs. McNeill Cook (a devout member of the Kirk of Scotland) how he had heard raps from departed relatives. He told how he had conversed with them and was told they were content, and for those on this level not to grieve or worry.

"Nonsense!" shrieked the pious Mrs. Cook. "It is all the work of Satan. I will hear no more of such Devil-inspired wickedness. It is witchcraft . . . even worse—blasphemy. It is blasphemy!!"

But this only encouraged the lonely teenager to explore the world of spirits more intensely. One morning, he hurried into the kitchen where his pious aunt was preparing the luncheon meal. From out of nowhere came yelps and screams. The voices bounced from the floor, ceiling and woodwork.

Mrs. McNeill Cook screamed. "Ye have had consort with the Devil. Ye have been possessed by the Devil. Depart! Begone with ye! Take your Devil with ye! I'll have no Satan in my house!!!"

She threw his clothes at him and, literally, drove Daniel from her house. Later, she brought in several clergymen to exorcise the Devil from her abode.

Now, the young man had to fend for himself. From the start Daniel Dunglas Home genuinely believed he was a medium. He would hold séances with groups at no charge. Generally, they offered to pay him for his services. By presenting the appearance of being honest and sincere, and by stressing the rule of a "love offering" and the "offering of the heart," he actually netted more money than those mediums who requested stated fees for their services.

At a typical séance, with groups sitting around a table, little fingers touching, the table would begin to shake. Voices and strange whispers would be heard from all parts of the room. Daniel, an invalid in his youth, had many days and weeks and months to master the art of ventriloquism, which was basic to a successful séance.

With some deft acrobatic ability, it was also comparatively easy for him to lift a table with his knees, giving the appearance that it was done by invading spirits. "See" he would call out to the group. "Over there . . . it is a spirit glow. A soft spark . . . no, it is turning into a pink cloud . . so soft, so fluffy . . . it has come from beyond . . ."

The power of suggestion was so strong, that many of those gathered would concede that they did see such light. The rapping was little more than a parlor trick.

(Just place your fingers on the polished top of a table. Press hard. Let one finger slip a slight fraction of an inch. A rap is heard. Doing it another way, place the heel of your shoe against one leg of the chair in which you sit. Slip it down a slight fraction. Again, you will hear a rap.)

There was another way in which Daniel Dunglas Home astonished fee-paying clients: he was able to bring back sounds of the departed without touching anything or doing anything noticeable. He would simply go into a trance and shortly after the room would become filled with rappings. Aside from the other two methods mentioned he often fastened a small wooden bolt or fishing sinker on a black silk thread. He let it drop through a crack in the woodwork or into a hole in the wall. The heavy weight would then be propelled by wind so that it let loose with a series of rappings purported to be "voices" or "sounds" from the Beyond.

Just how could Home hoax someone into believing that intimate details were revealed to him by a departed relative? He would seize upon basic facts, embellish them, and then employ such strong powers of suggestion that the living relative not only believed them, but was so convinced that he often repeated his discovery to others.

Home always insisted that the lighting in a room be ghostly. By positioning mirrors in a certain way, a single jet flame could give the impression of ghostly faces. As for hands, such apparitions could be created by sketching an imprint upon a mirror that reflected into a dimly lit room. Daniel Dunglas Home would secretly put on a luminous glove and it would appear that a severed hand was moving across a table.

Daniel was clever. By refusing payment for his services, he could not legally be charged as a hoaxer or impostor. Rather, he developed a reputation as a medium who communicated with the departed on a "love offering" basis. Always, a vase or bowl stood on a mantlepiece. Here, gracious guests would place their so-called "love offerings." Quite often, he would clear $500 to $1,000 for an hour's séance. He never took the money from the vase or bowl in anyone's presence; it would have been blasphemy to count money received for his spiritual gift. But when he was alone, he counted his receipts eagerly. His talent had helped him create a very profitable business venture.

In this age of spiritualism, mediums would often meet and discuss their gifts. That was how Home met a pair of very wealthy spiritualists, Mr. and Mrs. Charles D. Parker. They were connoisseurs of art, and experts at communicating with the Beyond. It was a fortuitous meeting. They began to introduce Home to members of the nobility, and that was how he happened to be called in to conduct séances attended by royalty and the crown heads of Europe.

This gave him needed credits. Furthermore, the crown heads rewarded him handsomely—so handsomely, in fact, that he could soon afford to purchase the former palatial residence of a Serbian king. He invited the Parkers to be his permanent guests and he now had a home base in the best part of London.

Home built a good, solid reputation. He was the dinner guest of the leading barons, marquis, princes and princesses from all parts of Europe. He openly disdained the taking of cash. Therefore, he was rewarded with diamonds (a medium's best friend), rare objects of art, paintings, trinkets, antiques and various forms of gold and silver. And, of course, the vase or bowl was always filled with money.

Because he was in such great demand, an introduction for a "sitting" was almost impossible unless one knew the right person. To keep in his good graces, royalists showered him with costly gifts.

On one occasion, he produced a pair of glowing spirit hands which moved about the table in the darkened room. This had been achieved by mixing a bit of phosphorous with olive oil, which he rubbed over his hands.

When the effect was accomplished, the hands vanished beneath the table. Here, Home quickly wiped them on the overlapping edge of the tablecloth which had been especially soaked in a soapy solution. His hands emerged, clean and normal, and the effect had been registered.

There was one near catastrophe. On one occasion, during a séance. he conjured up the face of a little boy who was claiming to be the son of Robert and Elizabeth Barrett Browning. The little boy, who claimed to have died in infancy, wished his parents well and wanted them to continue writing their brilliant poetry.

But something went amiss. After the séance, Home was informed that the Brownings had actually lost a child—but only through a miscarriage suffered by Elizabeth. A boy had *not* actually been born. Someone sought to protect Home by suggesting, "Perhaps they had a child out of wedlock."

His integrity challenged, Home had to hold another séance during which the "Browning boy" returned and said that he *did* belong to the married couple . . . and that he was the spirit of the child that would have grown into a boy.

But someone doubted him. It is said that this person had dared to reach out, seize the floating, glowing child's head . . . and, instead, "grabbed the rascal's bare foot, painted like that of a child's head!"

But it all happened very swiftly. The light was very faint. By the time Home wrested his foot free, it was hidden back in his boot. The lights went on and the astonished group preferred to believe Home.

Word of the medium's powers reached Paris. That was the time when Louis Napoleon (Bonaparte) was Emperor of France (1852-1870). His Highness commanded Home to conduct a séance. Home knew that this would erase all doubts and establish him as a genuine spiritualist.

When Home arrived, the Tuileries and royal courts of Paris were alive with pomp and glitter. Home knelt before Emperor Louis Napoleon and Empress Eugenie. In their private courts, Daniel Dunglas Home conducted a séance. The departed voices of previous emperors, as well as Napoleon, could be heard in a throaty whisper. Home was fluent in French and Spanish so it was easy for him to make use of his powers of ventriloquism.

The effect was so impressive that when Daniel returned to London, he was heavily laden down with jewelry and other treasures. By now, he was well on his way to becoming a legend in his own time.

Home met a Russian girl whom he wanted to marry, and plans were made. Alexandre Dumas, author of the *Count of Monte Cristo,* was one of Home's devout followers, and he eagerly accepted the invitation to be best man at the wedding. The bride, Alexandra de Kroll, was the daughter of a royal general of the Imperial Russian Army. It seemed as if this new tie would make Home the most successful spiritualist of his age. His wife believed in his authenticity, and he himself started to take himself very seriously.

But there were problems. They had a son who became ill with tuberculosis, which was contagious. The mother contracted the disease and eventually died. On her deathbed, the frail young wife whispered, as she held her husband's hand tightly, "I believe! I believe!"

Soon, thereafter, a new problem developed. A relative of Home's wife sued for custody of his son and his wife's estate. Daniel spent almost everything he had fighting the case. The estate went to the relative, but the sickly boy was allowed to remain with his father. The kindly Mr. and Mrs. Charles D. Parker remembered how good Home had been to them, and gratefully took the boy in.

Home was once again free to continue his work as a medium, and an opportunity soon arose to make a fortune. A wealthy widow of a member of Parliament had asked him to establish contact with her husband. He did so. Using ventriloquism, he told her, among other things, that Daniel Dunglas Home should be rewarded with $200,000. The wife quickly acquiesced, and paid him. It began to look as if things would be going in Home's favor.

But he had not expected the wealthy widow to double-check on him. She went to another medium who went into a trance, and he, too, contacted the dead husband. He told her that Home was a hoaxer and an impostor, and that she should get her money back.

A long legal battle ensued. The court ruled that Home had exacted monies from her under false pretenses, and that the money had to be returned.

The impostor continued to hold séances, employing all his tricks—ventriloquism, rapping and floating hands. In the darkness, he would sneak into an adjoining room. He would make noise as he raised a window. He would tiptoe down the hall, return to the séance room, go to the window, slip behind the heavy curtains, lift the sash, sneak out. Then he would come back again. The ghostly impression was made that he had floated from one room to the next.

The public seemed to forget the lawsuit that had been brought against Home. Even if there were some disbelievers, there were many who believed because they *wanted* to believe, and they paid well for it. Home's reputation did not suffer much, and he was called on to perform before the Emperor and Empress of France, King Maximilian of Bavaria, Queen Sophia of the Netherlands, Czar Alexander II of Russia, the Crown Prince of Prussia, the King and Queen of Wurtenberg, the Duchess of Hamilton. The list was endless. They showered him with gifts and money.

But he spent freely, and his lavish style of living consumed much of his wealth. In 1880, he married a society woman with whom he was very happy. His once ailing son regained good health. In his declining years, Home rarely gave séances. Life was good to him. He enjoyed his wife and his son. He predicted that after he died he would communicate with the living through other mediums.

But when the end came for Home, so came the end of a fabulous career. Hundreds of mediums tried to contact him. . . . They were unsuccessful.

7

BILLIE SOL ESTES

Poor Little Rich Hoaxer

HE BEGAN LIFE in 1910 as the son of a Clyde, Texas country preacher. Ambitious from the very start, Billie Sol Estes' earliest recollections are of his business ventures. He was driven by the need to achieve success. Nothing would stand in his way. And he used every bit of cunning within him to achieve that goal.

Obsessed with the idea of becoming a great financial wizard, Estes did not allow anything to distract him from his objective. He did not drink, did not smoke, and did not dance. His religious upbringing may have been partially responsible for some of the prohibitions that he placed upon himself, but to a greater degree it was his lust for money. He refused to waste time on such trivialities as liquor, tobacco and entertainment.

Estes was more than a hoaxer: he was also a swindler—a combination that propelled Billie Sol from poverty to riches in a career that was meteoric. True to his name Sol, the Spanish for "sun," he rose in a burst of glory, but like the sun at evening time, he plummeted into darkness and oblivion.

Basically, Billie Sol Estes employed schemes that appeared to be innocent and legal. He used the U.S. agricultural price-support program, for example, as part of a hoax to bilk finance companies so that he might garner at least $22 million.

One newspaper reporter said of Billie Sol Estes: "Without the loosely administered and jerry-built federal farm programs, Estes could never have prospered as he did . . . the farm programs seemed to be made to order for wheelers and dealers like Estes." Billie Sol was a creature of a society that had made itself vulnerable to victimization.

Before his hoax was exposed, Estes was considered an important government contact. In fact, at the age of 28, he was already a successful cotton farmer, and was named one of the ten most outstanding young men of the year by the U.S. Junior Chamber of Commerce. He had connections with top people in the Democratic Party, and knew many career public officials with whom he exchanged favors. His smooth talk and soft mannerisms won over even the most restrained and suspicious officials.

Billie Sol began his career during the Eisenhower administration. By early 1962, Eisenhower's New Frontier program was gaining a foothold. Billie Sol arrived on the scene, and using his heavy Texas backing, charm, and much money, arranged to be appointed to a special committee that offered advice about cotton to the Department of Agriculture. This was the beginning of his government involvement.

He started by building a financial empire with the government's official grain storage program as its base. He charged the government some eight million dollars for grain storage during the years 1959 through 1961. It was estimated that he had some 50 million bushels of grain in storage. This was legal; many corporations store materials for the government and charge for that service.

But, then Estes began his fraudulent activities. He sold farmers an easily applied liquid fertilizer called *anhydrous ammonia,* which helped crops grow at a fantastically rapid rate. Generally speaking, this fertilizer could be bought for $90 per ton wholesale, and resold for $100 per ton. To Billie Sol Estes, this kind of profit ($10 per ton) was a drop in the bucket. His ambition was to completely corner the fertilizer market. And *that* was illegal.

Being the hoaxer that he was, Billie Sol Estes set out to maneuver his operations so that they would appear to be legal.

Initially, he needed capital to acquire tanks in which to store the fertilizer. To accomplish this, he evolved a very complicated scheme. First, he borrowed money to buy tanks which he would sell to farmers and businessmen throughout the western part of Texas. He convinced them that they would make big profits. He guaranteed them that, in the event of any losses, he would take the responsibility. No one's investment would be in jeopardy. Billie then sold the mortgages on the tanks (at an irresistible discount) to a dozen finance companies. This money was, in turn, used to buy more fertilizer tanks from the Superior Manufacturing Company of Amarillo, Texas.

All along, Billie Sol was sustaining a loss on the liquid fertilizer he was selling. But he did not care. He made up for it in many ways, especially by charging the government a high price for storage. Slowly, the fertilizer market fell entirely into the palm of his hand. His profits were great.

Billie Sol had another scheme. He owned land which he wanted to put to use. He knew that if he grew cotton on the land, the government would pay him the guaranteed price. But to get this government-supported price, he needed a "qualifying acreage allotment" from the government. Since he had never before grown cotton on this land, he could not obtain the allotment. The government kept such allotments to a minimum so as to avoid overproduction of cotton, which would glut the market and bring down prices.

So began another hoax. There were available lands which had the coveted qualifying cotton acreage allotment. The Department of Agriculture, which bestowed these subsidies, said that once such an allotment was made, it could not be transferred. It applied only to a particular parcel of land. It was not an allotment which belonged to the owner of the land, but to the land itself.

How could Billie Sol work it out so as to get an allotment transferred to his own land? He looked for a loophole and found one. If a farmer had land with this allotment, and it was seized by the government under the doctrine of "eminent domain" for a clearly defined public use, such as to build a highway or a schoolhouse, then the qualifying acreage allotment that had once been given to him for that particular land *could* be transferred to any new land purchased within 36 months. This was the only exception to the rule. No other type of transfer was allowed.

This was all the information Billie needed. He began his search and found some 3,000 acres in states stretching from Texas and Oklahoma to Alabama and Georgia. The land he and his people found was owned by farmers who said the government was going to seize it under the powers of "eminent domain." The farmers said that they were being forced to sell out and vacate the land.

Billie Sol moved swiftly. He advised these farmers "I want you to default on your agreement. Don't pay your mortgages. Instead, buy my land. That means, you'll be able to transfer your cotton allotment to my land. Then, I'll take over your mortgages and, with them, I'll also have your new land and the cotton allotments. It'll all be legal. You'll receive a good price from me for your land, much more than the government would pay you when it seizes your land. Sign the papers. Take the money. You can buy new land somewhere else for that money. I just want the allotments."

The desperate farmers agreed. And so it was that Billie Sol Estes started his first fraudulent activity which, according to a U.S. Department of Agriculture ruling, was later declared to be an "illegal scheme and device." But at the time, Billie Sol had many close associates in government positions and he was prepared for the complications which he foresaw. He was confident that with a few well-placed telephone calls, all problems could be overcome. Billie Sol Estes had more sef-confidence than common sense.

In the summer of 1961, Estes was named to the National Cotton Advisory Committee at the suggestion of Undersecretary of Agriculture Charles S. Murphy.

Murphy had worked in the White House under President Harry Truman. He was also the spearhead of the Johnson-for-President drive in Washington, D. C. When Johnson was elected vice-president, Charles S. Murphy was designated the No. 2 man in the Department of Agriculture.

Billie Sol and Murphy worked closely together. It was Murphy who used his influence to push through the Estes appointment to the Advisory Committee. Several top government officials were unfavorably disposed towards Estes and his activities, and tried to block his appointment, but to little avail.

Estes was looked upon with suspicion and was actually charged with being involved in illegal manipulations of cotton acreage allotments. Officials filed reports in which they declared that their findings regarding the business dealings of Estes "were sufficiently derogatory in nature to recommend against his appointment to any public office."

There was an addendum:

"Since the matter has been referred for consideration of prosecution, it appears advisable to drop his name from consideration until the matter is cleared up."

Later reports stated that Billie Sol Estes had acquired a set of inflated and false financial statements from many farmers. It further charged that Billie Sol had used the credit of these farmers for the purchase of fertilizer tanks. He would use their financial statements to prove that they were financially sound and, hence, good risks.

At this point Billie Sol Estes escaped prosecution because the U.S. Attorney in Texas had examined the case and found that there was insufficient evidence to warrant federal prosecution. And despite the fact that Billie Sol was not Simon-pure (although not guilty of any official crime) his friend, Undersecretary of Agriculture Charles S. Murphy, saw fit to name Estes to the National Cotton Advisory Committee.

All this time, the public was unaware of the background or various activities of Billie Sol. But there were some government officials who wanted to investigate the alleged hoax, about which talk never ceased. In particular, a few officials with the Commodity Stabilization Service (C.S.S.) demanded the cancellation of Estes' allotments, pending further investigation.

Just as there were those who wanted to investigate Billie Sol, there were many other high-level political appointees who considered him a good man and wanted him to succeed.

To placate those who accused him of fraud, and to present himself as an honest citizen with nothing to hide, Billie Sol appeared with his attorney before the officials of the C.S.S. He was questioned intensively, but Billie Sol, with his smooth manner and soft talk, was successful in convincing the committee that he was not at all a hoaxer. He presented himself as a financial expert, putting his knowledge to work, and doing things for profit, but within the law. "There's nothing wrong with making a profit. Our system is based on profit," he reiterated several times.

It worked.

To begin with, the Agricultural Stabilization and Conservation Service simply requested a study of the Estes cotton allotment. Upon investigation, everything appeared to be legal. Billie Sol's manipulations were so complicated and confusing and so saturated with acceptable loopholes and legalities, that it was well nigh difficult, if not impossible, to accuse him directly of being involved in any kind of illegal scheming.

But Billie Sol was an astute man. Cunning as he was, he foresaw a problem looming on the horizon and the possible need for a special favor or service. He would make it his business to renew old contacts and to cultivate new friends to serve his purposes.

The record shows that one of his methods of ingratiating himself with men of power and influence in government was to be generous with contributions. He contributed to the political campaigns of men like Texas Democrat Senator Ralph Yarborough and Representative J. T. Rutherford—men representing the Pecos district in which Billie Sol owned many properties.

Billie Sol was generous to nonpolitical individuals as well. Often, he would give gifts of clothing to needy people . . . and sometimes even cash. It was discovered later, however, that some of the cash filled the coffers of those not so needy—as for example when a little gift of $1,000 was delivered to Assistant Secretary of Labor Jerry R. Holleman. Holleman, a former president of the Texas A.F.L.-C.I.O., was also considered to be quite "solid" with President Lyndon B. Johnson.

Much later, when Holleman was asked about the gift, he freely admitted receiving it. "Sure, I needed a little extra to keep up with the high cost of living in Washington," was his excuse for accepting it. Considering that his salary as Assistant Secretary of Labor was a mere $20,000 a year, some observers of the Washington scene were able to find it in their hearts to condone Holleman's action.

Billie Sol was generous with other political friends as well. It was reported that in January, 1962, he withdrew some $40,000 in cash from the First National Bank of Pecos and passed much of this on to political friends. It was confirmed that he spent $6,000 for 60 tickets to the $100-a-seat birthday celebration of President Johnson's New Frontier.

Billie Sol also loved to entertain, and did so graciously and lavishly. His generosity emerged on one occasion in particular. He attended then-Secretary of Labor Arthur Goldberg's lavish dinner for Vice-President Johnson, and surprised a good many people when he offered to pay the bill. Some reports had it that Goldberg (who later became a Supreme Court Justice) accepted Estes' offer, but Mr. Goldberg was quite emphatic when questioned about it. "I paid for Mr. Johnson's dinner out of my own pocket," insisted Goldberg.

Billie Sol Estes was riding high, and it never entered his thoughts that a small, almost insignificant source would trigger his downfall. He had always assumed that if he could fool the experts, smalltimers would never trouble him.

Early in 1962, a small semiweekly newspaper in Pecos, the *Independent & Enterprise,* looked with suspicion on the strange, meteoric increase in the Estes fortune. The editors knew that Billie Sol had connections with members of the Democratic Party in Washington. They had heard rumors about "legal" machinations, and about the manner in which Billie Sol acquired mortgages on liquid fertilizer tanks. On an impulse, hoping that a scandal lay buried somewhere in all the maneuverings, they started to dig. A good scandal could boost the circulation of their paper, and help them considerably.

The editors started to search the mortgage records in City Hall. One of them, young Oscar Griffin, discovered that there were a great many mortgages placed on storage tanks for anhydrous ammonia. It seemed to be an excessive amount; and a small town did not need that many tanks. Suspicions were aroused.

Oscar Griffin soon found that Billie Sol Estes had placed mortgages on over 33,000 liquid fertilizer storage tanks in 11 counties. "That was enough anhydrous ammonia fertilizer to accommodate the entire state of Texas," he said. "The full sum obtained through these mortgages exceeded some $30 million!"

Something was wrong.

Oscar Griffin was an investigative reporter. He had found discrepancies and began to dig more deeply.

For example, the western part of Texas needed approximately 300 tanks. Why were there 33,000 storage tanks? Were there actually that many storage tanks . . . or did they exist only on paper? If 33,000 storage tanks did *not* exist, then Griffin was surely on to a multi-million dollar mortgage scandal that could ruin many decent Pecos people along with Billie Sol Estes.

Oscar Griffin had to inform the public that a real possibility existed that a great hoax was being perpetrated. He prepared a few articles, and they appeared in the Pecos *Independent & Enterprise*. But they caused hardly a ripple. Oscar Griffin was a good reporter, and he made no wild accusations, neither against government officials, nor against Billie Sol.

Instead, Oscar Griffin merely presented all the facts, and did no more than *suggest* that something might be amiss, and that a serious examination of Estes's mortgage dealings would help dispel any suspicions.

The Pecos newspaper kindled a tiny flame, and at first attracted no more than local interest. But the full impact was soon to come. Local merchants and landowners became alarmed. The various money houses that had lent millions of dollars to Billie Sol grew apprehensive about the safety of their loans. But there was no immediate panic; there was no run on the banks. Those who held mortgages on various liquid fertilizer tanks explained to the satisfaction of the public, the soundness of their investments. They were examining every charge very closely, they said, in a step-by-step manner. The investigation would be thorough.

Soon, members of financial institutions from all over the country who had been in any way involved with Estes sent representatives to Pecos to find out what was going on. They sincerely hoped that none of what they had been hearing was true. They wanted to meet with Billie Sol and discuss it with him personally.

One of the money men declared that, no, this nice young local boy from Pecos was not a hoaxer.

"We dispatched some of our own representatives to verify the serial numbers of the fertilizer tanks pledged as security," he said. "But I think that what happened here is that Billie Sol hoaxed us much as the old Texas cattlemen used to hoax the so-called city slickers in cattle mortgaging."

Slowly, the awesome truth was revealed. There were only about 200 fertilizer tanks . . . not 33,000 as claimed.

What about the serial numbers on the tanks that had been verified by the representatives? Whenever they had come around to do their checking, Billie Sol quickly switched the serial numbers on the two hundred tanks he did own so they would correspond with the numbers on the particular mortgage being verified.

At a Texas court of inquiry, one associate admitted that he knew of Billie Sol's scheme. Since this associate had his life's savings tied up with this fertilizer charade, he asked the hoaxer about it and was told confidentially, "Oh, just forget about it. Don't worry. These money people know balance sheets but they don't know hoaxes."

Billie Sol added, "Some of these people love to be hoaxed. I recall knowing a man who needed a lot of money for a ranch or something. He went to a Kansas City bank and offered his cattle as security.

"The bankers agreed, saying they'd have to come out to inspect the cattle; this rancher drove them around in circles to a few water holes. This was open country and only the rancher was familiar with it. He kept driving around, showing the same cattle to the banker. The 'count' added up to the amount that had been offered as security.

"The rancher got the loan!"

This same approach and method was used with fertilizer tanks.

There were occasions when money houses would send their agents to verify other serial numbers. Billie Sol had extra sets of such plaques in his home office. He would send out his associates, in advance, to the field to do the tag-switching. The agents would be driven around in circles, and would look at the same fertilizer tank that had had its number changed a dozen or more times. The agents never suspected that they were looking at the same tanks.

In the meantime, Billie Sol carefully continued monthly mortgage payments and rental charges on the imaginary tanks. Everything looked good. After all, he reasoned, no business-man would pay money for mortgage payments and rents on non-existent tanks. Billie Sol paid some $500,000 in rentals. He paid another $500,000 on the mortgages. It was a small invest-ment that paid off in money received from the government.

But the Pecos *Independent & Enterprise* unearthed the records on the number of actual tanks in existence. Soon, the mortgagers began to suspect that their "properties" or "security-collateral" did *not* exist.

The hoax was fully exposed when a Dallas lawyer, representing the Pacific Finance Company, made an unannounced visit to Pecos. The lawyer came with a list of serial numbers and made his own tour of the fertilizer tanks. He found that out of 230 numbers, only three existed!

The lawyer also visited the local manufacturer of the tanks, and was told that only a few had been made.

Outraged at the obvious fraud, the Dallas lawyer confronted Billie Sol and said plainly, "Where are all the tanks?"

"There aren't any," was the reply.

The lawyer was furious. "This is a hoax. A fraud! You can be charged with civil as well as criminal penalties."

Billie Sol showed little emotion. "Yes, I do understand that the money I raised by mortgaging nonexisting tanks is illegal. But look at it this way. If you cause trouble now, everything will collapse and you'll never get anything. But if you cooperate with me, you should be able to break even, or come out ahead."

To convince the lawyer, Billie Sol started dropping many names. He showed a card which stated that he had donated some $100,000 to the Democratic Party. He said that he had a monopoly on the entire anhydrous-ammonia fertilizer business in West Texas because of price-cutting. All he needed was time, and he would make it good.

But the exposé had begun. Other creditors demanded justice.

Many meetings were held during which Estes admitted the fraudulent mortgages and then added craftily, "You'll have to cooperate with me . . . or you'll be wiped out."

On one occasion Estes is said to have bragged that he had cancelled an F.B.I. investigation by making just one call to Vice-President Johnson. And on still another occasion, Billie Sol was quoted as having told some of his creditors that if they pressured him, he would scoop up all liquid assets and fly to Brazil. The man was crafty, and the U.S. Attorney knew there was little time to lose.

On March 29, 1962, the government filed charges against Billie Sol Estes for illegal interstate shipment of fraudulent chattel mortgages on nonexistent fertilizer tanks. That same night, F.B.I. agents went to Billie Sol's $150,000 home in Pecos and placed him under arrest.

Under normal circumstances, he would have been imprisoned. Bail was set at $500,000. But Estes used what influence he had to have the bail reduced to $100,000. He raised the money and was set free.

On April 1st, Billie Sol wired the National Cotton Advisory Committee that he was resigning.

Several days later, his trial was under way. More than just the unveiling of a hoax was at stake. Many politicians and government officials had been involved in the scheme; many were questioned; many fell into political disfavor and many admitted that they had received gifts of cash and clothing from Billie Sol. Department store receipts, gift certifications—all were produced in court.

The scandal rocked the nation. Many important politicians and government officials were forced to resign. The Kennedy administration was visibly embarrassed by the scandal. Republicans seized upon it and compared it to the Teapot Dome Scandal.

President Kennedy was eager to have "clean" government, and, through the office of Attorney General Robert F. Kennedy, a directive was issued meting out swift justice to anyone involved in the scandal.

The trial was held in September, 1962 and, when it was over, Billie Sol Estes was convicted of fraud and was sentenced to an eight-year prison term in the federal penitentiary of Alcatraz.

He appealed.

The U.S. Supreme Court overturned the conviction on grounds that television coverage of the trial had denied Billie Sol Estes due process of law.

The hoaxer thought he would surely walk out scot-free.

But the ordeal was not yet over.

A U.S. district court found Estes guilty of mail fraud and conspiracy. He was sentenced to a 15-year prison term, which he still serves.

So ended one of the great swindles of modern times. Billie Sol Estes, the man who fooled some of the biggest experts in the country, could not fool everybody. A local newspaper editor turned out to be the best expert of them all.

8

XAVIER RICHIER

The French Doctor Who Robbed the Wealthy

XAVIER RICHIER WAS BORN IN PARIS, France, in September, 1910, of humble parents. He was an only child and grew up in a caste system which would have required him to follow in the footsteps of his baker father. He knew hardship and privation from his very early years. His father labored long and hard in the small bakery in the back of a tiny store in Paris, while his mother sold bread and rolls in the front of the shop. The small family slept in a small bedroom in the rear of the store. It was all the home they knew.

Xavier would see many elegantly gowned Frenchwomen walking along the streets of Paris. Escorted by smartly groomed men, they often came into the family bakery to buy sweet rolls and muffins. He felt envious. When he thought of how long and hard his father worked to earn a few pennies, the contrast only served to emphasize the wealth of the women who would come to the store to buy the breads and muffins that his mother would wrap up for them.

For as long as he could remember, his mother, prematurely aged with fine lines creasing her once-lovely skin, had only worn one or another shabby dress. Xavier often conjured up visions of how his mother would look if she were wealthy, garbed in exquisite gowns, smartly coiffured, with painted fingernails and lips to match, and shimmering jewels on her fingers, and around her neck. But it was only a dream, and Xavier knew that the only way he could help his mother or father was by continuing to deliver bread to the better homes of Paris.

In the very early hours of the morning, young Xavier would venture forth into the Paris streets, carrying any number of bags containing breads, rolls and muffins. Each bag bore a name and address.

Young Xavier would make his deliveries on foot. There was no money available to ride the trolley car. He knew, from over-hearing talks between his parents, that while they did have many wealthy customers, their margin of profit was very small. His father had often said that while the wealthy liked to *accumulate*, they did not like to share or distribute any of their fortunes. They paid so little for the baked goods they purchased, that the Richier family could barely survive. But the Richiers were content when they were able to pay their bills and eat modestly.

Always, young Richier would deliver bread to the servants' entrance in the rear of the house. It was rare that the maid would let him so much as set foot in the kitchen. He was never permitted to speak to anyone, except for exchanging a few necessary words. Most often, he made his deliveries without uttering a syllable. The maid or cook would take the bag, note the attached bill, pay the money and all but push the lad out of the doorway.

Xavier's most vivid memories were of some of the lowest servants sneering at him. He was, after all, a shabbily dressed delivery boy. The nature of the caste system became clearer to the lad; and it created an emotional scar from which he would never recover.

Often, as Xavier peeped through the window or open door of a lavish home, he could see rare paintings hanging on the walls, exquisite furniture and collections of jewelry and art works. He was awestruck.

He did not necessarily resent the wealthy millionaires for owning such treasures. More than that, he resented the way they *worshipped* their possessions and considered them *more* precious than a human being.

Like many lonely youths, Xavier Richier retreated into a world of fantasy. He dreamed of the time when he, too, would be wealthy. In some of his fantasies, he imagined himself taking away those rare and exquisite treasures from their imperious and haughty owners. He longed to teach them that nothing is forever; nothing is permanent.

Xavier wanted more than to just steal the antiques of the

rich. *He yearned to match wits with them.* He wanted to ridicule them. He wanted to destroy their self-created illusion of superiority. So it was that the boy's hopes of a new life were planted.

Xavier Richier was sent to a local school but, because he had to help out his parents both before and after school, he had little time to make friends. He did not have the leisure to join the clubs or participate in the recreational activities offered by the Paris school. Xavier became increasingly introverted. He daydreamed, read, or, for companionship, played with the family cat. On a few occasions, when the cat became ill, the boy would nurse it back to health. When the family acquired a dog and it, too, became ill, he showed a unique talent for being able to heal it.

By the time Richier was about 13, he devoted as much of his spare time (which consisted of a few hours between working in the bakery, delivering bread and attending school) to animals. When a neighboring storekeeper had a sick dog, it was young Xavier who healed it. One early morning, when he found a wounded dog lying on the street, after having been struck by a bicycle rider who left the scene of the accident, young Xavier paused to look over the whimpering animal. He returned to the bakery with his undelivered rolls and breads—and the limping dog beside him. His father was disturbed that the deliveries had not been made. He berated the boy, told him to hurry and make his deliveries, since they needed this day's money to pay for flour and other supplies, not to mention the rent. Xavier was told to leave the dog in the bakery; he would care for it upon completion of his chores.

When the boy made the deliveries, he was greeted with scoldings for his lateness by many of the maids and cooks in these elegant homes. When he explained that he had paused to help care for a sick dog, one maid shouted that she did not care if the animal lived or died—that delivery of the rolls was more important.

Hearing this, Xavier Richier became all the more determined to avenge himself upon the wealthy who considered rolls more valuable than life.

When he returned home that day, he discovered that the

dog was gone. It had died, his parents told him; and they had disposed of it.

The boy wept. He blamed the wealthy for their callous attitudes. He would take vengeance.

Richier liked the science of healing and soon enrolled in a biology class in school. By the time he was 16, in 1926, he knew that he wanted to be a physician. He talked it over with his schoolteachers who arranged for him to be granted a scholarship to the Paris Medical College. His parents were, needless to say, very proud. They were poor and humble and they did not want their only child to follow in their footsteps. They insisted that he now devote all of his time to studying medicine.

The boy studied long and hard hours in the Paris Medical College. He went through his internship in the St. Cecelia Hospital in Paris and in 1936, at the age of 26, became a licensed physician. All that now remained for Richier to do was to open up an office. This he did. Various physicians attached to St. Cecelia Hospital liked his unique talent as a doctor and recommended patients to him. They even advanced small amounts of money to Xavier Richier, M.D., to help him establish his practice.

The young doctor was now eager to repay his parents for all they had done to help him. He wanted his father to close up the bakery. Soon he would save enough money to buy a home in which he hoped his parents could live in comfort and luxury for the rest of their lives.

But fate struck a bitter blow. In 1936, some four months after young Xavier became a physician, his father was struck by a car while delivering a basket of bread. The time had not yet come when Xavier earned money enough to support himself and his parents; and it was still necessary for the older Richier to work and make his own deliveries.

The father died on the way to the hospital. The owner of the speeding car, an influential and wealthy importer, had been hurrying to an antique auction, anxious to bid on a valuable piece of furniture. As soon as he showed identification to the police at the scene of the accident, he was released and continued on to the auction gallery where he bid and won the coveted antique furniture. While the importer was bidding, Xavier Richier's father died of a brain hemorrhage.

Left alone, Xavier's mother could find no solace and, in January, 1937, she succumbed to a heart attack.

Now Xavier Richier was all alone, and he felt his entire world collapsing. He had struggled through medical school in the hope of becoming rich enough to help his beloved parents live in comfort and happiness for the rest of their lives. Xavier had been completely devoted to his parents and he had few friends. Now that both were dead, he was more embittered than ever.

Xavier Richier was determined to avenge the deaths of his mother and father. He blamed his mother's heart attack on the strain caused by his father's death. And he resented the ease with which the careless, wealthy importer who had caused his father's death, was then able to walk out of court, all charges dropped, because he had been able to afford costly legal services.

The Paris courts ruled that the baker had crossed against the street light; that the accident was his own fault. Xavier Richier was furious at the callous decision of the court.

Dr. Richier was a courteous, reserved man. He was known and well liked by physicians at the *Faculté de Médecine de Paris* where he took postgraduate courses and additional training. He conversed with his colleagues at meetings and worked with them on research in the laboratory. But very little, if any, personal talk was ever exchanged.

By 1937, Xavier Richier had saved enough from his growing, lucrative practice to purchase a house on the outskirts of Paris. He never invited anyone to his home. When fellow physicians asked him why he never attended any of the social functions held in the homes of hospital personnel, or why he never asked people to come to his home, he would say, "I live my own life in my own way. I prefer to leave others alone. I prefer that they leave me alone."

Xavier Richier, M.D., soon concocted a very clever scheme. He acquired a set of books on antiques, read them through very thoroughly and made many notes. Soon, he felt sufficiently well versed to give a lecture on art and antiques. This was step one of his scheme. He would announce in some of the local Paris newspapers that he would be giving a talk on the joys of antique and art collecting. A small room in a meeting house would be rented for the occasion; and the lecture would be free. He would make certain that all those who attended the lecture knew that he was more than just a lover of fine art. He was a *physician*.

Those who attended his lectures were wealthy, lived in elegant homes; were art enthusiasts and were eager to listen to any talk about treasures and collecting. The time would come when they would require the services of a physician, and they immediately thought of the art enthusiast who was also a physician. It was easy to relate to Dr. Richier. They had much in common with the doctor. And so, Xavier Richier gained entrance to some of the wealthiest Parisian homes.

By day, he was a highly respected physician. By night, he became the mastermind of a unique art theft ring. While he, himself, never stole an art object, he directed others in the theft, paid them handsomely and safeguarded the stolen valuables in his newly acquired country home in Lievin. Here, in this northern French town, Dr. Richier could bask in the beauty of his acquisitions. Rarely, if ever, did he sell a single item.

His hoax consisted of matching wits with his victims. He had endeared himself to as many as 100 wealthy people. When he visited a wealthy patient, he made a mental blueprint of the patient's home, roughly sketched its layout and noted whatever priceless antiques and paintings he saw there. He would then try to assess their value and plan a robbery. Never did he participate. On the contrary, he always expressed sympathy to the victim over his or her loss. He even speculated as to how the theft might have been executed, all the while deriving great pleasure in knowing that the stolen objects were in his own home.

Richier's scheme was carefully thought out. He gathered together a group of cohorts, all of whom were medical students who had failed the difficult examinations and had been dismissed from the Paris Medical College. Since Dr. Richier lectured at the college, he knew which students passed and which had failed. He then made the acquaintance of the students who had failed, expressing understanding of their feelings of bitterness. He invited them to visit him in his office, and he said he would help them out of their dilemma.

In his office, he cleverly talked them into wreaking vengeance upon the society that had wronged them. The method would be simple, but effective.

The doctor outlined his hoax to his newly-found friends. He explained that when he, Dr. Richier, received a call from an ailing person who resided in a luxurious mansion or on a large estate, he would drive to the patient's home together with one or two of his associates. He would introduce them as his assistants. He would then proceed to examine the patient while the associate excused himself for one of a variety of reasons. The associate would walk through the house, noting what valuables were there, familiarizing himself with their location and, on presentation pads, make rough sketches of the layout of the house.

Upon the associate's return, the doctor would excuse himself for a few minutes. He, too, would examine the valuables and make quick notations as to their possible worth. When he returned to the patient, he, too, would be armed with a knowledge of the layout of the house.

As Dr. Richier and his aide drove away from the patient's home, they would discuss how to execute the robbery.

On one such visit, in the early 1950's, two of Richier's assistants accompanied him to the Château de Menars, near Bourges. It was known to be one of the most lavishly furnished homes in the countryside. The Château de Menars was owned by Jean-Louis Frontenant, one of the richest French wine merchants.

The trio came upon a collection that was deserving of display at the Louvre: furniture from the royal palaces of the fifteenth, sixteenth, seventeenth and eighteenth centuries; walls covered with rare tapestries brought in by merchant ships from all over the world; priceless vases, paintings, and statues; cases containing rare colorful gems. Seeing such treasures on the first visit, Dr. Richier told Jean-Louis Frontenant that he would have to return for another visit, to examine the merchant once again, so that he might better determine the nature of his ailment.

Two days later Richier returned, this time accompanied by two of his aides, who were well equipped with cameras. Dr. Richier entered one of the bedrooms and examined Jean-Louis

Frontenant; at the same moment, his aides were outside, taking picture after picture. In all, they took some 50 pictures in color of various art treasures in the house.

By now, Dr. Richier was aroused with excitement. This would be his greatest hoax. For the past dozen years, he had used this ruse to take various art treasures from various homes throughout Paris and surrounding environs. His home was filled with these valuables. But none would match the wealth that was in the Château de Menars. He wanted these possessions . . . or at least as many as could be carried away.

Dr. Richier now dispatched his aides to some of the leading appraisers in Paris. They were instructed to show the color pictures and get estimates of value. The doctor wanted to know if the objects in the Château were indeed worth stealing. When his aides returned with the estimates of value, the doctor decided that, yes, they would proceed with the robbery.

To the home of the wine merchant, the Château de Menars, the trusted aides returned a few evenings later. They were familiar with the layout, having accompanied the doctor on his visits to the patient at least seven times. They knew through which window to enter. They had carefully unlocked the window when they had been inside the last time, three days earlier.

Quietly, they took those objects they had decided were the most valuable. Then they made their exit from the same window through which they had entered. They carefully closed the window, but were unable to lock it from the outside. They gambled on the chance that no one would ever know it had been unlatched.

The very next day, Dr. Richier telephoned the patient to express his regrets, having heard the news on the radio:

"I think it best I come to see you now. This tension may raise your blood pressure. I will bring medicine with me."

Arriving at the home, alone, he used a ruse to go to the room where the missing objects had been. He quietly latched the window from within.

Police were at a loss to figure out how a thief had gained entrance to the house, knew exactly what to take, and left without leaving a single trace or clue. "It's as if the thief knew every inch of the house; as if he had lived here. He was so familiar with the house," said one police officer.

There were no fingerprints. No footprints. The thieves had worn gloves on their hands and socks over their shoes.

The hoax had inflated Dr. Richier's ego. He had taken revenge on the very wealthy who had spurned him in his youth and had taken the life of his father. By this time, his medical practice was extremely lucrative. He could afford to pay his aides handsome sums of money for their efforts, as well as for their silence.

Should the aides wish to blackmail him for more money, Richier carefully pointed out, they were his *accomplices,* and hardly in a position to do so. If they put the finger on him, they would be exposing themselves as well. They chose silence.

From all of his robberies, Dr. Richier accumulated antiques and objects of art worth close to two million dollars. He arranged them in his modest home, filling each room with various objects. His living quarters resembled a museum.

To further add fuel to the fire of his hoax, Richier often volunteered to help the police in their clues. Naturally, all such clues were meant to sidetrack the authorities.

Like other hoaxers and impostors, Xavier Richier, M.D., had become overly confident. Three days after the robbery at the Château, he visited a patient who lived in a beautiful mansion that had once been the residence of a member of royalty. There he saw an exquisite Ming vase. He whispered to an aide to photograph it.

Meanwhile, the doctor made the usual sketches of the layout of the house, noting its entrances and exits. Then he returned to examine and treat the patient and chat with him a bit.

Richier's aides took the photograph of the Ming vase and showed it to no less than ten different appraisers in and around Paris. Two days later, the mansion was robbed. Nothing was taken, except for the Ming vase.

The newspapers told of the robbery. As the appraisers read about it, they remembered the men who had shown them the pictures of this now stolen vase. They remembered that the same men had a few days earlier shown them pictures of other objects—the objects that had been stolen from the Château de

Menars. Several appraisers called one another to discuss the thefts; they described the men to each other, and were sure that these men could be linked to the robberies. They notified the police.

Common sense told the police one important fact: there was only one way that a photograph could have been taken of the objects in the Château de Menars and the Ming vase. Someone had come into the house and taken the photograph. They asked the two victims for a list of their most recent visitors.

Both lists had the same person as a recent visitor: the doctor. Also included were the doctor's aides, their names unknown.

So it was that the hoaxing doctor was apprehended.

Xavier Richier, M.D., was summoned to the stationhouse for questioning. He complied. He made an innocent appearance. When asked for the names of his aides, he began to fumble and falter. He now looked and acted suspicious. Under intensive questioning he broke down and admitted that he was the mastermind behind the hoax.

Where were these treasures?

He said they were at home.

The police went to his home and discovered a veritable treasure, a cache of the world's most valuable artworks, paintings and antiques.

Xavier Richier and his aides were arrested and imprisoned in Paris. The hoax that had plagued the ailing wealthy of France was now uncovered.

On March 3, 1953, the Supreme Court of Paris, France, issued life sentences to the doctor and his aides. All of the stolen treasures were gradually returned to their rightful owners.

It is said that Dr. Richier was not the least bit contrite over his apprehension. *Paris Match* of that date quoted him as saying, "I fooled the experts, I fooled heads of police departments. I have no regrets for what I have done!"

9

JAMES LANDIS

The Swindler of the U.S. Mint

THE U.S. MINT, housed in a heavily guarded, old brick building, is charged with the responsibility of printing paper currency. This currency is as valuable as the gold in Fort Knox, and America's most expert thieves and impostors have employed one ruse after another to gain access to it.

So safe and secure is the Mint that its officials have openly boasted, "Billions upon billions of dollars have been printed throughout these decades. But all we have lost is about one hundred dollars, and that has been due to clerical mistakes, misplacement and pilferage. Nobody can ever steal the money we make at the Bureau of Printing and Engraving."

Whether or not money could indeed be stolen from the Bureau was to be tested by a master impostor who would eventually go down in history as the only man who succeeded in doing so.

The hoaxer was James Landis, an employee of the Bureau of Printing and Engraving. Landis was average-looking, youngish, polite, efficient on the job, and possessing a good attendance record. His more intimate co-workers said that Landis was a sad person; his eyes were mournful. But inasmuch as he performed his work efficiently and honestly, no one gave a second thought to this side of his personality.

James was born in 1900, in Milwaukee, Wisconsin. He received a good education in Milwaukee, including several years of college. He had helped organize a Little League baseball team, and had participated in a number of other social activities in his home town. He worked as a printer but felt that opportunities were limited, so he uprooted himself and decided to move to a bigger city where opportunities might be more lucrative.

He came to the nation's capital in 1923, inquired about employment opportunities, and soon got a job at the Bureau of Printing and Engraving. He married a local schoolteacher, had two sons, joined local charitable organizations and actively participated in community religious life. James Landis appeared to be devoted to God, country and family.

But if Landis was devoted to God, country and family, he was dedicated to a goal more important than all three: he wanted to be a millionaire. As he later explained, "I could see myself clerking along in this job, as undistinguished as the millions of paper bills coming from the printing presses. I would be a nonentity, a nonperson, good only for face value. Good for nothing else. It was a frightening feeling. I wanted to have a lot of money that would earn me good interest. With that interest, I could take my wife and children to a South Pacific island and live a life of luxury and comfort.

"We could be free to travel the world over, visit all those places you usually only read about; we could go to the best restaurants, the best resorts, the best hotels.

"We could have everything that money could buy—and then some.

"So, looking at those millions upon millions of crisp bills coming off the presses of the U.S. Mint, I decided that I had to do something. I didn't want to become like those bills . . . one just like another. But I did want what those bills could give me—*luxury!*"

Landis had begun to reveal the motivation peculiar to most hoaxers and impostors: the need to succeed even if by illegal means, and the desire to do so by outsmarting experts and authorities. As the need to accomplish his goal grew stronger, James Landis set about to swindle the U.S. Mint.

James Landis' job at the Bureau of Printing and Engraving was a very ordinary one. He transported currency between the vaults and the packing machines. Now that he was determined to perpetrate his hoax, he carefully scrutinized the way the money was handled. He knew that newly minted $20 bills were assembled in stacks of 4,000. Wooden blocks were placed at either end of each stack. A machine would then take these "bricks," as they were called, to a special banding machine. Here, two steel bands were placed around them lengthwise and welded. Once the bricks were so banded, they were moved along a conveyor belt to another machine that wrapped them in heavy brown paper.

A special machine affixed a Treasury seal to one end of the finished package. A label stating the serial numbers of the bills, the date, and the number or initials of the packer was also glued onto the brick. Each brick, worth $80,000, was transported to a special vault within the Bureau's red brick building. Soon, they would be shipped to a Federal Reserve Bank.

James Landis noted that the Bureau sent inspectors daily throughout the plant to open the packages, verify the amount of their contents, and to record additional vital statistics, such as the amount of the money and the face value.

Once the inspection was completed, the brick would be closed and returned to the packing machine. The initials of the inspectors and the date were added to the outside of the brick.

To the ordinary eye, the inspection looked routine, but James Landis noted that when Bureau inspectors broke open the bricks, they would discard the wooden blocks, unbroken steel bands or Treasury seals into the trash. Also in the trash were various little scraps of paper and pieces of tags that had been torn open during the inspection process.

Landis rummaged through the trash. He saw a piece of wrapping paper, a wooden block and some Treasury seals. He realized that it would be possible to assemble these odds and ends and create bricks of his own, so, little by little, Landis collected as many scraps as possible and smuggled them out of the building. At night, while his wife busied herself with the children, Landis started to practice duplicating the bricks.

It took him close to three months before he came up with an imitation brick of money that appeared to be perfect. He could now proceed with his scheme. He would have an imitation brick of money ready to be substituted for the real brick; it would have to be a perfect switch.

He continued to perfect his imitation bricks of money. He knew that each label on the brick had its own number. Each morning, as the inspectors examined the bricks, they would attach a label with a specific number. How could he attach a label to the false brick if he did not know, in advance, what the number was to be?

Landis noted that the affixed numbers were not in numerical order. He could put on a label with any number and it would undoubtedly be passed through. But he needed *real* labels. He was able to obtain these from trash baskets and bins. Many times, inspectors would tear off a label from a master roll only to find that it had ripped in half. The inspectors would throw away the label and take a new one. So Landis went through the trash baskets, took out torn labels and glued them together so perfectly that they could pass for brand new labels.

So it was that the plan began.

On the morning of his planned hoax Landis would switch the real bricks with the false ones. He came to work on schedule, carrying with him a paper bag containing two counterfeit bricks. According to regulations, all packages had to be checked in a special room. Landis was supposed to check the bag and be given a receipt. He would be able to reclaim his possessions when he left the building after work. This was the daily routine.

Landis was prepared for this. But it was the Christmas holiday season and he knew that the guards would be somewhat lax. As Landis entered the building, the guard glanced at him routinely. Quietly, Landis walked to the checking booth with the seeming intention of checking his bag. Out of the corner of his eye, he saw the guard turn to another worker.

At that instant, Landis walked quickly down the hall, up a flight of stairs and into a men's room. In the corner of the room sat a huge wastebasket lined with a burlap bag. Landis reached into the burlap bag, and quickly inserted his own paper bag containing the bricks. He smoothed out the burlap bag knowing that the basket would not be emptied for at least another day.

He breathed easier as he made his way to the locker room to change into his working clothes. As he had every other day, Landis reported for duty in his slot, exactly on time. He began to work. First, he carefully cleared out the vaults, so that others would be able to work inside of them. He would soon carry the bricks, in serial sequence, from the machine that fettered them to the machine that wrapped them. When he completed loading the platform that would carry the bricks to the wrapping machine, he would have less than fifteen minutes before having to repeat the loading process.

There were many other workers around but all were involved in their tasks and paid little heed to what James Landis was now doing. He bent over, as if to pick up a piece of paper which he would then discard. He walked past the wrapping machine, and as he stared at the stack of newly-packaged $20 bricks, his heart pounded with excitement. He began to work with such lightning speed that he amazed himself. In a flash, he grabbed a pair of the $20 bricks, wrapped them in a sheet of paper and fled to a storage room that was rarely used, at the far end of the floor. There, he quickly unwrapped the two bricks and carefully tore off the package ends upon which the labels were affixed. He placed them in his pocket, and, using a pair of pliers, prepared to cut the steel bands.

Landis knew that the severing of the steel bands would cause an explosive noise. To counteract this, he put the unwrapped brick between both ankles. He then squeezed the pliers until the steel bands broke. Only a muffled sound could be heard. Landis' heart thumped as he gazed upon $160,000 worth of crisp $20 bills.

The money looked different to him than it had through all the years he had worked at the U.S. Mint: this money belonged to *him*.

Nervously, he continued his work. He removed a pair of brown paper bags from his pocket and stuffed them with the $160,000. He shoved the bags beneath a low platform in the abandoned storage room.

Breathing easier, he returned to the packing room in which he worked. It had all taken less than nine minutes; no one had even missed him.

Encouraged, and more determined than ever to continue his hoax, he proceeded to perform his normal activities for several hours—until his "coffee break." Then, quickly and quietly, he walked to the men's room where he had hidden the dummy bricks early in the day. From his pocket, he took the genuine labels and placed them on the radiator flanges. He waited until they were perfectly dry. He removed the dummy bricks from the bottom of the wastebasket and took the bricks and labels into the toilet booth. He locked the door. Using glue from a tiny bottle which he had pilfered from the packing room, he secured the labels to the bricks.

Landis looked at his work: it was perfect. But there was something yet to be taken care of. Downstairs, the real bricks were in a state of constant motion. The counterfeits had to be inserted in exactly the same spots from which the stolen bricks had been, before being removed nearly three hours before.

Landis stole a special rotary stamp out of the packing room. He would stamp a new date on the label of the false bricks. It would look as if the inspector had already checked, rewrapped and returned the bricks. He would then add a forged set of inspector's initials. With this plan carefully thought out, he returned to the packing room.

With him, in the paper bag he had brought in the morning, he carried the counterfeit bricks. A few seconds later, he had made the careful switch by depositing the fake bricks in the spaces previously occupied by the real bricks. He properly stamped the fake bricks. To all outward appearances, they looked real. They looked as if they had passed inspection.

For the balance of the morning and throughout the afternoon, James Landis continued with his routine work. Knowing that his plan had worked smoothly thus far, he felt strangely at ease.

When the work day ended at 6 P.M., Landis went into the locker room, changed into his street clothes, draped a spare pair of work pants over one arm, and sneaked into the storage room. He gathered the two bags of real currency that he had earlier hidden beneath the platform.

But a problem arose. Landis had several paper bags, but they would not be large enough to hold both the $160,000 and his work pants. And he would need the work pants to complete his plan successfully. So he stuffed most of the money—nearly $130,000—into the larger paper bag and placed the work pants on top of the bundle. He then filled the smaller bag with $30,000 and hid it beneath the platform to be taken out the next day.

Landis knew that the storage room was seldom, if ever, used; he felt sure that the money would be safe temporarily.

He headed for the building exit, prepared to be stopped by one of the guards charged with the responsibility of inspecting all packages. As Landis passed one of the guards he opened his bag, pulled out one leg of the work pants and nonchalantly continued walking. The guard nodded, then turned to the next man. James Landis walked out into the street and headed home with his treasure. He anticipated greeting his wife, who knew nothing of his scheme.

Later, he said, "I worked under the belief that it would take a very very long time before anyone caught the loss. Meanwhile, every single day, I would take out several bricks of real money, substituting the false bricks.

"I felt I could continue for a year. You see, the bricks are stored in the vaults of the Mint for at least two months. Afterwards, they are shipped to any of the twelve Federal Reserve Banks.

"In these banks, the bricks are stored for several more months.

"Then, they are shipped to local banks. More delays. Finally, when they are opened, the loss could be discovered. But all in all, it could take as long as a year before the fake or blank white paper would be discovered."

But when the money loss was discovered, wouldn't the authorities release the serial numbers? Wouldn't the money be "hot" and risky.

"Yes," was his answer. "But I didn't take the stolen money and stash it away. No, I started to spend it. Oh, not on wild parties or the horse races. I would use the $20 bills for every little purchase. Then, when I changed these 'hot' bills for good ones, I put the other cash in a vault.

"By the time the loss would be discovered and serial numbers released, hundreds of thousands of $20 bills would be cashed in, all over the country . . . even the world.

"They could never trace them back to me." Landis felt quite secure because so many hands touched the bricks during the process, that fingerprints could never be identified as his.

James Landis knew enough of the law to realize that when the discovery was made, the Secret Service would begin an intensive investigation. But it would be a case of going around and around in circles. The "hot" money would already be in circulation.

Landis decided that if he kept stealing an average of $100,000 or more per week, he would need help in spending or exchanging it. He looked to a very close friend of his, Claude Armstrong, a co-worker at the Mint.

Why he confided in Claude and trusted him is unknown. As with many clever hoaxers, in some respects Landis was very naive.

He offered Armstrong a share of the loot if he would agree to spend the bills and accumulate the change. In this manner, James Landis would be able to work more quickly. Claude agreed.

Before long, Landis and Armstrong grew more greedy. They let four other co-workers in on the scheme.

"We divided the hot $20 bills amongst the six of us. We all made small purchases with these bills. The change or 'good' money would then be put into a special box which we would divide up later on. If all went according to plan, the six of us could net about a half million or a million dollars each . . . within one year or so.

"Then we could make plans to resign from the job. We would do so slowly, so that we would not call attention to ourselves. It was all so perfect."

But there was a slight flaw. In outward appearance, Landis's imitation bricks seemed perfect. But when touched, there was a difference. Originally, when the banding machine slipped on the steel bands, a great deal of weight was added to each brick. Landis' homemade bands were lighter . . . at least three pounds lighter than the original eight pounds per brick.

At it happened, one morning an inspector on a routine check picked up two bricks to examine. He found a discrepancy in their weights, and concerned, he notified his superior. Together, they opened the bricks. Arbitrarily, the inspector selected two of the false bricks . . . and slips of paper . . . not money—spilled out before their eyes. They were shocked.

Secret Service detectives spread the word to banks and merchants. They were instructed to ask for identification from anyone offering a $20 bill. The serial numbers of the stolen bills were provided for them. Landis and his associates tried to cash in some of the bills at a local food store. The merchant made a quick check of the serial numbers and saw they were some of the stolen bills. The merchant excused himself, saying that he had to go to the rear of the store for change and immediately contacted the Secret Service. Within a short time, the police had arrived and arrested Landis and his associates. But not before close to one million dollars had been swindled from the U.S. Mint. Some of the money was still in the vaults of the criminals . . . but not all. While Landis was frugal, his associates had spent "their" money wildly.

"It was a good try," was all James Landis said as he (along with his cohorts) was led away from his tearful wife and children to serve a ten-year sentence in Alcatraz. "For a while . . . I almost had it . . . a perfect hoax for getting money . . . all we wanted . . . forever and ever. . . ."

It was a hoax that rocked the very foundation of the Bureau of Printing and Engraving. It nearly worked.

10

CLIFFORD IRVING

The Howard Hughes Hoaxer

ON DECEMBER 7, 1971, the McGraw-Hill Book Company
in New York issued a press release to the media. At first glance,
it appeared to be just another press release heralding the publication of a book that promised to take the world by storm.
But upon closer examination, it became clear that this book
was bound to make front-page news. It was, after all, an autobiography of the mysterious and elusive multi-billionaire
Howard Hughes.

Howard Hughes, a billionaire involved in real estate, air-
lines, hotels, tool manufacturing and other assorted enterprises
had successfully avoided the public's scrutiny when, at the age
of 51 in 1957, he made his last brief appearance and vanished
from sight.

Everyone talked about this "bashful billionaire"; his whereabouts were the subject of a perpetual guessing game. On the
one hand he was involved in many national and international
activities, political and otherwise, and on the other hand he
lived the life of a recluse.

As soon as the news release appeared in the press, the public
could hardly wait for the book to appear. The world had
always been fascinated by this mystery man, and the opportunity to get to know the *real* Howard Hughes promised to be
a treat. Although the book was announced as an autobiography,
the actual writing, according to the release, was done with the
help of a professional writer, Clifford Irving.

McGraw-Hill explained that Howard Hughes would celebrate his sixty-sixth birthday on Christmas Eve, 1971, and that
a close bond of friendship existed between him and Clifford
Irving. The two had met approximately 100 times "in various

motel rooms and parked cars throughout the Western Hemi-
sphere." During these meetings, Clifford Irving had tape-
recorded the remembrances of the bashful billionaire, and was
then to fashion it into an exciting book.

The book would contain a massive 230,000 words. It would
reveal just about everything there was to know about Howard
Hughes. McGraw-Hill reportedly paid close to one million dollars to both Clifford Irving and Howard Hughes for publication rights. *Life* magazine had purchased the rights to publish
several installments of the book.

Press interviews were set up with Clifford Irving. Irving
described his meetings with Howard Hughes, a man who had
not been seen or heard from in 15 years.

McGraw-Hill explained exactly why Howard Hughes sought
to break his self-imposed silence. Quoting from what the publishers claimed was part of the Introduction to the forthcoming
book, Howard Hughes revealed:

"I believe that more lies have been printed and told about
me than about any living man—therefore, it was my purpose
to write a book which would set the record straight and restore
the balance. . . .

"Biographies about me have been published before—all of
them misleading and childish. I am certain that in the future
more lies and rubbish will appear. The words in this book—
other than some of the questions which provoked them—are
my own spoken words.

"The thoughts, opinions and recollections, the descriptions
of events and personalities, are my own. I have not permitted
them to be emasculated or polished, because I realized, after
the many interviews had been completed and transcribed, that
this was as close as I could get to the elusive, often painful
truth.

"I have lived a full life and, perhaps, what may seem a
strange life—even to myself. I refuse to apologize, although I
am willing now to explain as best I can. Call this my autobiography. Call it my memoirs. Call it what you please. It is
the story of my life in my own words."

These were the first words in the Howard Hughes book, as
written for him by Clifford Irving. It was considered *the* interview of the century. Ever since 1957, hundreds upon hundreds

of journalists from all over the world had requested an interview with Howard Hughes. But every attempt was unsuccessful. There was no end to the telephone calls and trips that reporters and writers made to the many residences in which the recluse was said to reside, but to no avail. The one place that was usually besieged was the Brittannia Beach Hotel in Nassau, Bahamas, where Hughes was known to occupy the entire ninth floor. But no one—until Irving came along—ever scored. "There is no record of a Mr. Hughes listed here," was the usual response.

So, when it became known that a Hughes autobiography was about to be published, it became one of the most exciting stories of the century.

Who was the miracle man, Clifford Irving, who managed to interview Howard Hughes? And how had Irving managed to become close friends with Howard Hughes—a man who, reportedly, had no close friends?

Clifford Irving was born in New York on November 5, 1930, the only child of a mother who was said to be aloof and distant. His father was a successful cartoonist. He had created "Pottsy," a popular comic strip which depicted the activities of a plump and happy policeman. It ran for years in the *New York Sunday News.*

As a youngster, Clifford was an average student. He seemed to do well enough in school. He graduated, in 1947, from the High School of Music and Art where those who knew him reported that he was popular with the girls, and was good at football.

His college years were spent at Cornell University, where his desire to write emerged. He studied all the creative arts and was well-versed in music, art, ballet, and opera, in addition to all types of literature: novels, poetry, nonfiction. Ernest Hemingway had greatly influenced him and Irving's later writings seem to bear this out.

Clifford Irving was named president of the *Pi Lambda Phi* fraternity in his senior year. At the age of 20, he married a lovely girl whom he had met on campus, Nina Wilcox. "They were a golden couple," was how some friends put it. "They looked and acted the part of being prince and princess. They had everything going for them."

But two years later, they split up. Now Clifford decided to put his education to use. He travelled across America, worked at odd jobs, and finally ended up working for a New York newspaper. He also began writing his first novel, *On a Darkling Plain*. He put in a great many months of work, writing and revising. He sold it to Putnam, in 1956, for a modest sum.

Clifford Irving was encouraged. He wrote a second novel, *The Losers*, which was not very successful. But he had now discovered the Balearic Islands and Ibiza, a settlement near Majorca, off the coast of Spain. Here, in this sun-splashed paradise of the Atlantic, where many artists and writers congregated, he met an English girl, Claire Lydon. They fell in love and married.

But the marriage had problems. There were suggestions of infidelity. It might have ended in divorce had not a tragedy occurred. While the couple was in California, Claire was out riding with the wife of a novelist friend. The car skidded and went off the road near Monterey. Claire was killed together with her companion.

Clifford felt the effect despite the strained relationship that had existed with Claire. He escaped by throwing himself into his work. First, he produced a low-key western, *The Valley*, which was accepted by McGraw-Hill. Then followed a fourth novel, *The Thirty-Eighth Floor*. And although his writings had been accepted for publication, Irving was moody. He was not receiving the recognition he craved and felt he deserved.

He started to travel. During his travels, he met a lovely English girl, Fay Brooke. She became his third wife.

Clifford Irving now started to socialize with the Hollywood moguls, hoping that they would purchase the film rights to his books. This would provide for him the great leap forward—from obscurity to fame and "celebrityhood."

But there was an artificiality about Hollywood that did not appeal to Irving, so he and his third wife, Fay (with a young son, Josh), moved to Ibiza. There, basking in the warm sun, and relaxing in the balmy climate, the writer was able to examine himself more closely. He wanted to be "big." He wanted to do something very big. But the more he contemplated his prospects for the future, the more confused he became. He was irritable, and his wife found it impossible to live with him. In 1965, they divorced.

Two years alter, he married another girl. She was an artist living on Ibiza. Edith Sommer. Edith was a lovely, refined girl. Her father was a Swiss businessman, and he provided her with a comfortable annuity. She had been married once before, and was now eager for a stable and durable marriage. She was convinced that Clifford Irving was the man who could give her the life she so desperately craved. And so Clifford Irving and Edith Sommer became man and wife.

On the island, Clifford became friendly with another writer, Richard Suskind, and the two of them decided that it would be nice to work together. While their friendship was maturing, Clifford wrote his next novel, a book entitled *Fake!* It was a study of a master hoaxer and impostor, an art forger, named Elmyr de Hory. This book got good reviews and Irving was offered good advances for future books. As it turned out, de Hory wanted to share in the royalties of *Fake!* which was his biography, and he filed suit. Clifford Irving's publisher, McGraw-Hill, put a hold on all future books submitted by Irving until the suit was resolved.

At this time, Clifford Irving and Richard Suskind decided to collaborate on a book. It was to be a work that would startle the world. They had both been to Las Vegas and heard much about the Howard Hughes mystique. Any library would yield thousands of newspaper stories, pictures, articles, and books about Hughes. But in all their research they could not find an autobiography of Howard Hughes that had been published in book form. They were convinced that the time was ripe for a book about the man of mystery.

Clifford Irving started the project in 1968 by writing a letter to his publisher, McGraw-Hill, in which he stated that he had contacted Howard Hughes. The letter said:

> I sent a copy of *Fake!* some time ago to Howard Hughes, and to my surprise received a note of thanks and praise from him. Some wheels are beginning to turn in my brain. Do you know if there is any biography of Hughes, or anything in the works for the near future? Let me know, but please don't mention it to anyone.

The editors took the bait.

Before long, Clifford Irving was seated in the offices of McGraw-Hill showing letters he had received from Howard Hughes (signed H. R. Hughes) and discussing the proposed book. Hughes had reportedly said that he was displeased with the inaccurate biographies written about him and wanted to write one to clear up all the errors and mistakes.

The publishers were ecstatic. They hastily agreed to pay $100,000 with the signing of the contract, another $100,000 when the research was completed, and then a big $300,000 when the manuscript was completed.

McGraw-Hill wanted Hughes to sign the contract, and for them to witness it. But Irving said that Hughes was still shy of the public and would not permit it. He said he would take the contract to Puerto Rico, where Hughes was temporarily staying, for his signature. This was done. He returned with the contract, signed by Howard Hughes.

The contract contained clauses in which McGraw-Hill agreed to keep the project in the strictest confidence. It also contained a clause explaining how Clifford Irving would pay Hughes:

> The money will be deposited as designated verbally or in writing by H. R. Hughes for deposit in any bank account by H. R. Hughes . . . and shall be paid (by Clifford Irving) within 15 days after receipt of payment from the Publisher.

It appeared that Irving had such a good relationship with Hughes that the billionaire was satisfied with being paid by Irving.

It was all part of a carefully calculated plan. No news was to be given to the press until the book was finished and all financial transactions were complete. This meant that no one, not even the *real* Howard Hughes, would know of this hoax until all the money was received by Clifford Irving.

McGraw-Hill attempted to protect itself in one way. Since they had no direct contact with Hughes, they wanted assurance that the right person was being paid. The checks were, therefore, made payable to H. R. Hughes.

In the weeks that followed, letters supposedly written by Howard R. Hughes were delivered by Clifford Irving to McGraw-Hill. These concerned the handling of the biography and the subsidiary rights sales. There was little doubt that Hughes was participating in the book, and that everything was proceeding according to schedule.

At one point, when McGraw-Hill had some doubts and misgivings about the project, they asked handwriting experts to verify the Hughes signatures on the letters they had been receiving. The experts checked specimens they had available from authentic sources and compared the handwritings. Yes, the experts said, Hughes did write these letters.

Checks made payable to H. R. Hughes were later deposited and cashed through the Swiss Credit Bank.

The manuscript was finally completed in 1971. It was given to the publishers, who went over it line by line. There was no doubt about its authenticity. The little phrases, the nuances, the small catch-words, every detail (which the authors had carefully researched) was absolutely authentic. The publishers were convinced they had a best-seller on their hands, and they congratulated Clifford Irving and Richard Suskind for the fine job they had done in preparing the book.

When reprint rights were offered to *Life* magazine, *Life* called in one of their favorite journalists, Frank McCulloch, who had interviewed Hughes in 1957. He read through the entire book. He felt it was authentic. But then, the strangest thing happened. McCulloch received a telephone call from Howard Hughes, who, in his familiar, nasal twang, said that he had read the book, and that it was a hoax. He denied ever meeting Clifford Irving or Richard Suskind.

When confronted with this charge, Irving said that it was untrue. He said that the man who called McCulloch was not Hughes, but an impostor. McCulloch was admittedly baffled. The book appeared to be authentic. Who other than Hughes could have known all the details included in it?

But by now, *Life* was cautious. It brought in a team of experts to pore over the book. Bit by bit, minor errors were unearthed. Various facts appeared either to be exaggerated or avoided. There was a strong suspicion that the book was not as represented.

McGraw-Hill was startled. Had it been duped?

As Clifford Irving and Richard Suskind basked in the warm Ibiza sunshine, New York publishers and attorneys searched for more clues to prove that these writers were frauds, if indeed, they were that at all.

Handwriting experts began to doubt the authenticity of Hughes' signature on letters and checks. Howard Hughes, himself, was forced to break his silence. For the first time in 14 years, on January 7, 1972, in a statement made over the telephone, he declared that the book was a fraud. Voice experts taped his trans-world telephone call, and verified that it was indeed the voice of the billionaire.

Soon, they learned that a bank account had been opened under the name of Helga R. Hughes. Checks payable to H. R. Hughes had been cashed through this account.

Who was Helga R. Hughes?

Helga was Edith Irving, the wife of the author.

The legal battle began.

Clifford Irving, Edith Irving and Richard Suskind were issued summonses, and with their lawyers they came to New York to face the charges.

Why did they think they could get away with such a hoax? After all, it was obvious that after the book was published, Howard Hughes would deny its authenticity.

Clifford Irving later told the court that he had assumed that since Hughes had vanished from sight for at least 15 years, he might have died. On the other hand, if alive, he would not want to cause a stir; that might necessitate an appearance in court—and rather than making a public appearance, Hughes might prefer to remain silent. After all, other books had been written about him, and he probably disliked them. but took no measures to challenge them.

Irving based all his actions on this one premise: Hughes wanted anonymity. Hughes hated to travel. He did not want to attract anyone's attention. He was a recluse and wanted to remain one. Irving gambled that Hughes would remain true to what seemed to be his lifestyle, that he would remain silent. If all this were true, Clifford Irving would be accorded his place in the world; he would be the biographer of Howard Hughes, and the author of a best seller.

It was all a gamble—and it failed.

Close to one million dollars had been swindled by Clifford Irving and his associate hoaxers. The Irvings were placed on trial in 1972 in New York. Federal authorities charged them with having perpetrated a hoax on the McGraw-Hill Book Co. After intensive questioning and cross-examination, both admitted their guilt. Each was sentenced to a three to five year prison term, *not* to be served concurrently. Clifford Irving served his term first, and was released on parole in late 1974. Edith then began her prison sentence; she was released on parole in early 1975. Rather than resuming a life together, the Irvings decided on a separation, although they did not divorce.

Both Clifford and Edith were determined to continue in their chosen professions: writing and painting. He began work on a book, unpublished as of this writing, which will tell the detailed story of his scheme.

McGraw-Hill lost a great deal of money from the affair. That which was not spent by Irving was refunded. But more than money, the highly respected publishing firm lost a great deal of prestige.

As for Irving, although his plan failed, he did receive worldwide attention. For a while at least, he had become an important figure. Basically, this is what had been missing from his life, and for a brief moment, he found it.

11

ALCEO DOSSENA

Duplicator of Masterpieces

ONE OFTEN FEELS A COMBINATION of intimidation
and adoration when looking at the rare paintings, sculpture
and sacred art objects on display within the hallowed walls of
imperious and haughty museums. The directors of these museums are considered to be several notches "above" all others in
the field of artistic endeavor. Sometimes even the artists themselves are accorded less respect than the art directors who
decide whether or not their creations are worthy of display.

No one at the Boston Museum of Fine Arts ever suspected
that one of their treasures, purchased for over $100,000 in
September, 1922, was a fake. When the Italian Renaissance
sculpture, the "Mino Tomb," was purchased, the museum was
extremely proud of its latest acquisition. Some of the world's
greatest scholars and art connoisseurs flocked to Boston. All
pronounced it a work of rare beauty. The "Mino Tomb" had
undergone extensive tests and examinations before its purchase.
After exhaustive research, scholars who considered their decisions inviolate vouched for the "Tomb's" authenticity.

Directly after the Boston Museum of Fine Arts had for-
warded payment for the purchase, it received a letter from
London. The letter came from Sir Eric Robert Dalrymple
Maclagan, head of the famous Victoria and Albert Museum.
He addressed his remarks to the director of the Boston Museum,
Mr. George Harold Edgell. In essence, Sir Eric wrote that he
doubted that the "Mino Tomb" sculpture was authentic. In
fact, said he, various sources had claimed that it was a fraud,
an imitation; Sir Eric promised further investigation.

So it was that the Boston Museum found itself the victim
of a shameful scandal, a scandal which had actually begun
years before.

In June, 1919, a meeting of the museum heads was held in the Hofmuseum of Vienna. Directors of the world's leading art institutions were chatting about the various items available for sale, exchange or loan.

The director of the Hofmuseum, Dr. Gustavo Gluck, told of a lovely new piece of art that he had heard was available for purchase:

"It is a beautifully carved memorial tomb of a Princess of Italy. It was created by Mino da Fiesole. You know him as the very talented 15th century Florentine sculptor. It would be quite an acquisition."

The director of the Boston Museum, Philip K. Fletcher, arched his eyebrows. "Mino da Fiesole was a great artist and there might be room for one of his works in our museum. Of course, he was not the very greatest . . . but he did possess talent . . . and he could be worthy of a little space on our main floor." He would give it his consideration.

Dr. Gluck showed him various photographs of the sculpture which would come to be known as the "Mino Tomb." "It is not yet available, but it is being considered for sale."

So word began to spread throughout the art capitals of Europe and America that the "Mino Tomb" might be available for acquisition in the very near future.

Months later, Charles H. Hawes, associate director of the Boston Museum, was busy preparing several catalogues and special exhibits when he received a telephone call from a professor of fine arts at nearby Wellesley.

"I hear that the 'Mino Tomb' is available for purchase," said Professor Hawes. "We have several art enthusiasts who would be interested in financing such a purchase. They prefer to remain anonymous. Perhaps you would consider it?"

Hawes knew that the "Mino Tomb" dated back to the Italian Renaissance, a period during which many sculptures were created, few of which had survived the centuries. To possess any object from this period would be quite prestigious. And so, the Boston Museum began to entertain thoughts of acquiring the "Mino Tomb."

The Boston Museum requested a set of photographs of the "Tomb" from Dr. Gluck of the Hofmuseum of Vienna, who said he could easily have them prepared. Upon arrival and subsequent examination of the photographs, the museum curators were impressed. Except for a slight crack that extended through the central slab, the marble effigy of a reclining figure was perfect. Beneath the figure was a sarcophagus upon which she appeared to sleep.

Experts agreed that the slight crack in the marble only heightened the aesthetic beauty of the piece. Over the centuries the crack seemed to have become edged in a rich, golden hue. Whispering voices of past centuries issued forth from the statue. To merely observe the sculpture was to bridge the gap of time: to hold it in one's hands was to be one with the artists of the Italian Renaissance.

The Boston Museum began to think in terms of an actual purchase. They learned that the sleeping figure was currently owned by a Florentine dealer who was only mildly interested in selling the treasure. They would have to negotiate.

Originally, the "Tomb" had been offered to several Vienna museums—all had gently turned it down. They discovered that the custodian of the former Imperial Museum in Vienna, one of the most respected world scholars of Italian Renaissance sculpture, had expressed some doubts about its great value and authenticity.

The custodian said he had never before heard of the "Mino Tomb." While he was not, he hastened to add, ruling on its authenticity, he doubted that the sculpture was actually a work of the Italian Renaissance period. The lines of the face, he said, were not characteristic of the period; it looked too sentimental and even modern. This was not to say that the sculpture was a fake—but there was just a slight shadow of a doubt, and that was sufficient reason to preclude its acquisition by the Viennese museum.

In view of this, experts at the Boston Museum decided to investigate. They decided to determine for themselves whether or not the sculpture was authentic. They had confidence in their ability to determine its true value.

A group of experts went to Italy in 1920 to view the "Mino Tomb." It was housed in a famous old Florentine castle, the Casa Davanzati, known for its collection of Italian masterpieces. The top experts scrutinized it closely, examining its every detail. They agreed: the "Mino Tomb" *was* authentic.

Negotiations were held and a price of $100,000 was agreed upon. It would only be a matter of time and the Mino Tomb would be in the Boston Museum.

The art world buzzed with the exciting news of a new art discovery. While it was still in Italy, a few chosen experts were permitted to fondle this magnificent treasure. They reported that when loving fingers ran over the chiseled features of the marble lady, they could feel the brilliantly crafted planes that were so gentle that only an expert could detect them; the gradations were almost imperceptible. It was a work of holy art.

The Boston Museum awaited the arrival of the "Mino Tomb." In September of 1922, it became their own.

The reclining sculptured figure was that of Maria Catharine Savelli, the youngest daughter of a powerful Italian family. The Savellis owned the Castle Gandolfo which was later donated to the Vatican for use as a papal residence; in fact, two members of the Savelli family later became popes themselves. But fate, unconcerned with the family's power and influence, dealt the Savellis a bitter blow: Maria mysteriously and unexpectedly died. To immortalize her, Mino da Fiesole had created a sculpture to show that she was not dead, but sleeping eternally. It was called the "Mino Tomb."

Following Maria's death, the Savelli family endured one tragedy after another. Shortly before Columbus made his voyage to the New World, the Savelli family ceased to exist. With them went all records and information about the "Mino Tomb." The sculptor, Mino da Fiesole, remained somewhat obscure throughout the centuries. Only the silent memorial of the sleeping Maria remained.

About four years after the Boston Museum acquired the "Mino Tomb," a scandal erupted in Italy. An unknown sculptor, Alceo Dossena, filed suit against Fasoli & Palesi, a firm that hired him to create "authentic works of art" of the various classical periods. In his suit, Alceo Dossena charged that he had been promised payment of $100,000 for creating "works of art" (like the sleeping figure)—cracks, stains, and all—and that he had received less than $6,000.

Dossena also alleged that he had originally been told that his creations would be sold only for decorative purposes. He had now discovered, however, that his works were being passed off as genuine antiques, and were being sold for very high prices.

Dossena claimed that he had been duped; he wanted full payment. To prove his claim, he said that almost all of the sculptured works of art he had created had a microscopic flaw. He had chipped off a small piece of stone from each of his works and kept it for matching; and if it were ever necessary to prove that he had indeed created these sculptures, he was prepared to do so.

When Fasoli and Palesi denounced him as an impostor, Alceo Dossena countered with the claim that many of his works were being displayed in leading museums throughout the world. "Millions upon millions have been spent for ancient sculptures that I created in my *atelier*," he said. "The Metropolitan Museum in New York, the museums in Cleveland, Munich, Berlin and the Frick museums have my works of art. Many marbles attributed to the ancients were created by myself. Hoaxers passed them off as authentic."

By 1923, the art world was in an uproar. Museum directors started to carefully examine their recently purchased masterpieces.

The Cleveland Museum had paid close to $80,000 for two masterpieces of the "Madonna," purported to have been sculptured some five centuries before.

Quickly, the art experts had the masterpieces X-rayed. They were shocked to discover modern nails hiding behind the gilt. The X-rays also revealed that slivers (marble chips) were missing; Alceo had these chips in his *atelier*. The experts were stunned: Alceo was a forger!

But could Alceo Dossena be considered guilty of imposture? He, himself, had not sold these treasures to the public. He had created them on assignment for Fasoli & Palesi, who, in turn, sold them to dealers. The dealers passed them off as authentic.

Fasoli & Palesi denied knowing Dossena. They had, they said, acquired these masterpieces from private dealers. Dossena, they claimed, was a forger who, himself, sold these objects to dealers. The affair became more and more muddled. The scandal threatened to bring down the crown heads of the art world. The experts had been duped and would be disgraced.

John Marshall, a leading archeologist and expert in classical art was called into the case by the Boston Museum of Fine Arts which was concerned about the authenticity of its very recent acquisition, the "Mino Tomb." He was assigned the task of viewing various masterpieces and determining their authenticity. He was soon joined by Gisela M. A. Richter, curator of classical sculpture at the Metropolitan Museum of Art in New York.

No convincing proof existed as yet that Dossena had perpetrated a hoax. He had sold art reproductions to a *dealer*, not to the public. Marshall and Richter would have to visit art dealers and museums throughout the world to determine whether Dossena had indeed sold phony art works directly to the public.

They sailed to Europe and visited many museums in London, Paris, Vienna, Prague and Budapest. They met many private art collectors and from one of them did receive the missing fragments that had been carefully chipped from the finished masterpieces. This collector had obtained them from the floor of Dossena's studio, during a visit. He had kept them, thinking they were of value. The collector offered them to Marshall and Richter.

In the midst of the investigation, John Marshall fell ill and died. This left Gisela Richter alone to continue the search. She relied upon the copious notes that Marshall had kept, outlining the investigation. She continued on, until she reached Rome. There she talked with various dealers and learned that Alceo Dossena favored a wine that was served at a special sidewalk cafe. Richter visited the cafe; she spotted Alceo. When confronted, the angry Italian, gesturing wildly, argued that he was the victim of a conspiracy.

But only when Gisela Richter said that if he did not tell the truth, she would have him arrested on a charge of forgery, did he calm down. He feared arrest. He did not want to spend the rest of his life as a criminal in prison. So it was that he agreed to talk to Gisela Richter in his studio.

He told his story quite plainly:

"You see, I took photographs of every work of art I created before I sold it to those thieves. See? I have a method of time-staining. I know how to create cracks so they look weathered. I know how to smooth out the sculpture so that it feels as soft as silk. Yes, it is all imitation. But let me tell you, I sold them to Fasoli & Palesi as imitations—not as authentic discoveries. Those thieves were the ones who claimed they were authentic. I want them arrested!"

Newspapers all over the world headlined the story. But Alceo Dossena, far from being condemned, was hailed as something of a hero. Even if he had duplicated masterpieces, he was a genius in his own right. His *atelier* was soon crowded with patrons who paid enormous sums of money for his "re-creations." The wealthy Prince Borghese gave him a blank check for a portrait of his Princess to be carved in the mode of the Early Renaissance.

Members of nobility and royalty commissioned assignments which they would use to decorate their homes and estates. It became very prestigious to own a Dossena "fake masterpiece." Alceo, himself, was not considered a hoaxer; only his *works* were considered hoaxes—and everyone clamored for them.

But the directors of the Boston Museum were not very cheerful at all. Angered at having been defrauded in their purchase of the "Mino Tomb," they decided to call in new investigators. One expert examined the inscription on the sculpture. It bore the date 1430. The expert quietly announced: "It is a fake. If you had taken the time to look up Mino da Fiesole in the biographies of sculptors and artists, you would have noted that he was born in 1431."

The directors burned deep red for shame. If any of them had taken a few moments of time to research such a simple fact, they could have saved $100,000, and the shame that accompanies having been duped.

Further investigation confirmed that the size and shape of the lettering in the inscription was not yet developed at the time when the Mino da Fiesole was alleged to have been created. It could not be authentic; sculptures of such size and shape came into being only after 1500.

Investigators from museums in New York, London, Paris, Vienna, Prague, Budapest, Warsaw, Moscow, Athens and Rome were called in to examine the statue and to offer opinions about its authenticity—or forgery. The Boston Museum still hoped to save face by finding proof that the "Mino Tomb" was authentic. Still more exhaustive tests were made using chemicals, cameras and microscopes. Of all the tests, X-rays proved to be the most conclusive. The ultraviolet ray acted as a surface-finder. It was beamed on the "Mino Tomb" and the strange purplish glow revealed certain creases, certain grains of stone by which the age of the sculpture could be determined.

As soon as the first X-ray tests were completed, the experts removed a small cross section of marble. The marble was ground up until it was very fine, almost transparent. The resultant liquid was placed on a glass slide and inserted under a powerful microscopic lens. The age of the sculpture could now be determined: the clearer the marble, the newer it was.

Using another test, experts viewed a cross section of the marble through a beam of polarized light. They made photographs of its rainbow hues. By classifying these hues, they were able to determine the origin of the stone quarry from which the marble was obtained. The rest was easy. A determination could quickly be made as to whether or not the stone out of which the 'Mino Tomb" had been fashioned was as old as it was purported to be—or even if the marble was from the vicinity from which it was assumed to come. The experts concluded that the stone was fairly new, from the 20th century, and that it did not come from the site suggested. Such marble quarries in Rome had not even been discovered during the Italian Renaissance.

But there were still some museum directors from London, Paris and New York who doubted these conclusions. They refused to admit that they had been duped.

So, the investigators continued to probe more deeply. They took microscopic cuts from the sculpture's surface and projected these cuts on a large screen in the darkroom of a chemical laboratory. They then made comparative studies with specimens from real antiques and known duplications.

"We can determine whether or not a work of sculptured art is authentic by breaking down the surface crystal," they explained. "Then we measure the depth, intensity and the characteristics of the staining. Yes, there is a difference between old and newly cut marbles. It is like the difference between dirty and clean hands. An old work of marble has soot and dirt, gathered and accumulated throughout the ages. A new or forged work will not have much dirt. If it is faked, we can determine that, too."

Their examinations showed that, yes, the "Mino Tomb" was authentic. It had been created during the Italian Renaissance and had passed from one dealer to the other throughout the centuries; each one had helped to restore it. The statue had also undergone a heavy waxing to help conceal the reconstruction.

Alceo Dossena continued to tell his story. He claimed that he had come across an authentic statue from the Renaissance era in Italy. He purchased this statue for $10,000, which represented almost his entire life's savings; he considered it an investment. He put this authentic statue in his studio. Then, using the real statue as a model, he started to create forgeries or copies of "missing" statues that had reportedly been lost during earthquakes or other disasters over the past decades.

Dossena soon established himself as more than just a person who had found "lost" works of art. He wanted to be recognized as a sculptor. He created new works of art which he sold for handsome prices. He had an insatiable urge to continue hoaxing. So would frequently slip in counterfeits of "missing" art works with his original statues.

And so it was that dealers in Rome found their studios and showrooms filled with counterfeit statues of "missing" works, authentic statues that were Dossena's own modern creations, as well as some real statues that Dossena had purchased for resale at a profit.

Alceo defended his actions: "I am a sculptor and I sold whatever I could . . . original works of art, copies of lost art. I never said they were authentic works of art from the past. I told Fasoli & Palesi that I had a small, private collection for sale. They came to my studio, saw the statues, offered me a price and I accepted. I have receipts to prove it."

Indeed, each receipt said that payment was being made for several statues—and descriptions were made of each one. The description would merely say "Mino Tomb" statue, for example. When Dossena went before a Roman court, charged with forgery, he waved this receipt before the magistrate and declared:

"It does not say that the 'Mino Tomb' statue I sold was

authentic. It says that I *sold* a 'Mino Tomb' statue. You can go to any tourist shop and buy a statue of the Leaning Tower of Pisa, or a portrait of the 'Mona Lisa' but nobody says it is authentic or a forgery. I never said that what I sold was either authentic or a forgery. I labeled each item as to its name. If Fasoli & Palesi felt they were originals, that was up to them. If they wanted to know if it was an original or a duplicate, they should have asked me. They never did. Read the receipt. It says 'for a statue' and nothing regarding its originality.

"My position is that I sell works of art. I misrepresented nothing. I did. indeed, sell works of art!"

This was a problem that involved international law. Eventually, Fasoli & Palesi claimed to have sold the imitations to smaller dealers in Rome to do with as they preferred. No one did business with these smaller dealers; nearly all of them went out of business. So did Fasoli & Palesi.

Imitations in museums throughout the world were very quickly removed and disposed of.

Alceo Dossena enjoyed a thriving business as a self-admitted copier of some of the world's greatest masterpieces in stone. He was hired by museums to make copies of their great works—and he was closely watched every minute of the day.

He amassed a small fortune—much, much more than the earnings of the greatest sculptors of the past whose work he had copied.

Was he a hoaxer?

In his own words, "Whenever I make a hoax, it is known beforehand. If the art experts choose to be fooled—they deserve it!"

12

LORD GORDON-GORDON

The Man Who Hoaxed a Railroad
Magnate out of Millions

A THREAT OF INTERNATIONAL DISASTER occurred on a summer afternoon in 1873. A group of Americans (two would later become Minnesota governors and several would become congressmen) were seized in Canada by the Northwest Mounted Police; they were incarcerated in a Canadian prison.

The charge was conspiracy to kidnap. The near-victim was a highly distinguished subject of His Majesty, none other than Lord John Gordon-Gordon of Edinburgh, Scotland.

Because this crime involved citizens of the United States, subjects of Canada and one British subject, there was much talk of the outbreak of war between the countries. Only the intervention of President Ulysses S. Grant and the cooperation of Canadian Prime Minister Sir John MacDonald helped avert a serious confrontation.

Lord John Gordon-Gordon enjoyed the power and influence he possessed. He glorified in the success of his career. In 1873, he was enjoying a great honor: The officials and executives of the Northern Pacific Railroad had requested that he name future towns and cities throughout Minnesota. He was also asked to help reorganize the Erie Railroad together with Horace Greeley, the newspaper magnate, and the famous Jay Gould, the multimillionaire. If Lord Gordon-Gordon accepted the offer to satisfy his ego, he also did so in the hope of being able to get very close to millionaire Jay Gould.

Lord John Gordon-Gordon was the illegitimate son of a merchant seaman and a barmaid who worked in one of London's more seedy areas. Through most of his very early years, he managed to support himself by stealing goods from unloading ships. He rifled cargo, and sold the stolen goods to pawn shops and fences. As far as he knew, his name was John Anthony Crowningshield. But he would soon change his name as well as his identity.

In June, 1863, John managed to steal a trunk from a docked passenger ship, newly arrived from Scotland. He dragged the trunk to his lodgings, broke open the lock, and peered inside. In it were the finest clothes money could buy. The trunk obviously belonged to a real gentleman—perhaps to royalty, or to one associated with royalty. This gave young John an idea, an idea which led to a plan that would shape his future life.

The youth sold a few timepieces from the trunk so that he could hire an assistant. Several days later, he appeared in Edinburgh, Scotland. Impeccably dressed in garments of the latest fashion, he called himself Lord Glencairn. With him, was a "gentleman's tiger" a combination valet and secretary. It was the fashion of the era for a gentleman to be so accompanied.

Lord Glencairn's gentleman's tiger was decked out in buckskin breeches and long red boots, a blue satin coat sporting red velvet buttons, and a hat embellished with a huge cockade to proclaim that his master held a coveted royal stipulation. If clothes made the man, then Gordon and his tiger were true gentlemen.

Together, the two stopped at one of Edinburgh's leading jewelers. The gentleman's tiger presented the card of his royal master. Lord Glencairn smiled, looked over various items, selected a few choice items of gold and paid with a check. (He had banked monies earned as a bookkeeper for a local shipping firm.) The check was as good as were the precious baubles he had just purchased.

Once his credit rating was established, Glencairn continued to make more frequent purchases at this and other jewelry establishments. Within four months, he purchased some $100,000 worth of gems earned from commissions received as assistant to a commodities broker. Then he purchased another $250,000 worth of valuables. This last purchase was paid for by check; the check was worthless.

When the owner could not locate Lord Glencairn to have him make good on the check, the matter was turned over to authorities. They searched, but could find no trace of either Lord Glencairn or his gentleman's tiger. But they did discover the method of operation employed.

Lord Glencairn would purchase jewels, then pawn them and use the money to buy more jewels at another shop, and then pawn these, too. Thus, to all who observed his transactions, he gave the appearance of having money enough to pay for his purchases. Thus, he established credit within the jewelry community. No one could have imagined that he was pawning the jewels almost the same day in a city that was distant from Edinburgh, and would return the next day with money from the pawned jewels to buy new sparklers.

To all outward appearances, Glencairn was a man of considerable wealth. This was the impression he sought to convey, and he succeeded, for he was able to issue rubber checks which would be accepted without question. Lord Glencairn had done business with at least nine shops throughout Edinburgh, and had established good credit with all of them. By the time he had vanished, the nine shopkeepers had been bilked out of one million dollars.

We next meet this self-designated royalist in Minneapolis in 1868. Using the name of Lord Gordon-Gordon, he registered in one of Minneapolis' finest hotels.

As soon as he had settled down, Gordon-Gordon deposited $50,000 in a local bank. He began introducing himself to the leading citizens of Minneapolis, presenting the more affluent people with letters of introduction from some of Britain's leading statesmen and royalists. To have such a tall, lean, meticulously dressed gentleman of such stature in Minneapolis was considered quite an honor for the city.

Everyone admired his fine grooming, which included patent leather gloves and a high silk hat. They looked upon him with awe and curiosity. It was apparent that Lord Gordon-Gordon was a gentleman of good breeding and culture. He always exuded the soft, pleasant scent of the best cologne; his handsome face was clean-shaven; his thick sideburns were an indication of his English heritage; his fingernails were so well manicured, it was obvious that he had never done so much as a day's manual labor.

Several days after His Lordship's arrival in Minneapolis,

he announced that he was commissioned to invest in new railroads that were under construction. He met with Colonel John S. Loomis, official land auditor of the Northern Pacific Railroad. Gordon-Gordon explained that he had "a few million dollars in American money for investment in the railroad lands in this area. I am quite certain we shall be able to conduct business together, for our mutual advantage."

Needless to say, the authorities were eager to cultivate His Lordship's friendship and to use the much-needed capital he was able to provide. He was introduced to society as heir of the great Earls of Gordon, a relative of the Campbell family, and a collateral cousin of Lord Byron. A descendant of the bold Lochinvar and several of the ancient Highlander royalists, he was assumed to be extremely wealthy. Society eagerly accepted him.

Several leading citizens of Minneapolis decided to honor Lord Gordon-Gordon with a dinner, at which time he was called upon to make a short speech. He was rather a modest man and made little display of himself. Speaking quietly, he explained that, among other things, he had come to Minneapolis in search of fruitful land which could be used as a colony to relieve his over-crowded Scotch tenantry.

"I believe we can make use of as much as one million acres. We will not only purchase such acreage, if it is available, but will cultivate it and help build a thriving community. All building will be done by local labor at satisfactory rates. Needless to say, we want to be welcome here in Minneapolis. We do not wish to impose ourselves on anyone."

He had arrived at an opportune time. The Northern Pacific Railroad was anxious to push westward before competing railroads could claim new territories. Much capital was needed to accomplish this. Doubtlessly, the investment would reap huge profits for all participants involved. Therefore, the land auditor and commissioner, Colonel John S. Loomis, spared no efforts in wooing the wealthy royalist.

The Northern Pacific Railroad showed Lord Gordon-Gordon some desirable territory that he might want to purchase at a low rate. The royalist travelled in a set of expensive wagons; he was served by a retinue of personal servants; everything that he required for his personal care and comfort was provided for. All expenses were borne by Northern Pacific and all requests were honored graciously.

A journalist of the era wrote briefly of the luxury in which the royalist travelled:

"Two palatial wall tents were provided for his personal use, one of which had the best shining silver and the most delicate of china. These contained succulent viands that would have enslaved the palate of Epicurus. Imported juicy fruits from Mexico were handed to him on silver trays. So, too, were choice flavors from the Spice Islands and dry wines from the best of vineyards. The table was set for a festive royalist. Indeed, such was the situation of Lord Gordon-Gordon."

As he travelled about, Gordon-Gordon gave some Scottish and some American names to new towns. He also designated sites for a local school and a church for each of these towns.

Lord Gordon-Gordon toured for almost three months before choosing the sites he wanted to purchase. He signed the necessary papers. In all, he purchased close to one million acres. He then arranged to have his money transferred from Scotland to New York. He had to make a trip to New York (again paid for by Northern Pacific) where he withdrew the deposited money and saw friends whom he told of his forthcoming business ventures. He returned to Minneapolis in 1869.

It was a year of great turmoil. Internal wrangling had developed within the ranks of the Erie Railroad. Several important executives wanted to seize control of the corporation; with millions being invested, legal tricks were employed to divert some of the money to the pockets of greedy men. Several of them floated forged stock certificates in the hope of siphoning off a few hundred thousand dollars for themselves. When the forged certificates were discovered, the hoaxers, of course, pleaded innocence. They were unaware, they claimed, that these certificates were not authentic. It was rumored that many officials were threatened with removal from office.

One prominent victim of the hoax was the famous New York financier and railroad investor, Jay Gould (1836-1892) who had invested many millions in the railroads. Now, he found himself an embarrassed victim of a hoax. As a respected New York banker, to be hoaxed was a slur on his financial reputation. The newspapers told of the scandal, much to Jay

Gould's embarrassment. One avid follower of the scandal was Lord Gordon-Gordon. He devoured every single word in the local newspapers until he was well versed in the scandal as well as in Jay Gould's involvement. Now he started his plan.

Lord Gordon-Gordon decided to come to the rescue. He brought in a handwriting and printing expert who could distinguish between authentic and counterfeit certificates. Gordon-Gordon was then able to identify the guilty forgers and save the railroad many millions of dollars. The hoaxers were apprehended and brought to justice. Lord Gordon-Gordon helped save the Erie Railroad from ruin; he became a hero in the eyes of many jittery investors from the leading banks of New York.

While in New York, Lord Gordon-Gordon had cultivated the friendship of Horace Greeley, publisher of the *Tribune*. He realized that Greeley was very influential (he was soon to become a candidate for the presidency) and would be a good man to know intimately. John Gordon-Gordon and Horace Greeley had dined together on numerous occasions. Usually, the meals were sumptuous feasts served by liveried servants. The succulent foods were specially prepared by a chef brought in from Paris for the occasion.

During one such feast, when Horace Greeley was feeling good, he asked Lord Gordon-Gordon if he knew of anything newsworthy to relate. His Lordship said that, yes, there were several items that might be of interest. He confided to Greeley that he owned close to one million shares of Erie stock and that many of his English friends also had vast holdings in the corporation. (Gordon-Gordon had had the one million acres of land that he owned exchanged at the rate of one share for each acre. The railroad needed the money for the laying of its tracks.) "Because I own one million shares, I am in an excellent position. I have the majority voting power. I can control the election of the Board of Directors. Of course, I shall use my power wisely and for the benefit of the investors and the public. I dare say, it would be judicious if you could notify some other newspaper publishers of the predicted success of the Erie Railroad because of my huge investment and my devoted concern to the stockholders."

"Most interesting," said Greeley. "I believe I can share

this news with some other publishers. I know that A. K. Mc-
Clure of the *Philadelphia Times* would be interested. Then
there is my good friend, Thomas A. Scott, who owns a string
of newspapers throughout the Eastern seaboard. Yes, I am sure
they would give it good space."

Lord Gordon-Gordon smiled. "That would be fine, Mr.
Greeley. The American people should know that our country
is growing and that the Erie Railroad, under my direction,
will serve the people . . . and our country."

Lord Gordon-Gordon wanted news of this venture to spread.
This could attract additional investors.

Lord Gordon-Gordon wanted New York financier Jay Gould
to put money into the railroad. Gould was on the board of
directors of leading corporations and banks. It was said he
could easily raise three or four million dollars to invest in
suitable properties on the basis of a few words. Lord Gordon-
Gordon wanted Jay Gould to become part of the Erie corporation. He offered to sell his own controlling votes of Erie stock
shares to Gould, who would then be in a good position as
president of the railroad. As its president, Jay Gould would
want to see the Erie railroad continue its expansion westward
to the California coast, to the Pacific Ocean . . . and he would
easily arrange from his banking connections to have millions
of dollars poured in as an investment.

Millionaire railroad magnate Jay Gould later recalled in
court:

"I asked Lord Gordon-Gordon what interest he held in the
Erie Railroad. He replied that he personally owned some 30
million shares of stock. His close and trusting friends owned
an additional 20 million shares. He was in full charge. He
wanted the railroad to be kept under my management.

"But he asked if he could select a new board of directors.
He said, condescendingly, that he and Mr. Horace Greeley
and myself would approve of all the members. Then he told
me a bit about his background.

"Lord Gordon-Gordon told me of having celebrated his
twenty-first birthday by entering Parliament. He took his seat
as the youngest member of the distinguished House of Lords.
He told how Her Majesty, the Queen, had great faith in his

ability and discretion. He said that the royal family had entrusted many responsibilities to him.

"He told of having made several secret negotiations with Bismarck of Prussia and having helped avert several local wars.

"Later, I agreed with Lord Gordon-Gordon to centralize power. Stocks of the railroad were placed in the form of puts and calls. In this manner, Lord Gordon-Gordon accepted them. I began by signing a form handed to me, whereby I wrote out and delivered to Lord Gordon-Gordon, calls upon him for 20,000 shares of Erie at $35 per share, good for six months."

By now, Lord Gordon-Gordon had everything proceeding according to his plan. Other investors had been bought out. The royalist was given an unlimited expense account. This proved to be the start of the swindle of Jay Gould. Lord Gordon-Gordon said he needed at least one million dollars in order to consolidate all holdings and have ownership solidly placed in Gould's hands.

Gould agreed to have this one million dollars given to Lord Gordon-Gordon in return for a promise that he would repay it out of his profits.

Later, Jay Gould testified in court:

"Because he paid some money personally, and because the success of this new plan relied much on my good faith as well as his cooperation, I arranged to deposit with Lord Gordon-Gordon a sum of money and securities to pay for one-half of his expenses. This came to about $500,000. This was considered to be my loan to His Lordship, and he was to refund this money to me after I was installed as president.

"A short time later, Gordon-Gordon said he had erred. There was a need for about $40,000 additional cash so he could continue consolidating his holdings. He said it was costly to pay for all the legal expenses, hence the need for this money. While I could not find any error, I did not want to disturb our arrangement, so I saw to it that he received the cash without any further question. I also offered him additional securities.

"When I requested a receipt, he refused to do this or accept the money. He said that his integrity and honor were sufficient and that his word was as binding as his signature. He stood, up, and started to leave.

"At that time, I realized that if he left the room without taking this extra expense money, the entire venture could collapse. I hastily called him back to the table, told him that while most of my dealings required a signature, that he was not to take offense, that his good name and word would be sufficient. So it was that he took this expense money without giving me any receipt."

Very shortly thereafter, the value of Erie Railroad shares increased. The stock option that Jay Gould had given to Lord Gordon-Gordon at $35 a share, would soon be worth close to one million dollars. But Lord Gordon-Gordon said he would prefer cash right now, so he sold these stock option calls to Gould for one-half million dollars. Gould was confident that he would then sell them for one million dollars and net a big windfall.

Jay Gould paid in cash and securities to the tune of a half million, and received the calls which he expected would rise to one million.

It was here that the master hoaxer, Gordon-Gordon, showed his genius for manipulation. He took the one-half million and began selling the shares he owned in the Erie Railroad. He also sold shares he owned in other railroads. This caused a drop in prices. Jay Gould saw this and was suspicious, but could not trace any sale directly to Gordon-Gordon.

He knew that Gordon-Gordon was selling these shares; no one else had so many outstanding shares. Now Jay Gould discovered that Gordon-Gordon was selling shares entrusted to him in escrow and this was forcing a drop in price of Erie stock. Quickly, the millionaire railroad magnate went into action. He immediately telegraphed all brokers and instructed them to refuse to handle large amounts of certain shares without his prior approval. This would keep the price of stock from dropping further. He then tried to send spies into Lord Gordon-Gordon's suite to overhear any of his conversations, but this did not work. He could not find any real proof of Lord Gordon-Gordon's trickery.

Gould now recognized Lord Gordon-Gordon as a swindler. He called upon Horace Greeley to intervene. The newspaper publisher tried his utmost to convince the royalist to discontinue tainting his hands with filthy lucre. How noble it would be if Lord Gordon-Gordon would return all investments and quietly back out of the Erie Railroad and all such negotiations.

"Let me assure you," Greeley said, "that your return of the money and securities at this point will not influence Your Lordship's rights to request restitution in a court of law."

Lord Gordon-Gordon arched his eyebrows. "I beg your pardon, Mr. Greeley, but I cannot accommodate your request."

Horace Greeley declared flatly, "It would be most shocking if Jay Gould wanted to accost you in court. Perhaps you can return some securities now."

Not wanting a court battle, Lord Gordon-Gordon reneged and did return a few securities, but it amounted to less than one hundred thousand dollars. Approximately one million dollars was still missing.

Jay Gould was fuming. He knew he had been duped and was concerned about the loss of his prestige. He had to get back his money from Lord Gordon-Gordon and halt the drop in price of Erie stock. Quickly, Gould went to court and had a warrant issued for the arrest of Lord Gordon-Gordon on the charge that he had misrepresented himself and had taken money under false pretenses.

But it was going to be a bitter fight.

Jay Gould hired the best available legal brains, such as Elihu Root and David Dudley Field. Lord Gordon-Gordon hired General Dix and General Sickles, both of whom were known enemies of Jay Gould.

It was 10 weeks before the case was brought before the court. During that time, Jay Gould saw himself losing control of the coveted Erie Railroad. He was angry. If he wanted anything, it was to destroy Lord Gordon-Gordon.

The court trial was as tough as a prizefight: both sides kept punching; neither would let up.

Lord Gordon-Gordon, when questioned about his ancestry, did not reply on ground that the case was to be determined on its merits and nothing else. He stated merely that he owned large land holdings in the Minnesota region and was a gentleman of breeding.

The hoaxer made such a good impression, that when he was

viciously cross-examined by Dudley Field, the judge broke in
and said that a royalist should not be persecuted like a common
man.

As the trial wore on, it seemed as if His Lordship would
win. But the so-called royalist fell victim to his own hoax. He
had begun to believe that he was actually the personage he
pretended to be.

Jay Gould made a list of all the personalities Gordon-
Gordon claimed to know. He sent cablegrams to all of them.
Overnight, replies came pouring in. None of them knew Lord
Gordon-Gordon. None had even heard of his so-called royal
family. He was unknown in the British Empire!

Apparently, Lord Gordon-Gordon expected this to happen.
The next day, he did not appear in court. Instead, during the
night he crossed the border and moved to Canada. With him,
he took about a half million dollars in cash and negotiable
securities.

Now he could travel in luxury and style throughout Canada.
Since his hoaxes were unknown here, he could use the same
ruses he had used in the United States. For a year, he travelled
throughout the countryside pretending to be looking for property. New York authorities had notified the Canadian government about Gordon-Gordon and the Northwest Mounted Police
set out to find him. They finally apprehended him, in 1873,
hiding out in a cabin in the woods. He had been recognized
when he came into a trading post on the outskirts of Montreal
and the authorities were notified to make the arrest.

Repercussions were heard throughout the world of royalty.
Although many believed Lord Gordon-Gordon to be a fraud,
others continued to believe him to be trueblood royalty.

The mayors and the governors of the various cities involved
went into a huddle. Extradition would be difficult. He was a
British subject. Extradition could be construed as kidnapping
and that would be a serious offense. What was to be done?

As fortune would have it, the story reached the newspapers
in Scotland. In Edinburgh, the nine jewelers who had been
hoaxed out of one million dollars read the story of Lord
Gordon-Gordon. His picture appeared in the papers. They
produced bounced checks which they said were probably written by him under the name of Lord Glencairn. All descrip-

tions fit. They cabled the United States. Now it was apparent that Lord Gordon-Gordon could be identified as an impostor and a hoaxer.

His Lordship was confronted with the accusations, and was quickly brought before a magistrate who read the charges and ordered him arrested and held on bail. He said he wanted to discuss the matter with an attorney. The attorney put up bail for Lord Gordon-Gordon, and put him up as a guest in his home. During the night, Lord Gordon-Gordon sneaked out of the house and vanished.

Perhaps Gordon-Gordon continued his hoax in another country, on another continent or under another name. Needless to say, he had hoaxed many people out of millions. Jay Gould managed to hold on to his Erie Railroad, but had lost close to one million dollars. He was lucky. Others had lost their life's savings.

Lord Gordon-Gordon had perpetrated a stock manipulation and forgery hoax that affected the entire railroad industry and the stock market. As a result, new safeguards were instituted to protect the public. All certificates were to be checked and double-checked by a special board of directors that would vouch for their authenticity. They had learned this simple method only after much financial loss.

13

JAMES ADDISON REAVIS

The Hoaxer Who Laid Claim to Arizona

ON A SLEEPY, SUNNY AFTERNOON in Phoenix, Arizona, a tall, quiet but crafty man alighted from his stagecoach. Brushing the sand off his polished boots and pin-striped trousers, he walked to the office of the *Phoenix Gazette*. He had arrived in the territory, he announced to the *Gazette* staff, to report on the area's progress—the development of its mines and lands—to his own newspaper, the *San Francisco Examiner*. As a courtesy, he requested that the *Gazette* include in its pages a notice of his arrival, noting the *exact* date: June 23, 1881. He thanked the printer/publisher for the kind favor and, with every seemingly good intention, promised to remember him in the future.

No one suspected that the arrival of this man, James Addison Reavis, would shake the foundations of the territory of Arizona and the United States itself. It would not be long before he would stake a claim, as had so many other prospectors and settlers before him. But Reavis would not claim a modest bit of ground; he would produce documents in the courts to prove that he was the sole owner of the entire territory of Arizona.

This would not be the claim of a crackpot. It would be backed by shrewd legal maneuverings that would require the help of some of the most knowledgeable lawyers in the country. And, as Arizona would soon find out, unless authorities acted swiftly and wisely, there would soon be established a "Kingdom of Arizona," and its first self-declared "king" would be James Addison Reavis.

The threat to the independence of Arizona came at a time when the West was dangerously wild, but was attracting many new settlers who hoped to acquire much wealth. The prairies, filled with huge herds of buffalo, welcomed countless immigrants who struggled across great wastelands in their Conestoga wagons, lured into the Golden West by tales which told of gold, silver, and endless tracts of fertile land that could be theirs for the taking. During the late 1800s, the rugged plains were infested with hostile Indians who resented the intrusion of invaders; the uprooted Apaches were united under Chief Cochise and stood ready to defend their lands.

As soon as Reavis saw that the *Phoenix Gazette* had indeed inserted a notice of the date of his arrival in its pages, he again boarded a stagecoach, this time for Santa Fe. Having arrived in this small, dusty, wind-swept settlement, he made his way to the U.S. Land Office, which had been established in Washington, D. C., to evaluate and investigate any and all Spanish land claims that had been filed according to terms of the Treaty of Guadalupe Hidalgo in 1848.

Reavis knew that the Treaty offered cash for land and had put an end to war between the United States and Mexico. He also knew about the Gadsden Purchase: James Gadsden (1788-1858), a soldier and diplomat, had arranged a treaty with Mexico in 1853, whereby he secured for the United States a tract of land south of the Gila River, which eventually became part of Arizona and New Mexico.

The Treaty of Guadalupe Hidalgo affirmed that Americans would recognize and protect Spanish titles to all land that fell within the borders of the territories ceded by Mexico. The United States officially guaranteed to recognize the very ancient land grants held by owners who had received them from the royal Spanish family before Mexico had seceded and become independent.

These Mexicans immediately appeared in the Santa Fe Land Office, armed with documents and papers from the Spanish Crown, in the hope of validating ownership of their vast properties. The Land Office would then proceed to research and investigate each royal document to ensure its authenticity. Because so many claims had to be investigated, the Land Office was in need of clerks and officials to deal with the expanding paperwork. When James Addison Reavis appeared and requested employment, he was promptly hired. He could read and write and cipher (a group of talents not too frequent in the Old West) and seemed intelligent and reliable. Reavis was not so much interested in the paltry salary as he was in learning as much as possible about filing claims.

Reavis was a cool, calculating man. He had one great talent: he could forge a signature, or an entire document, with such perfection that it would fool the most astute expert. He had discovered his talent a short time earlier when working as a supply clerk for a military outpost. He found that he could forge a bill of lading with such exactitude that when placed before the fort's commander it would be countersigned without even a second glance. When supplies would arrive, Reavis was able to sell them to needy settlers in the small village surrounding the outpost and keep the proceeds. As his talents increased, he soon found that he could forge various payroll records, pad bills and create records of nonexistent soldiers and officers whose salaries were large. This money he pocketed.

But this was only loose change to Reavis. He wanted to do more than just forge endless numbers of bills. He wanted to fabricate one great swindle that would enable him to live out the rest of his life as a gentleman of leisure. Although he was confident of his abilities as a forger, Reavis always feared being caught. So he decided to quit while he was ahead. He left the military outpost and started to travel through the growing West in search of a plan that would bring him a fortune. Reavis roamed the treacherous mountains and plains, side by side with professional gamblers, thieves, hoodlums and murderers. In a country still torn by the ravages of Civil War, jobs were hard to find. The only opportunity for making money was in the acquisition of land; everyone wanted land. And it was this that brought James Addison Reavis to a job with a real estate firm located in a small hotel in Santa Fe, New Mexico in 1881.

Reavis clerked at the real estate firm, earning some money and waiting for an "opportunity" to make still more. Quite by chance, he overheard any number of people in the Hotel Santa Fe lobby talking about the recently signed Treaty of Guadalupe Hidalgo. Many Mexicans were apparently losing their lands (which had been in their families for centuries under Royal Spanish grants) because they were unable to find the deeds. Reavis' ears perked up. He realized that if he could make his way to the territory of Arizona, he could take advantage of the Treaty of Guadalupe.

Reavis' boss at the real estate firm, a licensed broker, told him that the Union Pacific Railroad Company wanted to lay tracks over a stretch in New Mexico and Arizona, upon which stood several small homes owned by a local man. But the man's title of ownership stopped the railroad from carrying out its plans. The man refused to sell, realizing that the longer he held out, the higher the railroad's offer would be. The real estate man, Henry Perkins, told Reavis that if he could convince the man to sell the property, there would be a healthy commission for him.

This was a simple task for Reavis. He sat down at a table in his small room, dipped his pen in ink, and prepared a perfectly forged document to which he signed the stubborn landowner's name (he copied it from other papers in his possession). It was a "Quit Claim" deed in which the landowner irrevocably signed away all ownership to the property and all buildings thereon for an agree-upon price. Reavis naturally set a high price—$7,500—so that his commission would be sizable.

Reavis was starting to set the pattern which would soon establish him as one of the greatest hoaxers of his era. He did more than just forge a signature. He forged an entire document so perfectly that there could hardly be any question of its authenticity. Encouraged by his newly discovered talent, he began thinking in very grandiose terms: why not claim *vast* territories in the West as his own?

As soon as the "Quit Claim" deed was filed, Reavis collected his handsome commission. Many months would elapse before the real owner of the coveted property would become aware of the fictitious document. By that time, Reavis would have vanished into the Wild West.

No sooner had Reavis entrenched himself in the Land Office at Santa Fe, in the summer of 1881, than he began making expert copies of Royal Seals found on ancient Spanish documents and records. He took great pains to duplicate the colorful penmanship of the originals, including all the intricate curlicues as executed by royal scribes. Every detail was followed with such exactitude so as to dupe the experts.

Reavis devoted himself to learning the Spanish language, as well as its calligraphy. Not content with a knowledge of modern Spanish, he set out to master the language as it was spoken a century ago, at the time when the royal documents were written. He studied intensively, and soon became so adept in the language and its earlier style and idioms, that he felt confident of his ability to copy the necessary documents flawlessly.

Reavis continued to spend many long hours and days and weeks bent over a small wooden table in his little rented room, copying ancient parchments by the light of a kerosene lamp. He practiced and practiced, using up one quill after another as he imitated the artistic lettering found in yellowing documents. Often, he would write long letters to himself, imagining that he was an ancient scribe in a royal court. He was very self-critical. He would write and rewrite and rewrite, until he was satisfied that his documents rang true in every respect.

Never satisfied in his quest to become a master at copying, Reavis studied and read, acquiring more and more knowledge. He learned, for example, that the Spanish monarchs awarded vast stretches of land to their favorite settlers in the New World. He discovered that the monarchs measured land by leagues (any of various units of distance from about 2.4 to 4.6 statute miles) rather than by acres. He also found that documents were often more poetry than fact. The precise boundaries of grants were often rather vague. Continuing his research, Reavis found that Spanish grants for lands in California were more specific, and boundary lines were already established by those who had held them for many generations. But Arizona was part of the soon-to-be-called Wild West. The territory was vast and remote, rough and largely unexplored. Therefore, a royal scribe who was comfortably seated in his plush quarters in a Madrid palace would have no conception of this rough and wild country. He would use flowery phrases and vague boundaries in describing such land.

This gave Reavis a great idea. As soon as he had established his identity and family background, he would be in a position to take land inspectors to the property he claimed to be his own. He would just point out his boundaries as described in the vague, forged documents.

Reavis knew that in order for someone to claim ownership

through a Spanish nobleman, he must first produce proof that he was a descendant of that royal line. Using his fertile imagination, Reavis sat before his wooden table for most of the night and concocted an illustrious past that would, undoubtedly, have gained him entrance to the very bedchambers of the royal family.

Reavis decided that his most prominent ancestor would be a noble Spaniard who was a blood relative of King Ferdinand of Spain. He had his own dukedom and was the owner of vast estates in and around Madrid. Reavis named him Pablo de Navarre.

Pablo was the proud possessor of many knighted titles, and when Reavis got through with him, he also bore a long list of heroic designations which could be proven through forged documents. Furthermore, this nobleman came from a line of royalty: his mother and father had both been members of the court, and were blood relatives of several of the reigning kings of Europe.

Reavis worked out his ancestral line with great skill. He would not pretend to be the heir of *actual* historical personages; that would create the possibility that a rightful heir might challenge his claim. It was safer to fabricate a family. And Reavis' documentation was so detailed that it would be above suspicion.

Once he had established a strong base on which to build, James Addison Reavis continued to flesh out his claim. He had saved enough money from his work in the Land Office to finance trips to Europe and Mexico. He commissioned a tailor to provide him with a wardrobe befitting a nobleman. He mastered the classical Spanish dialect and grew long sideburns. Every motion, every gesture, every inflection was studied to give the impression that he was a member of nobility. When he felt ready, in 1883, Reavis travelled to the various monasteries and palaces of Madrid, Seville and Barcelona. He told the padres and monks that he was a theological student and asked them for permission to study the heavily guarded documents held in their libraries. He said he hoped to use this knowledge to convert the thousands of heathens in the Wild West to the virtues of Christianity. It was a convincing request.

Using his quill and parchment paper, he inserted his

adopted name, Pablo de Navarre, on some of the most ancient documents. The documents identified him as the owner of huge tracts of land in Arizona, by virtue of Spanish royal grants. These documents would be forged proof that the Spanish crown had given him almost all the territory in what was later to become Arizona and much of New Mexico.

Reavis soon established more than just a family name. He fashioned an entire generation of family members, gave them titles, included them in the higher circles of royalty, made them essential personages in the pages of history. He then added still another character to his story. He said that he had a half-brother, Juan de Peralta. It was this half-brother who had journeyed from Madrid to Arizona in 1851. In Arizona, he had purchased a huge tract of land. He had done this, according to forged documents, with a partner, one Rex Mooney. It was Rex Mooney (a law student) who had offered legal advice and was able to file documents in English. Juan de Peralta was not too expert in that language.

But Juan de Peralta loved to gamble. He needed more money. When he ran up huge gambling debts in the casinos and feared that loan sharks would kill him, he became hard-pressed and sold his share of the property to Rex Mooney for $15.000, which he used to pay off his gambling debts.

But Rex Mooney needed money, too. He had invested his $15,000 in a gold mine that failed to produce anything but mud. In order to recoup his loss, he sold the property to James Addison Reavis for $25,000. A short time thereafter, Rex Mooney was found dead in a small shack, just at the border between Arizona and New Mexico. It was said that he died of too much liquor. Official records suggested poison. This was at a time when border towns were wild brawling frontier places. Deaths by shooting were common. The law was the gun. Poison was often used to rid oneself of an enemy. The demise of an average citizen was little cause for alarm. After the facts were duly recorded, the incident was forgotten.

Whether Reavis poisoned Mooney or not will never be known. But it was a convenient death for Reavis, because he was now the undisputed owner of the Peralta Grant and could proclaim himself the King of Arizona. But he overlooked one small problem: Rex Mooney had a wife.

As soon as she learned of her husband's demise, she lost no time in travelling to Tucson. She claimed the Peralta Grant until Reavis showed her the documents which Mooney had signed, thus selling the vast territories. Mooney's wife responded by saying that there were other documents in her late husband's house to prove that he could *not* have legally sold the property to anyone without her approval.

Hearing of this, Reavis lost little time in going to Mooney's shack. He ransacked the house and under some floorboards, he found those documents which could have disputed his claim. Quickly he struck a match and, in a moment, the documents turned to ash. In one respect, this was a stroke of luck, because while searching the shack Reavis found more authentic documents proving that Rex Mooney had, indeed, owned such properties as grazing lands and ranches in the area—properties that had been deeded to him by various officials. He forged documents to say that all these properties were sold to him. Armed with this new set of documents, Reavis was set to claim sole ownership of more than just the Peralta Grant.

Mooney's widow proved to be an unexpected thorn in Reavis' side. When she demanded money, under threat of legal action, he quickly gave her a large sum to calm her down. But he could not get her to sign any documents releasing him from further claims. She was too clever for that. So he talked her into accepting a small percentage of whatever future profits he would receive from cultivation of the lands. Mooney's widow was satisfied—for the time being, at least.

Now, James Addison Reavis was prepared to finalize the project on which he had worked for so long. He prepared sets of certified official documents (one original and one duplicate), showing that Mooney had sold him all of his properties. With them in hand he walked into the offices of the surveyor general of the federal government in Tucson. Calmly, he announced that he was the owner of the Peralta Grant as well as all properties and lands throughout Arizona, including the growing cities of Phoenix and Tucson. He noted that he was now the sole and official owner of some 11,000,000 acres of this rich land.

In short order, the word spread throughout Arizona. Everyone was talking about the Spanish nobleman who claimed to be the rightful owner of the land on which they lived—and that he was the King of Arizona. It was as if a keg of dynamite had been set off in the Tucson town square.

Reavis posted notices on trees, on bulletin boards, in saloons—stating that as King of Arizona, he would consider every unauthorized person who tread on his property to be a trespasser. He advised the government in Washington that any deeds they had granted were illegal and that he would sue for damages in the amount of $100 million. He would, however, agree to a settlement for about half that amount so that he could take early possession of the entire region.

What about the many thousands who had worked hard to build homes or ranches? What about the many small and large storekeepers who were rooted in this region? What about those who ran cattle on open range land under written authorization from Washington? Still more important, what about the railroads that were already crossing this territory and those laying even more tracks? Would they all be considered trespassers?

What about the wealthy producing mines that brought forth gold, silver and copper? What about the future of this territory? If James Addison Reavis had an authentic claim, it meant that he could legally order every single person off his property, which literally meant everyone in the entire territory of Arizona. The territory was in an uproar.

Many oganizations established committees to deal with this seemingly just claim. The officials of the Silver King Mine, the heads of Wells Fargo and the rich bankers of the Southern Pacific Railroad Company entered into consultations with their attorneys. And, soon, the most brilliant legal minds of the nation were carefully examining all of the documents presented by Reavis. Then concluded that the documents presented by Reavis were authentic. And in their panic, they played right into Reavis' hands.

As soon as the big railroad and banking magnates realized that they were faced with a loss of their investments, they made an effort to settle with Reavis. It was better, their attorneys advised, than fighting what appeared to be a losing battle. They made partial settlements and, indeed, gave Reavis some $75,000 to $100,000—with assurances of more to come.

Now, James Addison Reavis had little doubt that he would

soon be the undisputed owner and King of Arizona. Encouraged by the payments he received, he soon set upon still another conquest: finding a wife.

There were several requirements. The wife had no need to be especially attractive or intelligent, but she had to be very young, about fifteen, and an orphan, either Mexican or Spanish. It was of utmost importance that this orphan girl had no ties, no connections, no involvements with anyone or anything.

With his newly acquired money in hand, he ventured forth to neighboring California, and began his search for a wife. By the time he had reached Baja, California, he was discouraged almost to the point of returning to Arizona. But, one night, as he left his small room in the village inn and passed the local saloon, he saw a slim, rather attractive girl. Maria Sanchez was her name. She worked in the saloon and in other houses, he learned—much like a slave girl. No one knew her origins. She was, no doubt, one of the countless thousands of children born to itinerant Mexicans who had been promptly abandoned. She would fit perfectly into Reavis' nefarious plans.

Reavis went to the owner of a small stable, in the rear of which the timid, homeless girl lived. Reavis told the stable-keeper that Maria Sanchez was not a homeless ragamuffin. Rather, she was the legitimate heiress to massive wealth, deeded to Reavis through royal Spanish grants. Reavis submitted documented evidence which the stablekeeper scanned (although he could read very little, if at all). Reavis then gave the man a handful of bills which was readily accepted. The waif was released to her newly discovered master.

Reavis moved ahead with precision. While he was a master hoaxer, he was not a rake. (He did not violate Maria Sanchez as might be expected.) He began by sending her to a convent school; the good sisters were asked by Reavis to help stimulate the waif's latent intelligence so that she could become his legally wedded wife.

Maria was registered in the adoption offices as his ward, and within twelve months, had undergone a Cinderalla transformation. Still very shy, it was now apparent that she was intelligent and lovely. She could now read and write both English and Spanish. And when she was suitably attired in fine silks, she gave the impression of being a child of royalty. She spoke and acted in the best of taste. Had she sat on the royal throne in Madrid, she would have been accepted as true-blue royalty.

James Addison Reavis was pleased. Now he began to plan the final act of his performance. Already, money was pouring into his newly opened offices in Tucson from those large railroad and banking interests who were hoping to satisfy his claims. Reavis used the money to outfit his ward in the finest of gowns. Then, he married Maria in full legal and religious splendor.

Now, as his lawfully wedded heiress, she could be Queen of Arizona. Almost immediately, after the wedding, Reavis hired the best available attorneys. They were instructed to spare little effort and expense in preparing his claim of ownership of the 11,000,000 acres of Arizona territory.

An amazing assortment of forged documents were offered in the courthouse before a judge. The townspeople of Tucson, the residents of the entire territory—not to mention the entire United States—were in an uproar. Who could challenge Reavis? If he won his case, this King of Arizona might claim ownership of still more lands. Furthermore, what if other heirs appeared and made claim to still more territories? The fear also arose that the Indians might revolt and legally claim the entire country as their own, and it would be difficult to dispute that they had indeed been the original settlers of the United States.

In the midst of it all, Reavis was calm and cool. He presented documents to the judge in the Tucson courthouse to show that, in 1788, the original De Peralta and first King of Arizona had a son. It was this son who inherited all of the vast territories now comprising the territory.

The lineage continued on, Reavis explained. The young De Peralta was an incompetent. He had ravished many women until he finally did marry, and then became the father of a child. This daughter, Maria de Peralta, married a wealthy arrival from the Spanish court and bore several children. To these children, the property passed. The lineage narrowed down to that of Isabella de Peralta. She gave birth to a child shortly after her husband died under mysterious circumstances. Isabella's daughter, also named Isabella, was the young girl who was now legally married to Reavis. Thus, it was Reavis who claimed ownership of all the territories originally granted to the first King of Arizona.

All the wills of the De Peralta family were "unearthed." Reavis offered these expertly forged papers, written in the Spanish language, complete with the idiom and style of the past two centuries. They were flawless. Top government experts were called in; they all pronounced them authentic.

In accordance with the law and with the terms of the Gadsden Purchase in 1853, any Spanish or American landowner who could produce authentic deeds signed by Spanish royalists or American realtors could keep their land. Since many squatters occupied land without any legal papers, they were evicted and had no claim to their land. But Reavis had documents from the Spanish royalists showing that he was the owner of the land. He owned more than a few acres. He owned most of this wild territory—almost two states.

Top Washington land surveyors found one loophole. They noted that if Reavis wanted to establish his claim, he needed first to establish his Arizona residency. He had not done so. It appeared that he had overlooked that technicality.

In court, Reavis calmly presented a newspaper. It was the *Phoenix Gazette*. Dated June 23, 1881, it contained the announcement of his arrival. The government's challenge of his residency qualifications were summarily dismissed.

By now, in 1885, dozens of landowners in the territory had grown frantic. They saw posted notices to the effect that if they did not want to be forcibly evicted from their properties, they could sign a "Quit Claim" for a reasonable sum of money. It was better than nothing.

Under a "Quit Claim" law, enforced by American courts, a squatter or anyone who could not show legal documents of ownership for his property, had a chance to sell out for a small amount of money. If he refused, he could be forcibly evicted by local marshalls. The courts preferred a small payment to avoid the hiring of marshalls and possible shootouts resulting from arguments. It was the easiest way to pay the squatters and have them voluntarily leave their properties.

In the meantime, while the Arizona and Washington, D. C. courts were kept busy with those trying to dispute Reavis' claim, the King and Queen of Arizona were growing immensely wealthy. In 1886, the queen bore the king two children: a prince and a princess. They all lived in regal splendor in a huge stately palacelike home in Tucson. The "royal family" later bought mansions in New York, St. Louis, Washington and Mexico. They would be the family's summer and winter castles, it was explained. The King of Arizona announced that as soon as the government acknowledged his rightful ownership of the territory, he would build a huge palace, and those who recognized his royal lineage would be made members of the royal court. Needless to say, he soon had many followers.

Meanwhile, even King Alfonso of Spain acknowledged that the lineage was correct and that the newly designated Queen Isabella had once lived in the royal court in Madrid, but had been mysteriously abducted at an early age. No doubt, the Spanish royalists were outraged at the terms of the Gadsden Purchase, the independence of Mexico, and the loss of their properties. They were eager to have an ally such as the King and Queen of Arizona. Diplomatic relations were established between Spain and the Kingdom of Arizona and the idea was proposed that a Spanish army be sent (as well as gold) to help the new Kingdom establish itself. The very threat of a foreign army entering American soil was enough to motivate Washington to immediately summon still more experts in the hope of finding a way to stave off the threat that was besetting the United States of America.

In the meantime, all documents that Reavis had filed continued to be verified as authentic by American experts.

Congress quickly and unanimously enacted a law in 1887 which established a new Court of Private Land Grant Claims, complete with plenary powers. Immediately, the new court examined some 385 different claims to land under royal Spanish grants. They did acknowledge that many were authentic: 68 claims were verified and less than three million acres of land were left in the hands of the current owners. The rest of the claims had no written deeds from the United States or Spain and had to be taken away to be sold at public auction.

One claim was too time-consuming for the court to handle. This was the Peralta Grant. And so, to supplement the work of the court, additional legal experts were called in. They again combed the documents for flaws. This time, they combined investigation with detective work. Chemists were summoned to verify that the ink and the paper were, indeed, ancient. Chemistry, like photography, were both in their infancy; Reavis never anticipated the possibility that his work would be subject to scientific testing.

Investigators were sent to Spain and Mexico to verify further lineage claims. While the claims were verified in Cadiz, Madrid, Barcelona and the various monasteries in which papers were filed, new flaws appeared.

The piercing eye of the camera revealed that some words on the documents had been erased. Others had been substituted. Furthermore, an aged monk in Cadiz acknowledged that Reavis had been to see him, to look over the precious deeds and documents. When asked to show these deeds, the monk searched and searched and was shocked to find that they were missing. Reavis must have stolen them. (These stolen documents were the ones with erasures that only the eye of the camera could reveal.)

Encouraged, American investigators then examined the documents even more carefully with the use of various chemicals. They discovered that many lines of the documents had been erased and altered. Furthermore, in some ten-page documents, there were several substitute pages written with different types of inks. For example, while the original Spanish documents were written in iron ink, the substituted pages were written in dogwood ink. While the originals required a quill pen, these altered documents were often executed using a steel pen. Chemicals faded some of the altered lines and were able to show which names and dates had been altered.

By now, the tireless researchers learned that while some of Reavis' ancestors may have been credible, many were introduced, fabricated and reversed so that his ownership by right of marriage or document could not be questioned.

In the Spanish archives, chemists found that birth register pages had also been altered, and that Reavis' copies bore these same alterations. Since royal scribes never altered records, it was obvious that Reavis (who was identified as having visited the archives a few years before) had made these shocking and unlawful changes.

With this new evidence, the Tucson Land Grant Court

challenged Reavis. In a court hearing, in March, 1890, the photographic experts and chemists presented hour after hour of documentation to prove that not only had the documents been forged, but that everything Reavis claimed was a fabrication.

Reavis had never dreamed of the invention of a device like the camera, or of new chemical discoveries that could prove him a liar. If he had, he might have taken still additional precautions. But he had miscalculated, and he was now defeated.

A month later, charges of forgery and taking money under false pretenses were brought against him. The court knew that the money he had spent could never be returned. Those who had signed a "Quit Claim" were told that the documents were false and that their lands were safe; they may have lost money, but their properties belonged to them.

James Addison Reavis was convicted and sentenced to an eight-year term beginning in April, 1890, to be served in the Phoenix Penitentiary. His wife and two children, absolved of blame, fled to Denver, Colorado, where she filed for divorce. Then she vanished. It is believed that one of her children, the son, changed his name and later became a distinguished member of the bar and a member of Congress.

The people of the territory of Arizona breathed easier; the entire country was relieved. Gone was the threat of a foreign power on their lands. Now, they could go about their business of developing, pioneering and cultivating the West.

What of the King of Arizona? Deposed before he was crowned, James Addison Reavis served his eight-year prison term. When he was released, he went directly to Phoenix; he was hardly noticed. He spent his time reading newspaper reports about himself and his great years of glory. It is believed that he, in 1899, after release from prison, tried still another hoax—that he had forged a document to prove that he was the rightful owner of a small piece of farming property, about ten miles north of Phoenix.

Early in January, 1900, the *Phoenix Gazette* reported that James Addison Reavis was planning to move to San Francisco. He boarded a stagecoach and rode out of Phoenix. He never returned.

14

ARTHUR BARRY

The Suave Thief of the Social Register

TO THE UNDERWORLD, a "second-story man" is exactly what the words imply: a thief who specializes in gaining entry to homes through the second floor.

A second-story man will usually select suburban homes which are not well guarded, to enter. He will sneak into a bedroom and proceed to comb drawers and closets for every valuable he can find.

One of the specialists in looting the homes of the very wealthy was a man of impeccable tastes. Unlike the common, everyday thief, this man masqueraded as a member of "society." This afforded him access to the homes of the affluent and made it possible for him to walk off with whatever his heart desired.

To the world-at-large, Arthur Barry was no different than any other member of the upper strata. Tall and well groomed, he oozed a magnetism and charm that easily won the heart of any society dowager.

He was meticulous to a fault. His polished fingernails were cleanly trimmed; his shoes polished mirror-smooth; his imported suits highly styled. He wore a diamond stickpin in his tie and his finger displayed glittering rings—all part of his booty. Barry's manner of speech was succinct, respectful and effective —a reflection of his schooling at Harvard and Yale. The education gained through his travels world-wide on the best of ships, and in the best of company, enabled him to easily converse about the fine foods and elegant restaurants found in every major city throughout the world. He held his audiences spellbound with stories of how he dined with reigning kings and queens, and with the leaders of society.

Because of what everyone considered his impeccable credentials, Arthur Barry was invited to the wealthiest of homes. When attending a party or social function, he would excuse himself and disappear to the second floor, where he would search room after room. Trying to locate the most lucrative treasures, he would rifle drawers and safes; then march down the steps and out of the house, his pockets filled with valuable pieces. After that, he would not be heard from again, and no one ever suspected that it was *he* who had robbed them.

Barry focused his attention on those listed in the Social Register. He once boasted, "If I have a very long lifespan, I would like to go through the entire list of the Four Hundred. It would be marvelous to hoax 400 of society's top people. They would be fooled into believing I was one of them. They would never believe I was an impostor. To tell the truth, there are times when *I* believe I am not an impostor."

Arthur Barry, born in 1901 in a city near Boston, Massachusetts, was the seventh of the 11 children of hard-working immigrant Irish parents. Arthur's later need to outwit the wealthy obviously stemmed from his difficult childhood. His parents were strict, often unfair in their treatment of him. For an unexplained reason, many of his brothers seemed to have received better treatment.

Barry's father managed to keep the family together, even on the low wages he received from the local brewery. His parents were unselfish in that they often went without meals so that the children could be fed. Arthur recalled that his mother wore the same dress for eight years. His father never owned anything but working clothes and "he worked about six or seven days a week, from early morning to late in the evening."

When he reached the age of 12 or 13, Arthur decided that he wanted to help out. He was too young to get a permanent job demanding a great deal of responsibility, so he decided to run errands for local townspeople. One townsperson in need of a messenger was known for his ability as a "peteman"—a master safecracker. The man, named Big Mike, had brought his know-how with him from Ireland. He was involved in a trade that required expertise in making explosives and shaping special tools. If his special tools did not work, Big Mike would use nitroglycerin to blow open vaults and safes.

Somehow, Big Mike took a liking to young Arthur Barry. He promised to teach Arthur how to make considerable sums of money. Arthur had only to do as he was told.

To make nitroglycerin, Big Mike heated water and dynamite in a bucket atop the kitchen stove. He put the explosive liquid into bottles and sold most of it to other safecrackers. A trusted messenger was needed to deliver the bottles. The messenger had to be careful not to drop the bottles in transport. If dropped, fatal injuries might result. Big Mike felt that Arthur Barry was such a lad, and he agreed to pay him $10 per delivery. Soon, Arthur was travelling by train to nearby cities, carrying the dangerous cargo with him. Who would ever suspect that such a quiet young man of 14, wearing knickers, was carrying a bottle or two of nitroglycerin in the shabby suitcase held firmly between his knees! He appeared to be such a fine, well-groomed, respectable person that many were moved to say, "Ah, if only there were more such fine boys."

But this type of work did not appeal to Arthur for long. Even at this young age, he had higher goals. Once, while riding the trains, he noticed the wealthy society people in their silks and satins and jewels. He liked that. He wanted to be a part of that life. Later, he reasoned, "They couldn't possibly miss a few thousand dollars. I needed the money for my family and myself. It was always so much more satisfying to me to be able to take the wealth from the wealthy, rather than the poor. But I had to learn my trade so I began with the poor."

Arthur Barry began his career in crime when he was about 16. He selected a middle-aged couple who ran a small shop. Each night, he observed how they closed the shop, and carried the day's receipts home with them. (Banks did not yet have night depositories.) One such night, after much surveillance, he broke into their home through an unlocked rear window.

Very carefully, he made his way to a desk and silently eased open several drawers until he found the bundle of cash. He scooped up the money, stuffed it into his pockets, stealthily made his way through the window, and quietly closed it as he left. He netted several hundred dollars from the robbery. When he was later asked about this second-story crime and the risk of the couple awakening, he replied blithely: "I had no fears. Sure, they could have awakened, but the cards were stacked in my favor. I was fully awake. They would still be sleepy, maybe in a state of shock. I knew every door and corner as they did. I could very quickly have vanished before they had a chance to sound any alarm. Before I rob any house, I study it and make a mental blueprint of it."

This was his very special talent. He would always make a careful study of the layout and arrangement of the house he planned to rob. He would be as familiar with it as its occupants. He had a fantastic photographic memory; after several glances, an image was embedded in his mind.

As time went on, Arthur's brothers and sisters drifted away from home and, to help out, he began giving money to his parents, saying that he had earned it from working along the docks and waterfront. All the while, his eyes were on the workings of the "high fallutin" society folks.

Arthur Barry wanted to do more than just pick up a few dollars as a common thief; he wanted to develop into a perfect impostor.

He began to formulate plans when he was 19 or 20 years old. Aware that many of the prominent members of society were in New York, Arthur made his way there in 1920, rented a small furnished room, and started to study the society pages of the newspapers. He noted announcements of engagement parties, weddings, and other special functions in rich areas along the North Shore of Long Island.

He carefully selected his victims. On the day of an affair, he would drive out to the Island, park his car near the estate, and change into formal clothes. He washed his face and hands with the water from a jug which he always carried with him. Then he would comb his hair, spray on some cologne, scrutinize his appearance in the rear-view mirror and, when satisfied that he could pass as a member of the wealthy social set, would walk through the gates of the estate when no guard was on watch. If there was a guard, he would walk to the back and would easily scale the wall or creep through the hedges. He was always careful to maintain an impeccable appearance.

Arthur Barry would then casually stroll over to the cocktail table, smile at some guests, pick up a canape, munch on it, and mingle with the crowd—as if he belonged there. Since such parties usually had 100 or more guests and because he was as well dressed as any of them, it was not difficult for Arthur to pass as just another invited guest.

The next step would be to seek out the host and hostess and tell them how wonderful the party was. They were, of course, pleased by the compliment. He would engage them in conversation, telling them of his world travels, and of the night clubs and restaurants he had visited. Actually, he had never left the East Coast of the United States. Being an omnivorous reader, and having a retentive memory, he could converse convincingly about faraway, exotic places. When he finished his story, there was no doubt in anyone's mind that this was a fine young man, one who was much travelled, and a fine addition to their social set.

After gaining the confidence of his hosts, Arthur strolled around the grounds, and casually entered the house. If ever in need of an excuse, he could simply state that he had to "freshen up" in the bathroom. Once upstairs, he quickly located the master bedroom. Inside, he would search for the places where jewelry might be hidden. He would stuff his pockets, then return to the lawn party and resume mingling with the guests. He would seek out the host and hostess once more, and brazenly talk with them about his skiing trips to Switzerland, silently laughing to himself as he felt the fruits of his efforts weighing heavily in his pockets. He felt gratified as moments later he walked away from the lawn party and casually strolled toward his car that was always placed out of view of the guests. Then he would be off to the "fences."

"I knew many fences in New York," he said. "It's easy to sell jewelry when you know the right fences. I had several who gave me top dollar, since I gave them top quality. In no time at all, I must have accumulated a half-million dollars!"

Arthur Barry was self-taught in manners, etiquette, and speech. He could fool not only the leaders of society, but royalty as well. And, indeed, he once *did!*

In 1923 he visited a speak-easy near Broadway, in New York's East Fifties. It was during the prohibition era when society was enjoying forbidden liquor and thrilling to loud jazz. Arthur Barry had read an item in a column which stated that this particular speak-easy catered to royalty. He decided to investigate. Asking around, he learned that on a particular night, the Prince of Wales would be a visitor.

Arthur Barry had no idea *how* juicy the plum would be that he would pluck from the crown head of Britain—but the challenge was great. He went to the speak-easy, found the prince, chatted with him idly about his own trips to merry old England, and asked how His Royal Highness liked New York and the reason for his visit.

The prince talked, perhaps a bit too openly. He was obviously under the influence of alcohol. Arthur Barry listened, very carefully, not the least bit disturbed by the prince's guzzling. Barry politely sipped from his glass while the prince swallowed large gulps.

A few days later, a second-story thief entered the home of Mrs. Joshua Cosden at Oyster Bay, Long Island, and disappeared with close to $500,000 in jewels. Some of these precious pieces belonged to house guests of the Cosdens—who happened to be Lord and Lady Louis Mountbatten—cousins of the Prince of Wales. It was suggested that this had been a "finger job" because the newspapers had made no recent mention of the Cosdens or their house guests. When the jewelry was fenced, Arthur Barry was some $350,000 richer.

Arthur Barry loved lavish living. He wanted to live the life of a socialite, and soon moved into an elegant and luxuriously furnished penthouse. His wardrobe was large and impressive, but he had no jewelry. He liked to dine in good restaurants, enjoyed the theater, and had an eye for the ladies. Money started slipping through his fingers. The would-be society king had to search out additional ways of financing his high living.

Arthur delved into the pages of the Social Register and acquainted himself with the names of the wealthy and influential. In addition, having studied the society pages of the newspapers, he became a frequent guest (self-invited) at the affairs of the well-to-do. On every occasion, he stripped their closets of valuable clothing and gems.

Barry almost met his Waterloo at the home of one very wealthy horse breeder in upstate New York. He learned that the society leader was to hold a lawn party in celebration of the victory of his special horse. Arthur Barry employed his usual tactics to become a guest, and then surveyed the upper floor. But, here, he came across a challenge he had not met before. This horse breeder kept the family jewels in a 200-pound safe in the bedroom closet!

Barry rejoined the guests and brooded, but his mind was active and his ears were open. The host was bragging that no one could ever carry away his safe. After a few drinks, he divulged that the combination was the same as the license plate of his limousine.

That was all Arthur needed to know. He continued to mingle with the guests, then managed to locate the family garage. In it, he found the limousine. Quickly, he memorized the numbers on the license plate. Already, he could feel himself fondling the precious jewels that were locked in the safe.

The problem now became how to gain entrance to the upper bedroom. There were too many people in the hallways for him to be able to sneak into the bedroom and have adequate time to open the combination lock. He would need time and privacy. Barry considered feigning drunkenness in the hope that he would be shown to the master bedroom to sleep it off. But, he realized that he would more likely be placed in other rooms.

The challenge was as intriguing as it was difficult, and Arthur became more determined than ever to open the vault and remove the treasures within.

Another problem arose: time was running out. At nightfall, the horse breeder and his wife announced that due to the lateness of the hour and because they had to rise early the next morning, the guests were respectfully invited to leave.

The problem became the solution.

Arthur Barry pretended to drive off after bidding farewell to the hosts and their guests. He returned quickly and waited. When the estate was blanketed in darkness, he managed to climb up to the second story and open the window of the master bedroom. (He had unlocked it while he was strolling through the room earlier in the day.) He entered the room in which the host and hostess were sound asleep. The heavy liquor the couple had imbibed was doing its work.

Barry opened the closet door. Quickly, he manipulated the combination lock. A hushed clock. The vault door swung open. There, in the darkness, he saw the shimmering treasure. Quickly, he scooped up the valuables and stuffed them into his pockets. Then he locked the vault door, closed the door to the closet, tiptoed down the staircase and out into the fresh air. Moments later, he was driving back to New York with one million dollars worth of jewelry stashed away in his pockets.

The suave impostor chuckled as he read the headlines of the newspapers the next day. The police, the detective bureau, private investigators—all were baffled as to how someone had actually whisked the treasures out of a locked vault, before the eyes of everyone at the party. No one ever thought to look at the bedroom window that was closed, but not locked, as it had been when the wealthy horse breeder went to bed that night. This clue to the fact that it may have been an outside job, escaped them. Instead, they suspected that a party guest had managed to open the combination safe and steal the jewelry. It was even speculated that the wealthy socialite and horse breeder may have faked the robbery to collect insurance money. Needless to say, such innuendoes almost brought ruin to the horse breeder. Even if his prize horse continued to win race after race, he would never live down the implications and suspicions stirred up by the incident.

Arthur Barry was elated! He had successfully carried out a plan that seemed impossible. His net gain, after the jewels went through the "fences," was close to $750,000.

For a while, Barry basked in the glory of his accomplishments. If Arthur had one weakness, it was the urge to display his success. Since he was the self-proclaimed "king of society," he would live accordingly. For one thing, this meant stylish dressing. He wore hand-tailored suits, which he discarded the moment new styles appeared. He moved from penthouse to penthouse, often spending small fortunes on new furniture and decorative pieces. He traded in one limousine for another, and even considered purchasing a Rolls Royce. This weakness for a life of luxury soon drained his ill-gotten resources. He was constantly in need of more money.

But Arthur avoided one type of indulgence: servants. He would not hire any servants out of fear that they might grow suspicious of his comings and goings. A clever servant, after all, might deduce that the jewel robberies headlined in the newspapers always occurred on nights when the master was gone from the house.

On a warm September evening in 1925, Barry read that the Hotel Plaza would be flattered with a visit by Mrs. James F. Donohue, daughter-heiress of the wealthy F. W. Woolworth. He read further that this socialite heiress would rent a five-room suite for an indefinite stay in New York.

Without delay, Arthur Barry sized up the situation. It meant that the heiress would be travelling with her furs, her finery and her jewels. Using his usual assertive technique, he telephoned the hotel to ask when Mrs. Donohue would be having her dinner party. He was given the information he requested.

On the evening of Mrs. Donahue's party, Arthur put on his best tuxedo and headed for the Plaza. He socialized with the guests, impressing them with his knowledge of fine wines and gourmet foods. Before the night was over, he had left the suite with close to $750,000 worth of jewelry. Included were a 10-carat diamond ring valued at approximately $50,000. He also took a family heirloom consisting of a rope of pearls valued at close to $350,000. Astonishingly, the rope was actually taken from a dressing room table in the bedroom of the heiress. She was soaking herself in a tub in the bedroom just a few feet away. She had gotten into her luxurious bath when she thought everyone had left. But Arthur Barry, the socialite impostor, had carefully and quietly returned to take care of business.

Arthur Barry always knew *what* to steal; he stole selectively. As one detective later stated: "The thief knew his pearls. There were four ropes in the drawer. One rope was real. The imitations are so good, they could fool an oyster . . . but not that thief!" Barry himself explained it sometime later. He said, "To tell if a pearl is real, just rub it gently across your teeth. A real pearl feels like sandpaper. It grates. A fake pearl is smooth and slippery."

But not all of Arthur's jewel heists were as easy to execute as the Donahue robbery. On one occasion, in 1927, he decided to do a second-story job in the summer home of the Wall Street billionaire, Jesse Livermore. It was a luxurious estate in Kings Point, Long Island and for this robbery, Barry would need a helper. He knew one man he could trust, a man who would follow orders.

Together, shortly after midnight, Barry and his assistant

managed to climb up to the second story of the lavish home. But they were unprepared for the insomniac couple who were lying awake in bed. They were not the Livermores, but house guests.

Barry spoke in a low tone. It was very dark and he could not be recognized. "Good evening. Have no fear. We shall not disturb you. We have come here to collect some of your little trinkets."

As the aide watched over them, Barry went to the dressing table, gathered up several wrist watches and bracelets which he could immediately feel were made of platinum and worth about $2,000 each. He knew there had to be more; this could only be an appetizer.

He tiptoed into the bedroom of the Livermores. The noise awakened both of them. Arthur Barry quickly cautioned: "No harm will come to you. Just remain in bed and let me take care of things. Now, you needn't reach for the telephone. The wires have been cut. Remain silent, I beg of you."

From their dressing table, he scooped up close to $100,000 worth of jewels. The Livermores were petrified. They clung to each other as they stared at the thief in the dark shadows.

Before he left, he doffed his hat and said, "Bye-bye and do keep well!"

Newspapers wrote of the bold, polite thief for weeks afterward.

Barry's escapades went on and on. He was later questioned as to whether he felt any guilt about his wrongdoing.

"No, not really. Haven't you often read of socialites who hide their gems and fake a robber to collect insurance? Furthermore, socialites can afford their loss. If they're in the Social Register, they *should* be hoodwinked. They can afford it. Who's the hoaxer? I wonder."

The impostor's undoing was a result of his involvements with women. He liked showgirls. It is believed that one of them, in a jealous rage, recognized the vague description of him in the newspapers, and notified the authorities. In 1928, he was arrested by New York police. He was tried and convicted. The jewels could not be returned; all had been sold.

He could not return the money, except for several thousand dollars; all had been squandered. His furniture and clothes brought little at the auction that was held, but it did help pay the fee for his attorney, who managed to win him a reduced sentence of 25 years in the Auburn, New York prison.

Arthur Barry served less than a year. In mid-1929, he shot his way out of prison and managed to reach Albany, where a close friend gave him new clothes, some money, and a second chance on the outside.

For several years, he remained a successful fugitive. He married a girl who knew of his past activities. They lived the lives of a happily married suburban couple, he a salesman of windshield wipers, she a housewife. There was one moment of suspense in their years together. That was on the night of October 22, 1932, when the always-feared knock on the door came.

He answered. But the police were not looking for the escaped Arthur Barry. They were searching the home and examining the background of every new resident of this small town near Flemington, New Jersey. The Lindbergh baby had been kidnapped!

Because of the intensive questioning, his background was exposed. One detective finally recognized him, and he was taken into custody.

This time, Barry was placed in solitary confinement for five years, and under extra heavy guard for the 12-year balance of his sentence. Upon release, he was much older and much wiser. He returned to his faithful wife who implored her brother, owner of a chain of restaurants in Worcester, Massachusetts, to employ him. He did.

Arthur Barry, the self-styled king of society, now worked as a counterman, thanking patrons who left a few coins as tips for filling their orders.

"I have no regrets . . . except that I was caught. Would I do it all over again?" He winked. "What do you think? Bring back Robin Hood and he would do it again. I feel no guilt, either. I took from those who could afford it. I didn't annoy the poor man on the street. No, I went right to the top of society . . . and I was a king among kings!"

15

ROBERT PAGE

The Insurance Swindler

IT TOOK FIFTEEN YEARS before Robert Page was apprehended. Up until that time, he had succeeded in swindling some of the top insurance companies in the United States out of a minimum of one million dollars. He did it for the "thrill" —and the price he paid was many years in Sing Sing, the New York State penitentiary in Ossining.

"I did it for the money," he said. "But I did it more for the feeling of power. Here I was, an average person, with a very modest school education, with no knowledge of law or medicine as is common among the shrewd insurance people. But even though I was far down the ladder, I reached the top because I could hoax my way to the tune of some one million dollars.

"Call me an impostor. Call me a hoaxer. Call me a swindler. But call me smart! Because I did deceive the experts. Nobody else could do it by himself. So maybe I am not so dumb after all."

Robert Page came from a family of modest circumstances. He looked very much like any other office clerk or bookkeeper. But, Page's outer appearance was deceiving. Underneath was an unusual man who was driven by a need to be recognized as such.

Page was very deliberate in his planning. "I did not hoax the top people without preparing for it. As you know, many a hoaxer is caught because he does not study his craft. I resolved to study the field so that I would be even more knowledgeable than anyone else.

"How did I do it? To begin with, I selected my contacts. They would be insurance experts. This meant I would have to read up on accident cases, on insurance law, on various court-room techniques. A few weeks in the library with these do-it-yourself books, and a working knowledge of technical words, helped make me so familiar with insurance accident cases, that I could pose as an insurance adjustor and hoax not only my 'clients' but insurance companies, lawyers and even judges. There were times when I would appear in a courtroom as an insurance attorney. I pulled off my hoax so perfectly, everyone was fooled . . . even myself!"

Robert Page's career began in 1934 when he had a slight accident in the downtown area of New York City. He had stepped off the curb, unmindful of the changing traffic lights. A taxicab zoomed by and Page was hurled to the ground. Many witnesses were on the scene, but when the police and ambulance arrived, no one volunteered to bear witness to the accident. Robert suffered several fractures, and endured a long hospital confinement during which he grew more and more confident that he would collect a tidy sum from the company that insured the taxicab.

When he was finally released, he appeared in court. The taxicab driver was represented by an insurance company which charged that Robert Page had foolishly and carelessly stepped off the curb without heeding either the traffic light or the honking of the taxicab. It was insinuated that he may also have been intoxicated. Page never touched a drop of liquor, but he was unable to prove it to the satisfaction of the court.

After much testimony and deliberation, it was adjudged that Page was totally responsible for his own mishap and that the insurance company could not be held liable for his negli-gence. The insurance company representatives left court with a victory smile on their faces.

Robert Page left court flat broke, unable to pay the seven thousand dollars of medical bills that he owed. He was without a job or the prospect of a job. A long hospital confinement had cost him his means of livelihood as a freight handler. He had hurt his back and could not work because of this spinal weak-ness. He was embittered. He stood outside the courthouse and was determined to get revenge.

After the trial, a spectator who had attended the courtroom

proceedings approached him. The spectator, Bernard Carver, introduced himself as one who had also been cheated out of an accident payment, and who had succeeded in avenging himself by employing hoaxes directed against insurance companies. Through such tactics, he had managed to make a rather comfortable living.

Carver confided in Page, explaining that he needed a partner, and Page was only too eager to join forces with the successful swindler.

The method of operation would be simple. The first step would be to wait on a street corner—especially one at which accidents frequently occur. Eventually, a drunken tramp would step off the curb and be hit by a car. The car would stop. The tramp would get up, shake himself and stagger away, too sodden to know what hit him. The car would drive away.

Then Robert Page would go into action. First, he would jot down the car's license plate number. Then he would file an official report of a hit-and-run accident so that it would be on record. The entire case would then be turned over to an attorney friend of Bernard Carver. The attorney would ask few questions. He might surmise that a hoax of some kind was being perpetrated, but he would be more concerned with his promised one-third of the settlement—the usual percentage collected by an attorney.

Then Robert Page would call police headquarters pretending to be the arresting officer. "This is Officer Smith, Badge Number 1563," he might say. (It was rare that a desk officer taking a call would bother to verify the number.) "I just witnessed a hit-and-run. Here's the license number. Can you get me the owner's name?" In a few moments, he would have the name.

Robert Page would then telephone the car owner. "This is the social service department at the hospital," he would say. "We have here the victim of an accident as our patient. Witnesses have given us your license number. There is going to be a very big bill for medical treatments. It looks like this poor fellow has developed a bone disease as a result. Would you give me the name of your insurance carrier. I hope you're covered, sir."

The frightened car owner would be most cooperative, and

would volunteer all sorts of information. Since he had been discovered as the culprit in the disastrous affair, he would be very frightened that the hospitalized victim might be seriously injured. The charges against him—leaving the scene of an accident—could have dire consequences. He would give Page the name of his insurance carrier and tell him the extent of his coverage.

Robert Page would then arrange to have a summons served, demanding payment totalling more than three-fourths of the insurance coverage. The insurance company would request that the victim be examined at a doctor's office. Page's partner, Bernard Carver, would then play another role. He would dress shabbily and appear in the doctor's office with a few X-rays that would supposedly show the extent of the damage. (It would be easy enough for him to obtain such X-rays. He would merely pose as a medical student, and make purchases at various supply houses that sell old X-rays to students for study purposes.) Carver would fabricate some kind of excuse so the doctor would not examine him at that time.

Page listened attentively to Carver's plan. He agreed to participate. Page did exactly as Carver had suggested. All went smoothly. They now had time to further develop their strategy.

Robert Page saw the hoax starting to pay off. "We waited a day, then telephoned the adjustor and said we would settle for $5,500. He readily agreed knowing that a settlement would mean that he would avoid the courts, which might have asked for an even greater amount. Now, we telephoned our attorney friend, and said that we had to bribe the adjustor at least $1,000 to settle with us for $4,500. This brought the actual settlement figure down to $4,500. We would split this sum with the lawyer who never knew that we had hoaxed him out of $1,000."

Robert Page quickly became adept at the art of swindling insurance companies. He used the same ploy a number of times. Because he provided X-rays, the "injured" person never had to be examined by the physician. Page always reached a settlement with the company; consequently, there would be no need for further negotiations.

Page's partner, Bernard Carver, loved to play the horses. He liked the "fast life," and money was spent as quickly as it was made. He also liked to drink—which made him somewhat unreliable. Page always feared that his partner, under the influence of liquor, might talk too freely, and, at some point, implicate him in a scene that was being developed. Because of this, Page decided that it was time to break up the partnership.

Once he was on his own, Robert started to accumulate extensive files of X-rays. He obtained them in the manner he had successfully used before: by posing as a medical student, and making the rounds of various medical supply houses located near the major New York City hospitals. Often, he would put on the uniform of an intern to make his purpose less questionable.

On each of the X-rays he would write an assumed name, knowing that insurance investigators were always checking to see if the claimant had a record of any previous claims with their company.

Now Robert Page was ready to line up people who would claim that they were hurt in accidents. As he explains it, "These were called 'floppers' and 'divers.' A flopper is a man who fakes being hit by a car who makes a turn at a corner. A diver is one who does more than just pretend to be hurt. He will crawl on the floor, even pretend to be unconscious. Soon, I had a number of these partners. We would go to a crowded street where there were many cars. Then I would have a flopper or diver run out, as if to cross the street, just as the car was turning at low speed. The flopper would let out a loud cry and flop onto the floor. He would get up and pretend that he was seriously wounded.

"In some situations, if it was very dark, I would have a flopper run out to brush against a car as it was driving along. The flopper would slam his hands against the door or fender. He would make a loud noise. Sometimes, he would even have a small plank of wood to slam against a fender and this would sound like a bad injury.

"Usually, I would net some $2,000 or $3,000 for each so-called accident. There were times when I made more. Of course, I was never very greedy. I did not want to kill the goose that laid the golden egg."

Robert Page made the acquaintance of several truck drivers who were only too anxious to earn some extra money. When they had revealed to him their various route stops, he would map out his plan. The flopper would be introduced to the driver. Then a street corner would be selected that was as distant as possible from the nearest telephone. This was important, since it served as a valid reason for taking the "injured" man directly to the hospital; rather than waiting in the street or a nearby store until the police or an ambulance would come. Such intruders might spoil the plan by saying that the man was not very seriously injured, and did not require examination.

The plan was worked out carefully. The "injured" was given an assumed name and address. (Because most were derelicts, this was not difficult.) Usually, Robert Page would slip some money to another derelict who would be willing to testify that the "injured" had lived with him. If ever an insurance adjuster came to the building, the derelict's "friend" would verify that he lived there. He would even say, "Sure, he's the one who got hurt in the bad accident." This would help the case considerably.

When Robert Page arranged for a derelict to do a flop act, he himself would wait until the police pushed through the crowd to ask what was going on. Then he would come out of the crowd, and, without anyone realizing it, would manage the entire scenario. He would make certain that an ambulance was called, and that the police filled out a report describing the accident in full. It was important that this be a part of the official record.

When the flopper reached the hospital, he would start complaining that his entire arm hurt—from the tip of his fingers to his shoulder. At this point, the hospital suggested that X-rays be taken. But the flopper was ready for this: he refused. He said he wanted to be treated by his own doctor. In effect, he refused medical treatment.

The intern was, in this way, only able to draw a general conclusion and would enter the case in the hospital report as a possible fracture. This now became part of the record, too.

Robert Page explained it this way: "My floppers were trained not to let themselves be X-rayed. If they did, the hoax would be discovered. Furthermore, the intern might possibly say there was no fracture, just an abrasion or a contusion. This was of such small monetary value, it was hardly worth the time or effort. So it was a rule that no hospital X-rays were to be taken, and the flopper would refuse treatment, and eventually be released. But it was entered on hospital records." He then added: "It has to be *legal*."

Within one week, the attorney would enter the picture. He would fill out the required forms and follow all formalities. He elicited only as much information as was necessary to prepare and present a case. He was concerned exclusively with his fee, and didn't care to know too much about the hoax. He never made mention of it, but did a thorough job.

The attorney would forward a claim letter to the owner of the accident-causing vehicle. One week later, an insurance company adjuster would normally telephone the attorney to determine the extent of the injuries. The attorney would reply, "It's a very serious injury. That is as much as I can tell you since my client has not given me a complete medical report. But why don't you arrange for a physical examination by your company's doctor?"

As soon as the insurance adjuster would agree, the lawyer would add, "My client isn't available right now, but he should be back in circulation in a few weeks. So I'll get in touch with you."

Now Robert Page began the next phase of his hoax. He contacted a physician who would agree to enter the case in his files. This was necessary to strengthen his case. He explained to the doctor the circumstances of the "accident" and then added, "I have quite a few of these accident cases. If we work closely together, it should be well worth your while. Now, may I suggest, doctor, that you first make out a record card for your files? It must show that you treated the 'injured' patient. Have no fear. You're not giving me anything in writing. I would like you to say that you have seen the accident victim —should the insurance company and the attorney call for more facts. That's all you have to say. Since this will take some time, I want you to be compensated."

The hoaxer slipped him a $50 bill.

Page later divulged that there were many physicians who agreed to take part in the scheme. After all, they had only to invest in an index card and a statement that the "victim" was one of their patients.

Robert Page lived up to the old saying that there is no

honor amongst thieves. The moment the doctor turned his back, he would steal some letterheads or slide some prescription pads into his pocket. He would use the stationery to prepare a complete medical report stating the nature of the injuries, the condition of the patient and specific dates of examination. With the use of a good first aid book and medical dictionary, Page was able to describe the injuries precisely and indicate the medication required. He could even record anticipated or suggested treatment.

Within a few weeks, the insurance company doctor called the attorney to examine the patient. Robert Page then found a vagrant who closely resembled the original one, briefed him on all details, and rehearsed him well. Everything was carefully planned so that this second vagrant would not make a mistake. Surprisingly enough, the derelicts were able to play their roles flawlessly.

When the "victim" was examined, the doctor first looked at the fake X-rays supplied by Page and then at the injured part. The injury had obviously "healed"; it had, after all, been several weeks from the date of the accident. But the X-rays were "proof" of the injury and this meant that there had to be a settlement made. On the average, a settlement of $3,500 could be arranged without much difficulty. Of this amount, Robert Page would net close to $3,000 for having expended very little effort.

At times, a fallen "victim" was brought to a doctor who insisted upon giving him a thorough examination. By some instinct, Page knew when this would happen, and worked hard to avoid it. One method he employed was to give the derelict a few shots of liquor, and force him to eat a large chunk of garlic. When he showed up at the doctor's office, he was so fetid, sodden and smelly, the doctor could hardly wait to get rid of him. He examined him quickly and hurried him out of the office, after hastily filling out a superficial report.

Whenever obstacles arose, Robert Page knew how to deal with them. By 1940, he had reportedly collected well over one million dollars in insurance settlements. He was always careful not to keep records that could be traced or seized. He avoided banks. Usually he would open an account and maintain it just long enough to cash some checks. Then he would close it out.

More often, he would go to check cashing agencies, produce false identification, and walk out with cash. His luxurious apartment was filled with any number of hiding places where cash was secreted.

"I kept all records in my mind," he said. "There was always the risk that a flopper would be recognized by a policeman or a hospital intern. I tried to avoid this by taking my floppers to different parts of New York City—and to different hospitals. But a risk always presented itself. What if an intern from a Brooklyn hospital was transferred to a Bronx hospital and recognized the derelict? Of course, a good excuse could be that 'all vagrants look alike.' My derelicts always had different names so there could be no such cross-checking. But it was a risk."

The hoaxer did not have his flopper get involved with just *any* car. He preferred small station wagons, or trucks. He was always careful to note the license plate of an approaching car. He explained why at one point, saying, "A very low license number suggests that the driver or car owner is an important person or public official. I didn't want to risk getting involved with them."

On one occasion, in 1941, a flopper decided to do a dive before a car approaching the Hotel Astor. The flopper moaned and groaned. The policeman approached, looked into the car, tipped his hat and called out, "Good morning, Your Honor."

Hearing this, Robert Page hurried over to the fallen flopper, and pretending to help him, whispered in his ear, "This guy's a judge. Say you're all right. Refuse help. Just walk away. You'll get paid just the same."

The flopper agreed, got up and said, "Oops, my fault. Didn't look at the street light. I'm okay," and just walked away.

Page would occasionally come across insurance companies that demanded that the victim be thoroughly examined. They wanted X-rays taken by their own company doctors. If this happened, the hoaxer would employ his powers of persuasion. Like most hoaxers and impostors, Page made a marvelous impression. His seeming sincerity coupled with a nice appearance and cultured manner of speaking would invariably achieve the desired results.

Page would arrange a meeting with the insurance company's agent and explain that his client was short of money. After some discussion, it was mutually agreed that an out-of-court settlement could be reached. In fact, the hoaxer would make it appear that his client was losing several thousand dollars by making this quick settlement; and was only agreeing to it because he was under extreme duress.

Robert Page learned that almost every insurance company was eager to make a settlement to avoid costly medical and legal bills. He used this information to great advantage whenever a company insisted upon a thorough examination. It almost always worked. The average representative was eager to save the company money by bringing the case to an early close. "I would make a nice settlement that avoided the risk of having the victim examined," he explained. "There were several occasions when the company refused to settle without first taking X-rays. I would say I would discuss it with my clients. Then I would manage to ease out of the case, even drop it—to avoid any risk of being caught."

Page was versatile. He would have his victims suffer broken arms, shoulders, legs, fractured ribs, and just about any other conceivable misfortune. He had endless numbers of X-rays on file that could be used to cover any eventuality.

He would never let his floppers know what kind of a settlement was reached. "Sure, they'd get mad. Many of my floppers thought I made as much as two hundred dollars per accident. To a wino or derelict, this was a lot of money. But I explained that I had to share the money with doctors, lawyers, insurance people—and very little was left for me. Sometimes, I'd tell the flopper that I made less than the twenty or fifty that he was getting. Actually, my average accident netted me some five or six thousand dollars, but I would not let the flopper know that I received even a fraction of this amount."

Strangely enough, a flopper employed by Robert Page was never hurt in an "accident." In fact, not a single flopper was bruised or so much as had his clothes torn.

One woman flopper, considered Page's best, was Rose Turner. She had originally been a pickpocket in the theater district. In underworld parlance, she specialized in clipping "binger bags," women's purses that have easy-to-open clasps. It happened that Robert Page and his criminal associate were on Broadway, near Duffy Square (a few blocks from Times Square), when they happened upon a robbery.

The associate recognized Rose Turner and told Robert Page of her history as a pickpocket. He speculated about what had happened. A crowd had seized Rose, her hand still on another woman's pocketbook.

The associate quickly received instructions from Page. He flashed a phony police badge at a young rookie cop who sought to take charge. In a low-key authoritative tone, he said, "I'm from headquarters. I'll take charge. You disperse the crowd. Give the other woman her bag. I'll bring this one to head-quarters. You can come in later on. Get the other woman's name and other facts."

The associate then walked Rose Turner to a safe distance, and got into a car where Robert Page was idling the motor. They revealed to Rose their true identities and then had dinner. Soon afterwards, the pickpocket was convinced to become a lady flopper.

Page was pleased with the new addition to his "family." He pointed out: "A woman victim seems to arouse more sympathy and it is always easier to get a good amount of money for an accident. But Rose liked to drink too much. That was the trouble. So after I used her a few times, I paid her off and we parted good friends."

One very special accident hoax in the Spring of 1942, which Page is fond of recalling, netted him a tidy sum.

"I heard that a basal skull fracture could bring top dollar, especially if the victim lost some of his functions. But I would need to put a flopper in a private hospital or pay a doctor a very big price to say he had treated such a patient. This would be very risky and extremely costly, especially with such an accident.

"So I contacted a close associate of mine at a hospital. I asked him to take a spinal tap of a deceased person. Then I cut my finger, and put some blood into the test tube filled with fluid so it would indicate a basal skull fracture. In the meantime, I arranged to have a doctor say he had treated the patient in his office. The doctor realized that this could bring in a lot of money, and kept insisting upon larger and larger retainers.

"You might call it a form of blackmail. . . . Well, I realized I had aimed too high. So as to avoid going broke, I decided to settle. The settlement came to $35,000, of which $10,000 went to pay the doctor and other people, and the smaller amount of $100 to the flopper.

"Afterwards, I decided to be careful not to get too involved because one mistake could bring everything crashing down on me."

For more than 15 years, Robert Page confounded the insurance companies. He was careful to live quietly and simply, and was able to throw off all suspicion anyone may have wished to direct his way. He had a nice apartment, drove a plain car, but was careful not to show too much wealth. He established a good credit rating by presenting himself as a salesman for a company. In fact, he did work at this trade in his spare time, and did earn good commissions.

By 1948, when his career reached its climax, he had amassed close to one million dollars. And his career might have carried on indefinitely had he not committed a small error.

A claim was presented against a car owner who had taken out insurance only one week before the "accident." The claim was filed in the name of one Ralph N. Lewis who allegedly worked for a small restaurant supply company. An investigator for the insurance company did something unusual. For no reason at all, he did not telephone Lewis, but walked into the restaurant supply company's office, asking to see Lewis.

Robert Page had arranged for a foreman at the company to say that the injured Lewis no longer worked there. Because of the injury, he was no longer employed by them. When asked for the injured man's representative, the name of Robert Page was given.

The insurance company investigator could not track down Page. He had several addresses for him, but at each place he visited, he was told that Page occasionally came in, that he received a lot of mail which was held for him, and that he picked it up from time to time.

This alerted the insurance company. Unable to find Robert Page, more than a dozen agents were put on his trail. Soon, the District Attorney entered the picture. Other insurance companies were notified. They produced records showing that they had made settlements with Page. A pattern emerged: X-rays were always provided by Page; settlements were always made, thus avoiding court proceedings; in all cases, the victim was never again seen.

Page was very closely observed. When he was found, the FBI, called into the case, authorized a telephone wire-tap. As fate would have it, among the first calls taped, Page was heard making appointments with doctors over the telephone. His conversations were clearly incriminating. This was all the evidence that the authorities needed.

In 1949, before the New York State Supreme Court in Albany, Page claimed to have used up the money he had fraudulently obtained. No amount of persuasion could make him divulge the whereabouts of the million dollars he had amassed. He was sentenced to a four-to-eight year term in Sing Sing. Upon his release, Page left the grounds, took a train to New York . . . and vanished from sight.

The million dollars was never recovered.

16

CHARLES BECKER

The Counterfeiter Who Fooled All the Experts

THE END OF THE NINETEENTH century was a time in history when everything appeared to be safe and secure. There was some hardship, to be sure, but the world was not yet embroiled in the wars that were to change the face of the earth. In this same atmosphere, young Charles Becker, alias Dutchman, began his illegal activities.

Charles Becker was a printer and an engraver, trades quite common to hoaxers. He was an artist, a master at his craft and as such, Becker could make engravings and counterfeit money that defied detection even by Pinkerton's National Detective Agency, Scotland Yard and the French Sureté. In the course of his career, Charles Becker manufactured and distributed millions upon millions of counterfeit dollars and securities throughout the world.

The United States Secret Service was baffled—and admitted it. One Secret Service agent tried to determine which of two $20 bills was authentic; one had been counterfeited by Becker. Only the serial number enabled him to do so.

"No wonder we can't find this counterfeiter," shouted the agent. "*His* money is better than the real stuff!"

The Dutchman was a perfectionist. He would work for months preparing counterfeit plates. If they were not completely satisfactory, he immediately destroyed them. On one occasion, he counterfeited nearly $200,000 worth of Bank of England currency. Upon completion of the job, he burned the entire lot, remarking, "When I crumpled the pound notes, the sound was different than crumpling genuine notes."

On another occasion, when he came to San Francisco, he had counterfeited what amounted to $500,000 worth of United

States goldbacks. He explained: "The counterfeit goldbacks just *smelled* different than the real ones."

Charles Becker, the master counterfeiter who was able to net millions upon millions in profits from fake money, had a true Jekyll and Hyde personality. He wanted to establish himself as a pillar of righteousness. During the work day he was gainfully employed by a legitimate enterprise. (He maintained that a man under suspicion would have several strikes against him if he could not show a record of employment.) He attended church every single Sunday and, ironically enough, was a member in good standing. He even solicited funds for the church.

The Dutchman was a clean liver and a lover of nature. He did not smoke, did not drink, ate modestly, and loved walking. He loved to sit amidst trees, in gardens, or by the seaside. Although he accumulated millions of dollars from his counterfeiting operations, the Dutchman spent very little—only for necessities. At the peak of his career, he had so many different bank accounts that it would have taken him days to cash them in.

Charles Becker was born in 1903, in Wurttenberg, a city in central Germany. He had little formal education, but read a great deal on his own. He became fluent in German, English, French, Spanish and Italian and was a voracious reader of the literary works of the greats of Europe and America. He loved classical music and art. Whenever he came to an unfamiliar city, he would acquaint himself with its culture by visiting many of its landmarks and cultural centers.

As is typical of most hoaxers, clues as to what possessed this man to turn to a life of fraud and deception can be found by studying his early childhood.

Charles was the only son of a Wurttenberg butcher. His mother was a chronic invalid. A younger sister was plagued by many ailments; she was not expected to live. His butcher father earned a good living but much, if not all, of his earnings went to pay hospital and doctor bills for his ailing daughter. Consequently, money was scarce, and there were days when Charles Becker did not know if he would be fed that night.

At one point, later in life, Charles remarked: "I always remember seeing my father running nervous fingers through his hair, even sobbing, as he sat at the kitchen table, under an oil lamp, trying to find ways to avoid the creditors. All I do remember of my childhood was insecurity, the threat of hunger, my father being put into a debtor's prison, and my mother or sister dying. I can never forget such memories, no matter how hard I try."

It was this childhood poverty that made Charles determine never to go hungry in adult life.

Becker gave evidence, early in life, that he might become a talented artist. By the time he was 10 years old, he was drawing sketches of his parents and street scenes of his native Wurttenberg. But he also showed evidence of being more than an artist. His work possessed a strange quality. With his pencil or crayon, he did more than paint a picture. He gave it a photographic reality, making the finished product appear almost like a reflection of the actual scene.

As he later recalled, "I could just look at someone's face, or any object, study it for a moment or two, and then I could copy it down on paper without having to look at it again. I suppose you would say that I had a photographic memory."

The idea of becoming a hoaxer may have begun when a friend once offered to give him a coin *if* he could duplicate his signature. Charles did so with such perfection that the townspeople of Wurttenberg were stupefied. Before long, Charles was copying other signatures for small fees.

When Charles was 11 years old, the Becker family was feeling the financial pinch. The butcher business was failing. His mother and sister (whom he loved deeply) were ailing, and they needed large amounts of medication. Young Charles was taken out of school to help support the family.

Having but one proven talent, he decided to make use of his artistic ability. He was offered an opportunity to apprentice with the town's only engraver, and he accepted it.

Charles did well. Within two years, he knew much more about the art of engraving than his master. His work was superior to that of his experienced teacher and everyone who visited the engraving shop began to ask Charles to do the work. Despite this, his employer continued to exploit him and pay him minimal, "slightly-above-starvation" wages.

Charles Becker continued to work in the engraving shop until he neared his twentieth birthday. At this time he began to think of his future. He thought of quitting because of the low wages. But since his master had the only engraving shop in town, he had little alternative. The expense involved in moving to another city was great and Charles had to save every penny he could, to support his parents and sister. He was trapped.

At about this time, Charles fell in love with an attractive blonde girl: Clara Bechtel. She was an impertinent type—arrogant, demanding, but very lovely. She told Charles, "If you want me, you have to prove it. Give me a ring and then I'll belong to you!"

Charles had no money to buy a ring, but he did have something else—a talent for duplicating signatures. Never before had he entertained the slightest notion of using his talent for deceptive purposes, but he was desperate. He loved Clara Bechtel; he wanted her. She might be the only possession he would ever have, and he did not want to lose her. So he succumbed to an unsavory impulse. He decided to sign someone else's name to a check.

Having seen the wealthy socialites of Wurttenberg parading around in their silks and finery, while at the same time mistreating all the lesser folk, looking upon them as if they were downtrodden dogs, he concluded that it would be no crime to fleece them. They treated their pet dogs better than they did the poor people of the city, so why not fool the wealthy folk? There could be nothing wrong in that!

The mere thought began to inflate Becker's ego. But even more important, the money would pay for a ring that would mark his engagement to the lovely Clara Bechtel. Without evaluating the consequence of his proposed action, he wrote out a check, and forged the signature of a leading citizen of Wurttenberg. The check was signed with such perfection that even Charles Becker could not believe it was a forgery. The check would be sufficient to buy an engagement ring, with a little spending money left over.

Becker took the check to a store in a nearby town. He assumed the identity of the signer and managed to carry off the purchase of a lovely engagement ring with the forged check.

Clara Bechtel was delighted with the ring. She and Charles became engaged. Everything looked rosy for a while . . . until the wealthy citizen discovered the cancelled check that had been forged. The jeweler of the nearby town rememberd the purchaser, and was able to describe him. The description fit Charles Becker. In no time at all, the Wurttenberg police found Becker and arrested him. The ring was retrieved from Clara and the engagement was broken.

Becker might have been imprisoned if not for the town's sympathy for Becker's ailing mother and sister, and for his father who had never done anything dishonest. Sympathetic Wurttenberg citizens convinced the jeweler that it would be wise to drop the charges. The jeweler agreed, and so Charles Becker avoided prison. But he immediately was fired from his job, and could find no other job in the entire city. There was no alternative but to leave town to seek his fortune elsewhere.

In the midst of this turmoil, his mother died. Shortly thereafter, his sister developed pneumonia and, after a lingering illness, died. Added to these tragedies, his father was stricken with a heart attack and he, too, died. Having a "criminal" son was, undoubtedly, a contributing factor, and Charles recognized this when. sometime later, he stated: "I blame myself for all that happened. If only I had had enough money to buy an engagement ring for Clara Bechtel, their lives would have been spared." This was an indelible scar that was forever engraved in his memory.

After a period of mourning, Charles took stock of his situation. It was a lack of money that had caused such tragedy; it was the uneven distribution of wealth. Becker resolved that never again would he be so impoverished. Never again would he suffer because of a lack of funds.

In 1924, unable to find work, and with debts piling up, Charles Becker did what many single men of the day were doing, he made his way to New York. He did so by working at odd jobs until he reached France. There, he hired himself out as a stoker on a passenger steamer to New York.

After a long and difficult journey, he landed in the city whose streets were reputed to be paved with gold. He searched for the gold and glitter, but what he found was slums, underworld crime and discrimination against foreigners. He discovered too, that wages in New York were sometimes lower than those in Europe.

He was in desperate straits when, one day, he met a new arrival from England. The fellow was a merchant seaman who had stolen the ship's cash box, jumped ship, and after having spent much of it on liquor and women, was now on the run.

The Englishman, Floyd Simpson, teamed up with the likable Charles Becker. From Floyd, Charles learned English rather quickly. Soon, they were breaking into Fifth Avenue mansions, stealing whatever they could carry off and selling the objects to fences. They managed to make ends meet with the small amount of money their life of crime was able to yield.

One night in 1926, the two men managed to gain entrance to a Park Avenue town house. As they closed the window through which they had just entered, they saw a policeman, coming around the corner. Both of them froze. The policeman, who hadn't seen them, might have walked on if nervous Simpson hadn't knocked over a vase.

Quickly, Charles Becker evaluated the tense situation. The policeman headed toward the entrance of the house. He would have to get rid of him. Simpson would have to hide before the policeman got there. The very moment that the policeman opened the door, Becker appeared and started shouting, "Officer! Officer!" He sounded hysterical. "Please you must help. Someone is being beaten and robbed around the corner. You must hurry!"

In a flash, the policeman followed Becker. When they got there, no one was to be seen.

"How many were there?" asked the officer.

"Three of them!"

With that, the policeman and Becker split up in search of the nonexistent robbers. This gave Becker time to sneak back to the house, join Floyd Simpson, and help him carry off the booty to a thieves' lair near the waterfront. Simpson congratulated Becker: "My boy, for a foreigner, you've got a great future ahead of you."

Becker smiled. *"We* have a great future ahead of *us,"* he corrected the Englishman.

So it was that they joined forces to pull the same acts in other cities across the Atlantic seaboard. Whenever a policeman suspected that someone was breaking into a house, Becker used the same ruse of yelling, "Help, police! Help, police!" Often, he would lead the policeman to a corner where a robbery was allegedly taking place. Other times, he would yell just enough for the policeman to come running, so that Simpson could get out of the house. At times, the young Becker would run so fast that a policeman would be unable to follow. This gave Simpson time to escape, too.

But this was just small pickings for Becker. He eventually told Simpson, "This isn't what I came to America for. I'm afraid we shall have to split. This is all too small. I cannot waste my life on small amounts." They parted ways in 1929, and Charles Becker began to make plans of his own.

He knew that he had the ability to forge and counterfeit. He knew that he was a master engraver, thanks to his apprenticeship in Germany. Why not put those talents to more profitable use? There was little or no competition. Counterfeiting required high skill, and the average criminal was not so gifted.

Becker planned and prepared for his further activity very carefully. He studied counterfeit money in various museums and money exhibits. He read as much as he could about the subject. He noted the mistakes of amateurs: terrible paper, green ink that was bluish, gold ink that was closer to pink. He was disgusted by such amateurish work; he vowed never to be so sloppy and unprofessional.

Already possessing a good knowledge of the art of making engraving plates for counterfeit bills, Charles now turned his attention to studying about dyes, bleaches and inks.

He got a job at a New York chemical plant, from which he stole small amounts of necessary materials. In his furnished room, he created a small laboratory. He decided not to buy any paper for his counterfeiting operation unless it was as good as the paper upon which real money was printed. He saved up a quantity of actual dollar bills, and then bleached them white— without destroying the paper. In the history of counterfeiting nobody had ever done this before. Becker had perfect paper— made by the U.S. Mint!

Charles engraved plates for $10 bills, and bought a small printing press. Night after night, the Dutchman busied himself with his work, but he was not easily satisfied. Every bill looked counterfeit to his expert eye. He would take no chance. After working for six months, he finally created an engraving and produced counterfeit ten dollar bills that met his standards. They were perfect specimens, he thought, and he decided to test them. He took a few to a bank and said boldly, "Let me have these in single dollars, please."

The teller scrutinized the bill.

"What's the matter?" he demanded. "Think it's a fake?"

"Oh, no. No, sir!" responded the teller. "It's just a habit with me. Now, how would you like these?"

"In singles."

"Very good, sir."

Encouraged by his success, Becker started to print more and more counterfeit ten dollar bills. He kept his chemical job so as to have a dependable source of supplies and to present an image of being a working member of society.

Before long, the Dutchman had accumulated about $50,000 in exchange for the bogus ten dollar bills. But it was still small pickings. Somehow. through the underworld, word of Becker's activities reached his former compatriot, Floyd Simpson. Simpson reappeared on the scene and warned Becker: "Better cut in some other folks, lad, or they'll squeal on you."

"Let them do what they will," retorted Becker. "I worked hard for myself, not for some blackmailers."

To be safe, he gathered up his equipment and sneaked across the Hudson River to New Jersey. There, he buried everything. In case those "other folks" mentioned by Simpson should disclose his activities to the police, Becker wanted to remove all possible evidence from the furnished room in which he lived.

Becker's thoughts now turned to making preparations for a gigantic hoax that would net him millions—not mere thousands—of dollars.

He happened upon a small, almost childish-looking man, who was appropriately nicknamed "Little Joe." Joe came from a prestigious family, but he tired of society balls and house parties and began to make friends with unsavory characters.

When Becker met Little Joe, he discovered that Joe had one weakness: he was a kleptomaniac. And it was this weakness that Becker used to his advantage.

"Little Joe, aren't you afraid you'll get caught?"

"Not me. All I take is small things, things I can stuff in

my shoes or socks. I dump empty wallets and pocketbooks in a hallway. I dump my wallet there, too. Then, in the middle of a dance, I start yelling that I've been robbed. My pockets are empty. All the loot is stashed down below. So everyone thinks I've been a victim with the others. That's all."

"That sounds good, Little Joe," said Becker. "I have been working on a plan to set up fake brokerage houses throughout Europe. I want you to go with me and help me. To begin, we'll need at least $100,000 in cash. So I'll print up some counterfeit bills. We'll cash them throughout the city. When we have enough, we set sail for Europe."

Becker now had to retrieve his buried printing press—which he did. He printed the bogus bills and again buried the printing press. Soon, the pair had $100,000 of real money in their possession. Before leaving for Europe, two more partners joined the scheme. One was Andrew Sawyer, an escaped convict who had been a confidence man. The other was Philip Carter, a close friend of Sawyer.

When the four arrived in London in 1935, the setting was laid for the start of a hoax that would shake the financial foundations of Europe. They began by buying a lovely brick house in the better part of London. Then, Becker quickly set his scheme into motion. He opened a small brokerage office on Threadneedle Street and hired several clerks. The firm was soon doing legitimate business in stocks and bonds. All who knew the foursome regarded them as honest men of finance. That was the impression Becker sought to create, and he was pleased that his plan was proceeding as designed.

In a locked room on the top floor of their brick house, the Dutchman started to arrange the engraving and printing setup. Little by little, they purchased dyes, bleaches, acids, inks. They made purchases separately, in different parts of London, in very small amounts, so as not to arouse suspicion.

Before long, Becker was ready to make his first counterfeit pound note. Again, he bleached authentic paper. After five months of labor, he was able to obtain what he hoped would be a perfect engraving. To most observers, it was perfect, but to the perfectionist Becker it was not satisfactory. The ink did not pass his own test. So he labored for several more weeks until the ink was pronounced "perfect."

The Dutchman now counterfeited the equivalent of $25 in American money. To test his ability, he took the counterfeit bill to a bank and told the teller that he had acquired it from someone he did not trust. He suspected, he said, that it might be fake. The teller studied it carefully, discussed it with another teller. Both pronounced it authentic. But the perfectionist refused to accept their verdict.

Boldly, he marched right into the offices of Scotland Yard. He presented the bill to their experts and asked if they could assure him it was genuine. The experts studied it carefully, and said it was a real bill.

This gave Charles Becker the confidence he required. He had hoaxed not only bank tellers, but the experts of Scotland Yard as well. He was ready to put his master plan into action.

He arranged to have Andrew Sawyer and Philip Carter set up their own brokerage house. Becker's brokerage house had many customers, and some overflow. Becker would steer customers to this bogus Sawyer-Carter, Ltd. trading house. The two principles were so properly garbed that they led everyone into believing that they were authentic brokers.

The scheme demanded a simple procedure. Valid securities were purchased with counterfeit money by Sawyer and Carter, at the *phony* brokerage house. The good securities were then given to Becker's *authentic* brokerage house and sold for genuine money. Becker accumulated the genuine money which was secreted away under assumed names.

Charles would never let anyone interfere with his meticulous craft. But a problem developed. The phony Sawyer-Carter, Ltd. unloaded the Dutchman's counterfeit money in return for real securities at a rate swifter than Becker could turn out the money. He was physically healthy, and was able to labor throughout the night, but the demand for 25 pound notes was so great that he could not meet it. There was only one solution: he would have to counterfeit bills of higher denominations.

He worked week after week until he was satisfied that he could successfully counterfeit 100 and 500 pound notes. Again, he tested these new bogus bills at various banks; they were pronounced authentic. Before long, the counterfeit money was passing through Sawyer-Carter, Ltd. at an average rate of $25,000 per month, a considerable sum for the time.

Charles Becker made a great deal of money from his own legitimate brokerage house, and he started to speculate in the stock market. These dealings were honest, and he succeeded in earning about one-half million dollars a year.

Now Charles wanted to *enjoy* his money; he wanted entertainment. He started traveling throughout Europe, stopping at the best hotels and dining at the finest restaurants in every capital.

He developed a taste for the finer things in life. While he had always liked women, they never satisfied him as much as did the joy of engraving bogus money. At times, he even slipped these women some of his bogus bills, and enjoyed a secret laugh of triumph.

By 1940, Charles Becker had stashed away millions of dollars. No one was the wiser. All of Europe was flooded with the bogus bills and the hoax appeared to have an endless lifespan. The Dutchman decided to expand. He followed the same plan in Paris; that is, he opened one legitimate and one illegitimate brokerage house, and the same monetary exchange continued.

Again, he needed associates. He had to find men whom he could trust to manage the bogus offices. He selected those who were confidence men, those who had prison records. They would fit right in with his plans. He even told some of them about his perfect counterfeits, and they agreed to work at very handsome salaries.

In Paris, Becker purchased an attractive home that had once been the residence of a prince. It was within walking distance of the Louvre. There he set up machines to counterfeit French money. He found it less challenging than previous undertakings because French money was not very meticulously made. He soon had his first high denomination franc bills rolling off the presses.

One of the men hired was a one-time bogus English nobleman, Clive Higgins, a character whose dubious past included being a swindler. Clive Higgins was soon set up in a plush office beside the Paris Bourse as the president of Higgins, Ltd. Investments-Securities.

Higgins frequented many sidewalk cafés and fancy restaurants. He had a natural charm, and was exceptionally suave. Before long, he offered to purchase somewhat depressed securities for a good price. He paid for them in counterfeit bills and then resold the securities for real money. The system continued until Becker and Higgins had accumulated many more millions of dollars in real money.

Becker decided to press his luck still further. He started counterfeiting securities. He created a French government bond that was verified as authentic by the official government bank! So, in addition to French franc notes, French government bonds now started to flood the market.

The Dutchman continued his business in London, opened a branch in Rome, then duplicated the method in Berlin. He started to travel from one capital to the next.

But a minor problem arose: the international exchanges were overburdened with bogus currency and securities. International economic balances became disjointed. Everyone was confused . . . but did not know the source of the counterfeiting. Since bogus bills and securities came from four European capitals, it was difficult, if not impossible to track them down.

This represented a threat to the safety of Charles Becker. He gathered together his associates in crime and said that it would be wise for them to pull up stakes quietly and to leave Europe.

The urgency was increased when the Paris newspapers headlined the scandal and announced that French government bonds were declared counterfeit. The Sureté confirmed that there were more issues of securities on the market than had originally been printed.

This created a panic. Investors did not know whether the securities they possessed were genuine or fake. Prices tumbled. There was talk of an impending financial crisis throughout Europe that would even affect America. But no one knew how to stem the tide; the criminal source was unknown.

Quietly, Charles Becker closed his various offices. By the the time he was ready to leave, he had nearly $3,000,000 in English bank notes secreted in safe deposit vaults throughout London. With this money, he set sail for the United States in 1945.

Back in the States, Becker managed to have the notes exchanged in the underworld—at a loss of some three-quarters of a million, but it was worth it.

He now decided to retire to the life of a gentleman. He purchased a small house and transformed the ground floor into a restaurant for a more elegant clientele. Everything appeared to be going smoothly. The hoaxer was ready to forget the past. Quietly, he would chuckle as he read of the panic overtaking the financial capitals of Europe.

But the hoaxer's laughter turned to tears.

The turnabout came by a strange quirk of fate. Becker went to Boston in 1946 for the purpose of purchasing some fine foods and liquors to be shipped to his New York dining establishment. Becker wanted to fool the experts still further. Masquerading as someone else, he ordered the supplies to be shipped to a nonexistent address after presenting false credentials. Then he said, "Oh, you must forgive me. I am so embarrassed. I have run a bit short of money. Perhaps you could spare a check for just $50. Add it to my bill. That is all I need. I'm known at the bank and can cash it there."

The wholesaler gladly gave him a check in the amount of $50. Charles Becker used a false name as he presented the check—which he had increased to $50,000—to a bank teller. The bank teller foolishly gave Charles the $50,000, but grew suspicious of such a large amount. After Becker left, the teller sent a messenger over to the merchant with the check. The wholesaler screamed, "Someone forged the check. It was for $50." Quickly, he described Becker, and said that he was from New York. Hardly had he boarded a train in Boston, for New York, when he was arrested.

When Charles Becker was convicted of forgery in 1947, in the federal courtroom at Foley Square, he stated that "the wholesaler was so wealthy, he should have been glad to share his wealth with someone less fortunate."

Ironically, Charles Becker had the last laugh. Even though convicted, he had never been apprehended as the counterfeiter who brought about the near collapse of the financial capitals of Europe. Only after his passing did some of his associates report the story. By then, it was too late for retribution. The hoaxer was beyond the reach of mortal man.

17

WILLIE SUTTON

The Masquerading Bank Robber

IN THE PLANNING AND EXECUTION of a robbery, no one was the equal of Willie Sutton. While he may have lacked the nerve of a John Dillinger or a Jesse James, he had something more valuable: theatrical style. Willie Hutton could don uniforms, evening clothes, business suits or working clothes, and give the impression that he was a legitimate member of whatever outfit he chose to represent. He might dress up as a night watchman, carry a lunch pail, flash identification, and march—without being questioned—through the gates of some of the country's most carefully guarded vaults or estates. The appellation "Willie the Actor," which he gained, suited him well.

The number of masquerades he employed was legion. Dressed as a bank messenger, he was admitted to the inner sanctum of a bank without hesitation. On various occasions, he disguised himself as a mailman, a fireman, and a chauffeur. His masquerades made it possible for him to slide past guards and to enter buildings or homes where treasures were his for the taking. He was, in fact, so effective and convincing an impostor, that many believed that if he had been so inclined, he could have become a successful stage actor. But Willie "the Actor" Sutton *preferred* the fraudulent life; to him it was much more challenging and rewarding.

Willie Sutton was not an average bank robber. He planned everything down to the last detail. He very carefully studied his chosen target before developing a plan of action; he scrutinized the habits of the guards, each of the employees, and even the police who patrolled the streets nearby; he studied the interior of the bank and thoroughly familiarized himself with its layout; he drew up blueprints showing each and every entrance and exit; he made a study of the alarm system and carefully investigated every safeguard installed by the bank. Nothing was left to chance. When Willie Sutton employed aides to execute a job, he insisted that they, too, study every detail of the plan, thereby leaving no room for error. This hoaxer was, in a word, a *perfectionist.*

Like a good many other hoaxers, he was not one who resorted to violence. In fact, he never carried a weapon of any kind. If ever he had to contend with a guard, he would overpower him and use the guard's weapon. Sutton was fond of saying, "I am not a hoodlum. True, I hold up banks, but I have never physically harmed a single person."

Sutton's life of hoaxing and robbing began in 1922 when young Willie served as an apprentice to a master bank robber, Doc Tate. The two met for the first time in a poolroom which young Willie often frequented. Willie enjoyed playing pool and talking with the assorted small-time thieves and robbers who assembled there. Doc Tate took a liking to young Willie, and before long invited the youngster to join him in a robbery.

Because a series of bank robberies had just been completed and banks were protected heavily in every area of the city, Doc Tate singled out a prosperous jewelry store in Wilkes-Barre, Pennsylvania. Willie and Tate formulated their plans. Every detail was worked out in advance. The jewelry shop was on the street floor of a hotel. Next to the hotel, a new skyscraper was under construction. Doc Tate told Willie that he had noted that there was only one night watchman on duty and that every night, at about midnight, the guard went into his little shack to relax or have a bite to eat. This meant that the scaffolding and construction site was unguarded at precisely that time each night. This bit of information provided by Doc taught Willie his first lesson in carrying out a hoax: be observant. Learn the habits and conduct of every person who will be involved in a particular escapade.

Willie and his teacher checked into the hotel—but not at the same time. After registering, each went to his own room, having arranged to meet later in the hallway. At midnight, they looked out of a hall window and saw the watchman climbing up the staircase to his shack. The two gangsters left the hotel from separate exits. It was pitch dark—a perfect night for the two thieves to climb the girder that would take them to the roof of the building of the jewelry store. Quietly, they forced open the skylight. This, too, had been carefully planned in advance. Everything was working as anticipated. The two now managed to let themselves down into the jewelry shop.

Then came the surprise. The vault was not an average one; it was a Mosler vault. True, the knob could be pried off. But, on a Mosler vault, the dial had a steel plate backing. The tumblers could not be reached unless they were drilled through. This was a very difficult and involved task and time was short.

But Doc Tate was astute. He smiled at young Willie and said confidently, "Yes, I anticipated such a possibility. There's no need to start weeping. We have all weekend. You know that this is Saturday night. It means that the jewelry shop will be closed until Monday morning. That should give us plenty of time to drill through the dial so we can reach the tumblers."

The two had prepared themselves with a small bag of tools to contend with any problem that might develop. In short order, Willie started drilling into the steel plate of the dial on the Mosler safe. The drill made a soft hum as it plowed its way through the tough plate.

They continued working for close to twelve hours, taking turns and resting occasionally. Suddenly, they heard a noise coming from the front of the shop.

Doc Tate held up his hands to silence Willie. Willie stopped drilling. Together, they tiptoed to the door, peeked through the keyhole, and saw two carpenters.

"Probably came in here to make a phone call or just goof off. Maybe we better leave," said Willie.

Doc Tate shook his head. "After all the work we've gone through, we can't leave," he said. "Besides, since we started drilling, we don't want the owners to come in on Monday morning and see what we did. They might suspect someone from the adjoining hotel and track us down. No, we're going to finish what we began. We have to get rid of those two carpenters."

"But how? We don't have any guns. You said we're not supposed to carry firearms because it would be too tempting to use them. You said we can't have any shootings because that would really get us in trouble."

Doc Tate had a plan and whispered it to Willie.

Moments later, Willie Sutton walked into the outer room. The two carpenters had just opened their lunch boxes and removed several cans of beer. They were surprised when they looked up and saw a neatly attired, slim young man.

"W-what. . . ?"

Willie had one hand in the right pocket of his coat. His index finger held stiff. "Okay, boys, everything will be fine. You won't get hurt. Just do exactly what I tell you. Don't make me use this."

The two carpenters stared, open-mouthed. They had every reason to believe that Willie had a gun in his pocket.

"We . . . we don't want any trouble . . . b-but . . . what are you doing here?"

The carpenter's partner snapped, "Shut up! Do as the man says, understand? We don't want no trouble!"

Willie smiled. He felt a surge of power. "Walk in front of me. Back in there," he ordered.

The two carpenters, with hands upraised, walked ahead of Willie Sutton. He ordered them to march into a back room where they were locked up. "Don't say a word or make an outcry," Willie warned. "If you do, we'll let you have it."

That little task finished, Willie returned to the room containing the vault. In less than 30 minutes the vault was opened. Quickly and quietly, as the huge door swung open, Sutton and Tate scooped up expensive necklaces, watches, stones, brooches and anything that they could pass through a "fence," without any trouble.

After filling their pockets, they unlocked the door to the room in which the two carpenters were incarcerated. Willie and Tate then made their way out of the jewelry room through a rear door and returned separately to their hotel rooms. They gathered their few belongings, and not having brought along suitcases, they were able to depart unnoticed, without even checking out.

Within a few days, the thieves fenced the stolen goods and cleared some $60,000 from the jewel heist. As for the carpenters, the newspapers reported that they were so scared that they remained in the room until Monday morning, never realizing that the door had been unlocked. The carpenters were unable to give any clues as to the identities of the robbers, and Willie and his partner-teacher were as free as birds.

Thus began the career of Willie Sutton. By 1925, he concluded that he had learned as much as he possibly could from Doc Tate, and the two broke up. Doc Tate was never heard, from again, but the hoaxing career of Willie Sutton was firmly set. He later recalled: "Doc Tate would always say that 'Genius is the capacity for taking pains . . . the recognition that nothing is simple and that success is possible when you struggle for it.' That applied to my profession. To become a safe-cracker, I had to work for it. Nothing would come easy to me. Before I would pull any job, I would begin by studying the outside of the building.

"I would always make a rough sketch, like an artist's rendering, of the building. Then I would go into the building, pretending to be a workman, a guard, or a messenger with checks to deposit. I would pretend to write up deposit slips, or just count a sheaf of bills, anything that would make it possible for me to loiter, without looking as if I were loitering.

"Once inside, I would make quick diagrams of the location of the vault, note the locations of burglar alarms and any visible wiring. You get so that you can develop an instinct about the location of all components. I would make quick sketches of these devices.

"Then I would note the different exits and entrances of the bank. With this carefully plotted-out blueprint, I would be able to make my robbery with the greatest of ease and, of course, perfection."

Everything was calculated very shrewdly and coldly. It was this training, under the tutelage of Doc Tate, that established the pattern for countless robberies—all of which were perfectly executed, without violence. Never was a robbery a hit-or-miss affair. It was set like a timetable that was very carefully followed. Not one moment was left unaccounted for. It had to work the first time. There would be no second chance.

As for his lifestyle, Willie Sutton enjoyed the best that life could offer. He lived at quality hotels, and enjoyed gourmet food. His clothes were stylish, without being ostentatious. He would frequent the best Broadway night clubs and theaters. By watching performances with particular concentration, he perfected his art of making proper entrances and exits. He studied the movements of the performers on stage. . . . It was as important to him in his career as to an actor in his.

Between 1930 and 1933, Willie Sutton worked for the infamous Dutch Schultz, but his assignment was rather degrading to someone with Willie's "talents." According to the impeccably dressed "actor," all he did was collect "policy" payments; he was a glorified messenger. Willie Sutton wanted to go on to "bigger" and "better" things.

In 1934, returning to the trade that he had learned from Doc Tate, Willie made his way into the vault of a Long Island, New York bank. Here he made his first mistake. In trying to save time—and thus beat the clock—he had used an acetylene torch, instead of a drill. But he was not fast enough. The torch was not faster than the drill. Willie was caught and was sent to prison.

But Willie learned from his errors. He knew that whenever a robber was caught, his complete *modus operandi* (M.O.) was studied and put in a special file. If Willie Sutton were to again use an acetylene torch, and escape, the records of the police would be consulted. His name would be listed among those who had used this method. Therefore, Sutton decided not to use the same method again.

One afternoon in the spring of 1939, as he walked along New York's Fifth Avenue, Willie saw a heavily armored truck stop before an impressive office building. It was shortly after five o'clock—the usual closing hour. Two of the uniformed armed guards went to the locked door of the building. They pressed the bell. Shortly thereafter, they were admitted. Willie found himself fascinated by the ease with which these armed guards could gain entrance to the locked building. The armored truck could have been parked a block away and they would probably still have been admitted. His mind began working and several hoax possibilities began to take shape in his mind.

Feeling confident that the security guard of the Fifth Avenue building did not actually know the identities of the two guards, he concluded that all that was needed to get into the building was a proper uniform. This led him to deduce that if he wore the right uniform, at the right time, in the right place, he could gain access and entry to almost any building, be it a jewelry store, bank, or an establishment that housed treasures that he would be more than willing to share with the actual proprietors.

Willie Sutton found a Manhattan classified telephone directory. He turned to "Uniforms." In a few minutes, he had jotted down the names of several firms that catered to theaters. "Willie the Actor" was now ready to play a role in a drama that was to be very exciting.

He began by contacting a former associate in crime, Jack Barton, and told him to rent a very small office on Broadway, and establish a school for actors, to be called the Oxford Dramatic School. Willie gave Jack enough money to pay several months advance rent and to furnish the office. He then had some stationery and business cards printed.

Once this was done, letters were sent to several costume rental firms which offered not only ordinary costumes, but uniforms of all kinds for theatrical productions. Willie used his new stationery bearing the imprint, Oxford Dramatic School, to notify a uniform company that they were going to put on several benefit performances and needed some costumes. In particular, they wanted one bank messenger's costume.

Within a few days, a reply was received. If the Oxford Dramatic School would send the actor to their premises, they would fit him with a satisfactory uniform.

With letter in hand, Willie Sutton walked into the showroom of the costume company, ready to present himself as the actor to be fitted. He could feel his pulse racing as he examined uniforms of every description. He could become a policeman, a fire chief, a Western Union messenger, a military officer, or even a judge of the Supreme Court. The badges on the costumes were so perfect that no one would ever suspect that they were theatrical props. Every uniform looked genuine.

Willie handed the letter to the company salesman, adding that he had been sent by the Oxford Dramatic School, and "I hope you have a bank messenger's uniform in my size."

"We have sizes for all actors. Try this one."

Soon, Willie was outfitted in a neat-looking, conservative, dark blue uniform with polished buttons. But more important, it looked so genuine that Willie felt confident that he could walk into the United States Treasury itself and not be questioned.

He paid for the rental of the uniform and left.

The next step was for Willie to select a bank that would be his target. He found one in Queens. It was small, but not *too* small. There were a few clothing and hardware stores nearby, as well as a pet shop, but, basically, it was a rural area. He began to plot out the routine of this particular bank.

He noted that promptly at 8:30 a.m., the first employee, a uniformed guard, arrived. This guard would open the outer bank door and station himself between it and a second locked entrance door. He admitted to the bank proper only those who presented identification cards or were recognized by him personally.

Sutton started to refine his plans. To begin, he had to find out the name of the bank manager. He telephoned, and using the excuse that he wanted to send a financial statement to the bank, he asked the switchboard operator for the manager's name. She gave it to him without question.

Then Willie visited the Western Union office on Broadway and paid for a telegram to be sent to his own bogus company, the Oxford Dramatic School. A few hours later, the telegram arrived at the sparsely furnished office. Willie steamed it open, threw away the message, and on a yellow sheet of paper typed the name of the Queens bank manager, and the name and address of the bank. He folded this yellow sheet of paper so that the name and address could be seen through the envelope of the Western Union envelope. Then, he sealed it. He held it up and examined it. He was satisfied. It looked like a legitimate telegram being sent to the bank manager.

Early the next morning, seated in front of a small mirror in his hotel room, he began to apply makeup to his face. This was the first time he tried this gimmick, but he knew he had to look a little older, a bit more florid, not as dapper as an actor. He was now ready to carry out his hoax.

Dressed up in his uniform, he approached the glass doors of the Queens bank shortly after 8:30 a.m. The guard had already arrived and was standing at the entrance. Willie Sutton rang the bell. The guard swung open the door and looked at messenger and his uniform.

Willie cleared his throat. "Here's a telegram for your boss." He offered the bogus wire and a note pad to the guard: "You gotta sign."

The bank guard took the pencil and pad handed him by the impostor. It was all carefully calculated. The bank guard held the pencil in his right hand and shifted the note pad to the other. At that split second, when both of the guard's hands were occupied, and he started to sign, Willie reached down and lifted the pistol from the guard's holster.

The guard turned red and began to shake. "W-what . . . is this?"

Willie flashed a smile. "Just behave yourself, sir, and nothing will happen. Now, just step back, if you please."

The bank guard obeyed. "Raise both hands," said Willie quietly. It had had happened so swiftly, so perfectly, the guard could do no more than follow instructions.

At that moment, as planned, in walked Willie's associate, Jack Barton. Jack closed the front doors and positioned himself obscurely near the entrance.

Willie knew what would next happen. The clock was ticking the minutes away. The employees would start arriving, one at a time, within minutes. Willie had watched the procession every morning for a week, and he knew how punctual the employees were.

"Now, sir," said Willie as he moved over to one side, the pistol pointed at the guard, "as the other employees start arriving, please open the door and admit each one. Do not try to make an outcry. I do not want to hurt you, so don't force me. Just do as I say, sir."

"Y-yes . . ."

True to form, the other employees arrived on time. The bank guard trembled, but he obeyed Willie's orders. He checked the identification of each employee. After each one entered, he relocked the door and waited for the next person to arrive.

When the first worker had entered the bank, he came face to face with Jack Barton. Barton aimed a gun at him.

"W-what . . . is this?"

Jack motioned toward a chair. "Please be seated."

The terrified worker obeyed.

Before long, six more employees had entered the bank, one at a time. Each one was surprised in the same manner. Each was ordered to sit down.

The very last man to arrive was the bank manager. Willie calmly pointed a pistol at him and politely said: "Sir, no harm shall come to you. All you have to do is open your vault. It would be sheer folly, sir, for you to refuse. In doing so, there may be harmful consequences for you and your employees. Why risk lives for the sake of money? Hardly a wise choice, you'll agree! So please open up your vault and we shall be out of the bank in a little while."

As Willie studied the reaction of the manager to his admonition, he began to sense that he might have underestimated this particular bank manager. There was a certain strength in the middle-aged man. He was the dedicated type of banker one often read about—one who would sacrifice his life for the sake of his firm. Something inside Willie advised him to beware; this man was the type who felt that the bank's entire reputation was now in his hands. He might do anything for the good of his institution and its reputation.

Willie reacted quietly and quickly. "Just think of your wife and children . . ."

He had to say no more. He could see the courageous stance the manager had assumed begin to falter.

"Very well . . . I have no other alternative."

"A very wise decision, sir."

While Jack Barton aimed his gun at the frightened bank employees, Willie Sutton, gun in hand, followed the bank manager into the vault. By now, it was 8:45. In only 15 minutes the bank would officially open for business.

Willie did not want to wait much longer. He didn't want to encounter the early morning bank customers. He was after big money, not petty cash from bank depositors.

"Please hurry, sir. I cannot delay too long."

The nervous bank manager obeyed. Within a minute, the door of the vault swung open. Inside were several metal boxes. Using his free hand, Willie opened them and scooped up about $250,000 in crisp new bills. He stuffed them into his pockets. Once he had taken all the money out of the boxes, Willie motioned to the bank manager.

"Please join your fellow workers." The manager obeyed.

Outside, as they all sat together, Willie said crisply, "Now, my associate and I are leaving. We're not alone. We have a third associate who is waiting outside. You are to remain here in your seats for at least ten minutes after we are gone. If you should decide to run outside, or run anywhere to a phone before ten minutes, my outside man will have to use his gun."

Willie Sutton knew that even if they telephoned the police immediately, it would take at least fifteen minutes before the screeching cars would reach the bank. But he wanted to allow himself and Barton as much escape time as possible.

Willie Sutton and Jack Barton then backed out of the bank. They slammed the huge glass doors shut and were on their way. Within seconds they were absorbed somewhere in the heavy traffic streaming along Queens Boulevard. Thanks to the smooth technique of this brilliant actor-robber, Willie and friend were one-quarter of a million dollars richer than they had been an hour earlier.

But Willie Sutton was not always as lucky. On various occasions, his careful planning ran into unexpected complications. On one occasion, in 1933, Willie miscalculated the working hours of a guard, and he was caught, arrested, convicted, and sentenced to Eastern State Penitentiary.

As a prisoner, he exhibited model behavior and before long was granted privileges as a trustee. Then, taking advantage of his limited freedom, he started planning an escape.

Willie calculated that a few of the cells on the prison's main floor were only 30 feet from the wall. He decided he might be able to dig a tunnel beneath the wall. He needed to be transferred to one of the cells on the main floor. But the warden and other prison officials knew that the cells nearest to the walls provided a possible chance for escape. They were, therefore, inspected daily. When Willie learned this, he abandoned his plan.

Another possibility remained. The cells at the very end of the block were occupied by prisoners who were awaiting release. These end cells were approximately 100 feet from the wall. Willie wanted to be placed in one of those cells. There was a slight chance that he could manage to dig a tunnel without being detected. The last cell on this particular block was occupied by a forger named Charlie Kerner. The two of them became friendly. Despite his imminent release, Charlie could no longer endure prison life, and would do just about anything to get out sooner. He would be glad to join with Willie "the Actor" in an escape attempt.

By now, Willie was making careful plans. He had been confined to Eastern State Prison for 12 years, sufficient time to study the construction of the prison; and he knew every inch of it well.

Willie knew that Kerner's cell measured 10 to 12 feet. The cell had an extremely thick concrete floor. It would be impossible to dig through the floor.

But the wall was another story. True, it was about five feet thick, but he reasoned that once they penetrated three or four inches, the rest of the concrete would be soft and rotting. He outlined his plan to Charlie Kerner.

They would bore through approximately six inches of the wall. The soft part would then crumble under their boring. At this point, they would start digging down. They would have to dig down about thirty feet.

The prison wall itself reached some 25 feet below ground level. It was 14 feet thick at its base. The wall was not made of concrete, but of stone blocks. There was no way of burrowing through stone blocks. Therefore, it would be necessary to dig underneath them.

This was a very slow, and tedious job. Willie recruited several hand-picked men who could be trusted. Each was serving a term of 30 to 40 years, and each was willing to do anything necessary to escape. The lucky part for Willie and his friends was that these men worked in various tool shops, and could lay their hands on a variety of tools and implements that would make it easy to dig and burrow.

Before long, all of them were working on the walls. As anticipated, the core of the cell was found to be rather soft, and it was easy to remove the dirt and rotting concrete. But how could it be easily disposed of? Willie had an idea. They would stuff the earth in their pockets . . . and later flush it down the toilets.

When they reached a depth of 15 feet, they came across the sewer system of the prison. They worked around it and, after six months of digging, an escape tunnel had been dug. They managed to crawl through the tunnel . . . and were almost free . . . when they came face to face with two prison guards.

It was a shock to all concerned. The guards ordered Willie to put up his hands. He started to run. The guard shot. No bullet hit Willie, but he tripped. He was apprehended, and placed in the isolation block.

Later, in August of 1945, the would-be escapees were transferred to a Pennsylvania prison. Here, Willie again carefully calculated an escape plan. This time, hacksaws were used to cut through the metal bars of the steel doors. Each night Willie and his cohorts waited until the night guards had made their last round. The careful sawing then continued.

When they managed to break free, they overpowered several guards, seized their weapons, and literally walked out of prison.

Outside, a prearranged contact was waiting to drive them to Philadelphia. As he was waiting, he heard the wailing of the prison sirens, became frightened and panicked. He drove off before the escaped convicts could get to the car.

Willie thought the end was near. Suddenly, he saw a small milk truck. The milkman was nowhere in sight. Willie realized that he had no keys to start the truck and that they would have to be driven.

Willie told what happened: "We all climbed into the truck and waited. When the milk driver returned, he was obviously astonished to see five of us in the truck . . . with a gun pointed at him. We told him that he would not be hurt. All he had to do was drive us to Philadelphia. He did so without any complaint.

"To celebrate, we started to drink milk. It tasted very good. The driver saw what we were doing, and said his company would dock his pay for all the quarts we were drinking.

"Not wanting him to lose money, I handed him a fifty dollar bill. A few months before, a friend had smuggled about a hundred dollars to me. Now I could spend it . . . in a decent way."

Once in Philadelphia, the six escaped convicts split up.

The entire police force had been alerted, and Willie was

forced to go into hiding. He secreted himself in the basement of a building where he found bags of discarded clothing. He exchanged his prison clothes for these. The next morning, he arranged for someone in Philadelphia to drive him to New York.

Willie Sutton settled in New York and pursued his career as a talented impostor. On one occasion, he assumed the guise of a New York fire inspector and called on a plush Fifth Avenue jeweler who made the mistake of turning his back as he took the "official" on an inspection of the premises. When they were alone in the back room, Willie deftly cracked the jeweler on the head. When the jeweler revived a half-hour later, $60,000 in expensive gems were found missing. The jeweler identified Willie from photographs, but the elusive hoaxer could not be tracked down. He had vanished.

The following year, two impressive-looking policemen walked into a bank in Havana, Cuba shortly before closing time. They chatted with the bank manager and were taken into the vault. Within 60 minutes, over $500,000 had been taken from the vault. Like the Fifth Avenue jeweler, the Havana manager also identified Willie Sutton from police photographs, but the elusive impostor was nowhere to be found. Willie Sutton's dream was to outwit everyone; and his skill as a hoaxer was second to none.

In 1950, he decided to undertake another caper. He programmed an expertly timed heist of the Manufacturer's Trust Company in the Sunnyside, Queens area of New York; and came away with about $64,000. Although the frightened clerks could not positively identify him, the police were able to piece the bits of information and evidence together. They deduced that Willie Sutton was the only thief capable of masterminding such a job.

The FBI distributed handbills with Sutton's photograph to almost every bank and department store in the country. Each posted the notice. Many smaller stores likewise pinned up Willie Sutton's photograph and his face became known to thousands upon thousands of people who had never before seen the face of the famous criminal.

Now began a strange set of coincidences. One of these handbills reached the clothing store of Max Schuster. His son,

Arnold, who worked as a salesman in the store, looked it over and shrugged indifferently. He might have forgotten it, except that his father was worried about robberies, and he posted the handbill above the desk in the rear office. Day after day, young Arnold Schuster saw the picture. It became engraved in his mind.

On Monday, February 18, 1952, young Arnold left his home, and boarded the subway for downtown Brooklyn where his father's clothing store was located. It was shortly before noon. The rush hour had passed and the train was no longer overly crowded. Arnold Schuster always bought a paper in the morning and buried his face in it during the train ride. For some unknown reason, on that particular day, he did not buy a paper. Instead, he glanced at subway advertising posters, and studied the faces of the other passengers. That was when he noticed a slim, neatly dressed man across the aisle. Arnold might not even have looked twice, except that being a clothing salesman, he was always interested in the styles of clothing worn by people. He noticed the fine cut of this passenger's garment. He studied him carefully, and noticed his wedge-shaped face and neatly trimmed mustache.

Arnold Schuster's heart skipped a beat. He grew tense. The passenger was Willie Sutton! It was the same face that had been staring at him from the handbill over his father's desk in the rear of the store.

Excited, Arnold stood up when the train stopped at Pacific Street. The dapper man was leaving. Arnold followed him. But Willie Sutton, always aware of being followed noticed Arnold Schuster tailing him. Willie walked casually into a filling station on Third Avenue and Bergen Street, just two blocks from the Brooklyn Police Headquarters.

At that very moment, a police car coincidentally pulled up to the curb. Arnold ran to the car and told the two officers that he thought he saw Willie Sutton.

Now, all three were on the trail. They walked over to the filling station and questioned the atttendant. "Yeah, I let that man borrow a battery to install in his car," he said, pointing toward Sutton who was walking away. "He'll drive his car back here to have his dead battery recharged. He's parked over on Dean Street."

The officers walked to the parked car and spoke to the neatly dressed man. Sutton vehemently denied that he was Willie Sutton.

Arnold Schuster frowned. Well, maybe it was a wrong guess. He went to a pay phone, told his father about it, and was advised to come to the shop and forget what had happened.

The cops, however, remained suspect. They developed a plan. One cop would watch Sutton; the other would call for help. They agreed that the resemblance was so close that the suspect should be taken in for questioning.

Young Arnold Schuster heard the news. News announcers said it was believed that there was a $75,000 reward for his capture. (It later turned out that only $75.00 was offered as a reward.)

The officers credited with the arrest were promoted to rank of detective with wage increases. They were ineligible for the reward.

But Arnold Schuster was not even mentioned. He had earned and wanted some of the credit . . . and the reward. He consulted with attorneys who suggested that he contact the police and put forth his claim that he was the man who had spotted Willie Sutton. The police apologized, explaining that in the excitement they had neglected to mention him. Also, not knowing his name, they were unable to find him. Arnold Schuster was feted and praised by Police Department officials and received the $75 reward money. He made several television appearances for which he was paid $750.

Problems arose for Arnold Schuster. Hate mail and threatening phone calls started to arrive at his home. The harassment continued and he had his phone number changed. Threats continued nevertheless. His father opened his store one day and found a note: "This is your last day."

On March 8, 1952, less than three weeks after Arnold Schuster had shadowed Willie Sutton, he called his mother to say that he would be coming home to have a quick bite to eat, because he wanted to change his clothes and go to a dance that night.

A short distance from his home, as he passed the house owned by a doctor, shots rang out. Inside the house, the doctor and his wife sat in their living room reading. When they heard the shots, they looked through their window, but saw nothing. The doctor thought he heard a car speeding away, but that was all. Then came a knock on the doctor's door. The doctor opened it, and a girl next door cried out, "A man is lying in the alley."

Arnold Schuster had been slain. Two bullets pierced his groin. Two other bullets went through his eyes.

Willie Sutton went on trial and was sentenced to 30 years to life for the Queens bank robbery. He served 17 years, and was freed in 1969. White-haired, ailing, and now nearing 70 years of age, he persisted in claiming that he did not know who had slain Arnold Schuster.

The killers were never found. Arnold Schuster's father, Max, sued the city for failing to protect his son. He was awarded $41,000. The police conducted an intensive investigation, and could say no more than that the killers were crack shots. They had many suspects, but none could be charged with the killing. There was no proof, and the case was labelled "inactive."

Before Willie Sutton died in 1970, he summarized his own life in these words:

"I prefer to think of myself as an artist, a showman, rather than a thief. I never hurt anybody. I never carried a gun. I didn't like to use a gun. If I did, it was only to threaten someone. I don't think I could ever shoot anyone. My greatest feeling of satisfaction came when I could hoax someone into believing I was something other than myself . . . and make a profit out of it. I suppose if I had to do it all over again, I probably would. Only I would take more time to polish my craft!"

18

GEORGE HULL

The Cardiff Giant Hoax

MANY SCIENTISTS EXUDE AN AIR of infallibility. Because of their years of training, knowledge of laboratory techniques and mathematical configurations, they often feel that they can offer conclusive proof concerning the validity of almost any presentation. To hoax men of science is the epitome of ego glorification to the dyed-in-the-wool hoaxer. When a hoax is successfully executed, the scandal that follows provides the impostor with a feeling of self-satisfaction, of superiority.

One such achievement dates back to 1871. A cigar manufacturer, who knew little more than the art of cigar making, succeeded in startling the entire scientific community.

George Hull was a middle-aged man who enjoyed a comfortable, albeit, uneventful life as a cigar manufacturer in Binghamton, New York. Like most people in their middle years, he began to contemplate his circumstance and his future.

"I kept asking myself: 'Will I continue to manufacture cigars until the very end? Will I continue to be just another cog in the giant wheel of life? Or will I do something to become famous—world-renowned and distinguished—so that I can go down in history as something more than just a tobacco man?'

"That was when I decided to do something. At first, I thought I would create a gimmick—such as the world's greatest and biggest cigar. But as I thought about it, I realized that that would just be something unusual that people would look at, talk about and soon forget.

"I wanted to make myself more famous than that. It was a rather perplexing problem; I could not find an idea that would startle the entire world.

"That was uppermost in my mind. So I kept thinking, kept searching, kept planning . . . but to no avail . . . until early spring, 1871 when I went out to Ackley, Iowa to visit my sister. That was how it all began."

George Hull visited his sister for several weeks, not knowing that it would be in Ackley that his giant hoax would begin.

George's sister was a religious woman. One day, she asked him to join her at a revival meeting being held by John Turk, a Methodist evangelist who travelled from town to town, village to village, exciting the lives of villagers with his tales of fire and brimstone.

George Hull was bored during the meeting, but he tried to feign interest. As he was about to doze off at one point, he heard the Reverend Turk read from what he said was his favorite passage in the Bible. It was Genesis 6:4 which told of giants having walked the earth.

Suddenly, a spark in George's mind was ignited. Giants once walked the earth!

As soon as the meeting had concluded, George Hull made his way to Reverend Turk, introduced himself, and said that he would like to know more about these giants. He asked several questions.

Reverend Turk beamed and rubbed both palms together in anticipation of a lucrative donation. "Oh, the Bible describes such giants, and I would imagine they were at least twelve feet tall," said Turk. "They might very well be double or even triple the size of modern man. God so saw to it."

Thence followed a brief sermon during which Reverend Turk sought to evangelize George Hull. But the latter was disinterested. He managed to ease away from the evangelist and did not see the anger on the face of the minister for not having graced his out-stretched palm with greenbacks; George Hull had something more important on his mind.

He lay awake in his sister's house the entire night. Innumerable thoughts raced through his head. *Giants had walked the earth!* George Hull would capitalize upon this Biblical quotation.

The following day, he went to the stone quarries near Fort Dodge. He searched for a slab of hard stone that would measure at least twelve feet high, four feet wide, and several feet thick. In a gypsum bed, he found just what he could use. As payment for this hunk of stone, George bought several barrels of beer for the quarry workers; he walked off with a paper certifying that he was the owner of this enormous chunk.

George Hull now needed to transport this huge block of gypsum. But inasmuch as it weighed five tons, this was not an easy matter. The railroad station was about 30 miles away and when Hull tried to transport the gypsum on wagons, they collapsed beneath the weight. He foresaw that crossing bridges would be a risky proposition.

When passersby saw that he was trying to move a five-ton gypsum block, Hull was forced to offer an explanation. He said simply that he was being sent throughout the country, by the government, to gather up mineral specimens from every state. These would be part of a special exhibit in Washington.

Eventually, Hull managed to have the gypsum transported to the railroad, and with it he travelled to Chicago. In Chicago, he put the gypsum in a barn owned by an old friend.

Every step of George's plan was carefully worked out. The next step was to hire an artist, then a good stonecutter. This he did, giving them simple instructions: "I want you to carve me a naked giant. That's all. Make him as well carved as possible. He should be so realistic and lifelike that people will travel the world over just to see him. You will be well paid for your work."

The artist and stonecutter nodded, then asked, "How is he to look? His facial expressions, that is?"

"Give him the look of having met death in the throes of pain and shock."

The artist and stonecutter began their work. They were among the best in their respective professions. George Hull, like any other astute hoaxer, would not settle for anything but the best. He paid top money for top quality and did, indeed, receive it.

The two men worked in harmony on the huge chunk of stone for nearly 20 weeks. They fashioned the features—the eyes, nose, mouth, fingers—to perfection. Even the toes and toenails and other details of the anatomy were carved with careful attention to detail. Hull insisted that the massive figure of stone be realistic and authentic.

To create the illusion that the giant had met his death in agony, the body had to be twisted slightly to one side. One foot was turned up, and while one arm was drawn across the giant's stomach, the other arm was twisted behind his back. Leg and body muscles were contracted as if it was death itself that was forcing him into this position. The effect was highly dramatic and realistic.

When the basic structure of the statue was finished, it stood some ten feet four inches and weighed approximately 3,000 pounds. To create the illusion of "real skin," the artists used needle-pointed hammers on this surface to simulate human pores; bluish streaks in the gypsum gave the figure the appearance of having arteries and veins.

The next task was to make the giant statue appear to be very old—at least 5,000 years old. This was accomplished by treating its surface with sulphuric acid which served to dull the stone and make it look as if it were many centuries old. To give it the appearance of having been buried underground for ages, the artist and artisan cut a pair of small grooves on the underside of the statue. This would convince onlookers that it had been eroded by water while buried in the ground for centuries.

When the gypsum man was finished, it was a masterpiece. It did look as if it had indeed been a giant that had walked the earth, just as described so vividly in the Bible.

George Hull paid both the artist and stonecutter a handsome sum; he also paid his friend for rental of the barn in which the men had worked. All three were sworn to secrecy. Like many hoaxers, George Hull had faith in the power of money—and in limiting his associations to just a few carefully chosen friends. He offered them good money, after his hoax had been carried out.

Ready now to continue with his hoax, he quietly arranged for the giant to be sealed in a crated box. The statue was labelled "machinery," and was shipped to a small suburb outside of Binghamton, New York. The crated giant was parked in a freight station while Hull tried to find it a home.

George was on good terms with one of his cousins, William Newell, a farmer who owned some good acreage near the small town of Cardiff, in the Onondaga Valley, a dozen miles south of Syracuse. Stubby Newell, as William was known, was not a man with the highest of ethical standards. But, while he was reputed to have indulged in shady machinations in order to increase his landholdings, Stubby would never risk breaking the law.

It was not unexpected, therefore, when George Hull approached him with the desire to buy something on his farm, for Stubby Newell to ask, "Will it put me in jail?"

"No risk of that! It isn't what you think it is. Just let me say that I want to bury this box somewhere on your farm and let it remain there for a few months. You'll be paid for it. The responsibility is entirely my own."

"Very well," said Stubby.

A four-horse wagon was used to pull the statue to a location near Cardiff. Now, it was up to George Hull, Stubby Newell and several other trusted relatives to help place the heavy object into the ground.

The conspirators labored hard and long. They dug a five-foot deep pit behind the barn and in it they placed the gypsum man. It was buried face up and covered with dirt. The ground was then seeded with clover. George Hull would now have to be patient for several months before he could make his next move.

But Hull's opportunity to further his hoax came sooner than expected. As luck would have it, a nearby farmer was plowing and unearthed some bones. The find was brought to scientists at Cornell University in Ithaca, New York, who declared them to be genuine fossil bones. Now, thought Hull, the discovery of his giant might also be acecpted as real.

George knew that if his hoax were to be successful, it would depend upon the way the statue was "discovered." He wanted the giant to be found in a natural way.

He approached Stubby Newell and said, "Suppose you start telling neighbors that your farm well is starting to run dry. You'll have to go to the expense of digging a new one. Now, this will be very costly, but you'll have to say that it must be done or you'll run dry." Then he let Stubby Newell in on the proposed hoax and offered him a 10% share of the profit of admission when the "giant" was put on exhibition.

Stubby Newell did so, displaying some rather good acting

ability. He hired two famous well-diggers, or dorsers, to ascertain where water might be located. They used a two-pronged hazel stick as they combed his property. Suddenly, the stick prongs pointed downward; they had found a source of water. (Stubby had previously soaked this area with water.)

"That's where there's water. You boys start digging," said Stubby to the diggers. Then, in need of money to pay for this work, he went to Syracuse to talk to some bankers.

All was carefully planned. The impact would be greater if the buried giant was discovered while Stubby was out-of-town.

When Stubby Newell returned to his farm (without having obtained a loan), he found a small crowd gathered around the spot where the well was to be dug. Then, he went into his act, as rehearsed with his cousin, George Hull.

"What's wrong? What's happening?" he shouted, pushing through the crowd. "Is anyone hurt? What's the trouble?"

"Look! Look!" the well-diggers excitedly answered. "After going down only a few feet, look what we found!"

With a look of genuine astonishment on his face, Stubby Newell stared at the huge statue that had been buried in his soil.

It did not take long for the news to spread throughout the entire area. Farmers left their chores to see the discovery; business people closed shop to have a look at what was called an unbelievable discovery. Before the week was over, the entire country was aware of what had been uncovered near Cardiff.

Stubby Newell next went to the general store in Cardiff and bought a large white canvas tent. Quickly, he set up the tent over the open hole in which the sleeping giant lay—as if it had for hundreds of centuries. He announced that for one-half dollar a person could enter the tent and look at "the eighth wonder of the world."

Stubby Newell, following instructions dictated by George Hull, had a ticket booth erected. He designated the spot where viewers were to stand. Then he had workmen dig a trench around the giant; it made quite an authentic and impressive sight.

Lying in the trench, bathed in the ghostly light of the tent, the statue most certainly did look like one of those giants of Bible times. The story went that when he died, he was placed in this pit, which was then covered by the shifting sands of hundreds of centuries, and finally turned into a fossil-like stone.

Newspaper reporters from the biggest and smallest cities of the country, and press correspondents from journals throughout Europe—all flocked to the farm to look at what was labelled the "Cardiff Giant," a link to the past, proof that the Bible was authentic.

It was speculated that the stone giant was a petrified man or, perhaps, an ancient statue. But no one dared question the authority of the many evangelists who hurried to the scene and exclaimed, "He is the giant foretold in the Bible."

In Binghamton, George Hull busied himself with his cigar manufacturing. A neighbor asked if he had read about the discovery of the Cardiff Giant on his cousin's farm.

Hull replied: "I've read about it, but have been so busy with orders coming into the cigar factory that I just haven't had the time to see it."

The excited neighbor told him what he had read and seen.

George Hull shrugged and puffed on his cigar. "I just don't believe it."

Soon, more and more regional and national preachers came to view the statue (at a reduced price). All pronounced that the buried man was, without the slightest doubt, a former living being who had survived hundreds of centuries. This, they explained, was proof presented by God that the Bible was authentic.

Soon, thousands upon thousands of Americans made the long journey to the insignificant hamlet of Cardiff to view the link with the past. Many who had previously doubted, again believed that God's word was the truth.

Now, George Hull made his move. He made his first visit to his cousin's farm. He was astonished at the thousands who paid fifty cents for a view. He said to Stubby: "We're playing to a full house. It's more like standing room only. Raise the price to one dollar."

In 1872, a one dollar price was comparable to a ten dollar admission price today.

Word of the Cardiff giant spread world-wide. Soon, railroads and other forms of transportation set up regular trips to the site.

It was estimated that George Hull was taking in several hundred dollars per hour from his scheme. He paid 10% to Stubby Newell for his services, and the others who were in on the hoax also received compensation. Among the latter were those who had designed and carved the giant, and those who helped effect the shipment and burial.

George Hull was a good hoaxer. He was also knowledgeable in the art of showmanship. He prepared a lecture which Stubby Newell delivered before the audience was permitted to walk down a special pathway, which led to the giant. After all, they were paying one dollar for the privilege, and were entitled to a lecture as well as a view.

Stubby Newell's speeches were changed as the popularity of the Cardiff Giant grew. Soon he was saying that through God he had been able to find this man who had lived in Bible days.

With the coming of winter, the snows made it difficult for tourists to come to the farm. So as not to lose revenue, it was decided to have the giant moved to a special exhibition hall in Syracuse. This was accomplished through the use of an elaborately engineered program of cables, pulleys and scaffolding.

Once the giant was securely placed in the exhibition hall, more and more scientists and archaeologists from the entire country arrived to view—and to question.

Some professors agreed that it was a true fossil. Among these was Professor James H. Drator, considered the leading paleontologist of the era, and head of the prestigious New York State Museum. Drator boldly proclaimed: "The statue is remarkable and it is authentic. It is a link between the past and today."

Another visitor was Dr. Andrew D. White, professor and first president of Cornell University, and later Ambassador to Germany and then Russia. White was the type of person who thoroughly questioned and researched whatever he saw or heard.

He arranged for a close friend to chip off a tiny sliver from the giant. He then employed the latest scientific testing methods available. When the results were in, White announced: "The sliver is pure and plain gypsum."

Dr. White did not make an outright statement that the Cardiff Giant was fake. He did, however, recommend that scientists and archeologists investigate the giant very carefully before making any conclusive statement.

While the Cornell University president was making his cautious pronouncements, another observer, famous New York sculptor Erastus Dow Palmer made the journey to Syracuse and declared outright that it was a disgrace for a museum to display such a fake. This giant, he said, although well-sculpted, was neither a fossil nor an ancient statue. In fact, he said, it was a recent creation. It had been buried underground for several months, and then brought back out again. "The Cardiff Giant is a hoax!"

The public was not yet ready to accept this bold charge. No sooner was this announcement made, when famed circus magnate Phineas Taylor Barnum—himself a hoaxer of no minor proportions—became fascinated by the statue.

Barnum had not yet begun his circus, which was later to gain international fame. At this time, he ran a museum in New York. As such, he was constantly on the lookout for new attractions. He was fascinated to note that on a typical Sunday, within six hours, some 3,000 people paid one dollar each to view the giant. After noting the debate over whether or not the Cardiff Giant was authentic, he decided to seek out the perpetrators of the hoax.

Barnum approached Stubby Newell: "I'll buy your statue."

Newell discussed the proposition with George Hull. "We don't want to kill the goose that lays the golden egg," Hull said. "Why should we sell it?" Tell him we prefer to keep this fossil where it was buried for thousands of years—in our area."

Barnum was not easily discouraged. He went to a local sculptor and said, "Make me a duplicate of the Cardiff Giant."

This proved to be the beginning of the end.

Months later, while thousands upon thousands kept lining up to see the Cardiff Giant, the master showman, Barnum, announced that his giant would be on display; admission, a mere fifty cents.

Furthermore, said Barnum, ". . . my giant is the *real* one. You can see it in New York. No need to go all the way up to Syracuse to see a fake. Mine is the one, the only, the original

Cardiff Giant—and it's all yours for the looking, at fifty cents!"

By 1893, a legal battle had begun. It reached the New York State Supreme Court in Albany which ruled that Barnum had every right to display a duplicate and that it would be up to the scientific world to decide which of the Cardiff Giants was authentic.

A fierce battle erupted in the scientific world. Some scientists claimed that both giants were hoaxes; others claimed that only one was a hoax, but could not decide which one; still others said that since there had originally been more than one giant in the world, the possibility remained that both were authentic.

George Hull prepared to go on tour with his statue. He travelled all along the Atlantic Coast, displaying the statue and continuing to maintain that it was authentic.

The Barnum duplicate statue continued to draw some crowds, but they eventually dwindled. P. T. Barnum, never wanting to admit defeat, maintained that his was the authentic Cardiff Giant. When crowds became sparse, he put the statue in a storage shed on the banks of Lake Erie, near Buffalo. In 1904, the shed was mysteriously ignited and dynamited. By the time firemen reached the scene, the Giant was destroyed. It was rumored that Barnum deliberately dynamited the giant so it could never be proven to be false.

By now, newspapers were seeking to expose the nature of the entire hoax. They learned that some payments had been made to Stubby Newell as well as to several Chicago sculptors. They also learned that George Hull had paid a visit to his sister in Ackley, Iowa and that while there had purchased a large block of gypsum. The newspapers published interviews with those who had been involved in the creation and shipment of the statue, including the sculptor himself.

But the public still preferred to believe that George Hull's Cardiff Giant was authentic. Even after Hull had been labelled an impostor and hoaxer, the public continued to pay money for the privilege of viewing the statue.

For almost a decade, the Cardiff Giant was an attraction. It made its final appearance in 1901 at the Pan American Exposition in Buffalo (where President McKinley was assassinated). It was then put in storage. It had lost its appeal; people no longer considered it to be an attraction.

In 1939, long after all the hoaxers had passed from the scene, the Cardiff Giant was acquired by the New York State Historical Society and placed on permanent view in the Farmers' Museum in Cooperstown, New York. There, in an open pit, the giant lies just as it did when "discovered" in 1869. Visitors, today, say that the statue has a smile on its face.

19

VAN MEERGEREN

The Magnificent Art Hoaxer

IN THE LATE 1930s, a lawyer from Amsterdam, Holland, was called to Paris to administer the estate of a Dutch businessman who had recently died. The late businessman had owned a fully furnished and decorated home in Paris—all of its possessions would be included in the estate.

The Amsterdam lawyer made a careful inventory of the furniture, personal belongings and little trinkets found in the house. He went upstairs into the attic and discovered a lot of useless rummage; he listed it all. It had to be included for the inventory to be complete. When he had almost completed the task, the lawyer pushed away some cartons, and noticed a gilt-edged, framed painting lying against the wall. Curious, he brought it downstairs into the sun-filled parlor. He gazed at it. The painting of Christ and the Disciples at Emmaus was truly beautiful but probably of minimal value.

A scrawled signature at the bottom of the painting, however, struck the lawyer's calculating mind. The signature looked authentic; maybe the painting had more value than he thought. On impulse, he decided to take the painting to Dr. Abraham Bredius, an art expert in Monte Carlo. Dr. Bredius was more than just an expert; he was also a world-famous collector. The world's leading art museums relied upon his judgment to select appropriate (and priceless) treasures for their collections. If anyone could determine the value of this painting, it would be Dr. Bredius.

After a few moments of scrutiny, Dr. Bredius pointed to the signature. Peering through a magnifying glass, the both of them saw the monogram: *I.V.M.* Dr. Bredius had no doubts. This was the signature of the great Jan Vermeer of Delft (1632-

1675) who used to sign his works of art with the initials I.V.M., standing for I. V. Meer.

Within days, the art world became aware of the discovery of this "new Vermeer" painting. He was one of the greatest old Dutch masters. The leading collectors and museums had vied for his works and this new discovery produced great excitement.

The highly respected British art journal, *Burlington Magazine*, headlined the find: "It is a marvelous moment in the life of an art lover to discover an unknown painting by a great master. The brilliant work by Vermeer is as pure and fresh as the day when it was painted some 300 years ago. It is a voice from the past. Here is *the* masterpiece of Johannes Vermeer that the art world has always thought of but never expected to see. Now it has come to life. It is every inch a Vermeer."

No sooner had news of this discovery spread than scores of the greatest critics, connoisseurs and buyers hurried to Paris to see for themselves this splendid creation on canvas. It was breathtakingly beautiful. Even the most astute and conservative art experts studied and acknowledged that this was "without dispute" the most "magnificent Vermeer ever created" and "surely the most precious." It was even likened in value to the crown jewels worn by Their Majesties of the Netherlands.

There were those who doubted the painting's authenticity and value. But the patriarch of art experts, Dr. Abraham Bredius, had given his stamp of approval to the Vermeer, and the majority joined him in approbation. All heralded this as the greatest art find of the century.

In the midst of it all, Bernard Hannema, the director of the prestigious Boymans Museum in Rotterdam, announced his acceptance of this work of art as authentic and offered some $270,000—about 550,000 guilders—as a purchase price. The entire world now agreed that if the Boymans Museum would pay such a sum, then the Vermeer was an authentic and price-less treasure.

Shortly thereafter, the Boymans Museum put the *De Emmausgangers* (as it was called in Dutch) on display. Placed beside the great works by Rembrandt, Franz Hals, Da Vinci and other masters of the art world, the Vermeer painting stole the show. Art lovers and curious average citizens thronged the halls of the Boymans Museum to gaze upon it. Because of the great interest in the treasure, the museum had reproductions of *De Emmausgangers* prepared for sale to millions of people throughout the world.

All the excitement over Vermeer's masterpiece had a curious effect: it precipitated a strange chain reaction. Shortly thereafter, several other Vermeer paintings were discovered and validated as being authentic and priceless. While Vermeer may never have had as great a reputation as other classical painters, he now was gaining rapidly in popularity. Some began to think of him as an even greater master than Rembrandt.

An Amsterdam art dealer, P. deBoer, joined with another expert, D. A. Hoogendijk, to offer some of the new Vermeer discoveries to the highest bidders. One painting, *Last Supper,* was sold to a private collector for some $800,000 or 1,600,000 guilders. A second painting, *The Blessing of Isaac,* was sold to a wealthy art lover for over 1,000,000 guilders. A third, *Christ's Ablution,* fetched an even higher price and was accepted for display in the exclusive Rijks Museum in Amsterdam.

All of this took place during a hectic era in Dutch history. It was the 1940s when hordes of Nazis roamed the tiny nation. Nazi leaders combed all museums and treasure houses and either bought or, frequently, stole as much as they could to be shipped back to Germany.

One Nazi "robber baron" was a wealthy German banker by the name of Herr Fritz Miedl. He managed to get his hands on a newly discovered Vermeer treasure, *Christ and the Adultress.* He claimed it as a Nazi prize and quickly put it up for auction; it was bought by a collector for $850,000. The collector, who said he was a patron of the arts and a true lover of classics, was a man named Hermann Goering, the infamous Nazi murderer. The corpulent Reich Marshal was delighted with his new art treasure—a stolen work of art that was purchased with stolen money looted from victims of the Nazi holocaust. Goering placed it in a special room of his estate near Berlin. Everyone admired this great Vermeer as a true masterpiece worthy of display in a Nazi home.

There the painting hung until the end of the war. After the liberation of the Netherlands and the surrender of Nazi

Germany, Allied forces searched Goering's home and the Vermeer painting was confiscated and put with other treasures for evaluation and return to their original owners.

Immediately, Dutch authorities claimed rightful ownership of the Vermeer painting. Furthermore, they demanded that the gangsters who participated in this Nazi crime should be punished. A search was made for Herr Fritz Miedl. He was nowhere to be found. Spies did track him down to Madrid, Spain. But they were unable to arrest him. As the invited guest of Generalissimo Franco of Spain, Miedl could not be extradited. But Dutch spies learned that Miedl did not work alone; he had associates.

Investigations now unearthed another name: Hans van Meergeren. A very speedy investigation led to the man's arrest. Identified as a Dutch artist who had arranged to sell the painting to the Nazi beasts, he was promptly charged with collaboration with the enemy of the Dutch people.

Hans van Meergeren did not deny *some* of the charges. He said quite simply that he had, indeed, been the one who told the Nazis of the whereabouts of the precious Vermeer painting, *Christ and the Adultress*. And, yes, he had arranged to sell it to Hermann Goering. Yes, he had dealt with Nazi conquerors. Yes, he had certainly dealt with Dutch Quislings. But could he be charged with collaboration for selling a *worthless* painting or two?

Instantly, the art world was in an uproar. Did van Meergeren say that the paintings were worthless and that he was innocent of selling art treasures because, in truth, they were not treasures at all?

Slowly, the truth was revealed. It was substantiated that Hans van Meergeren was an artist of little reputation. He had sold many of his own paintings for small amounts of money but had little hope of gaining recognition. The only way that he could gain world-wide recognition as an artist of great talent would be for him to forge paintings and pass them off as classic treasures. Indeed, that was just what van Meergeren had done.

Every "newly discovered" Vermeer painting was a forgery. He, Hans van Meergeren, had painted them all and affixed the familiar monogram—I.V.M.

The art world was astonished. Was it possible that the *Emmausgangers* was a forgery? It was unbelievable. The Boymans Museum refused to accept the hysterical confessions of a man they said was senile and not in control of his own mind. More and more art experts were called in to authenticate the paintings. They all verified them as authentic Vermeer masterpieces.

Dutch investigators said that van Meergeren was trying to dupe authorities by claiming that the paintings were forgeries. But van Meergeren was adamant. He went so far as to say that he would paint a "new Vermeer" right before the eyes of art experts and the Dutch police. Accompanied by the police, van Meergeren was escorted back to his studio and, under their watchful supervision, painted a "Vermeer." He did it expertly, right down to the monogram. It was a breathtakingly beautiful painting, the style of which was distinctly Vermeer; the art experts had to admit that they had been duped.

Now that the art hoaxer was winning his claim that he had not sold any *treasure* to the Nazis, but a few worthless paintings, he presented still additional proof of his alleged innocence of crime. He had even "forged" the paints, he said. He had expected that art experts would eventually examine the paintings under X-ray and microscope to verify the age of the paints. Therefore, he decided to "forge" the paints as well.

Van Meergeren created green from genuine lapis lazuli; he created radiant red from the dehydrated bodies of Mexican insects; and added white lead to brighten up the various colors. He even used mud to create darker hues and shades. These were the same methods that had been used by Vermeer.

As further evidence of his "innocence," the master forger, van Meergeren, then showed the authorities certain art books as well as a historical photo-library encyclopedia that he had acquired to help him create what would look like an authentic Vermeer.

There were still many art experts who refused to believe the word of van Meergeren. They maintained that the *Emmausgangers* was real. The canvas was authentic; it was genuine seventeenth century canvas. Surely he did not fake that as well. Van Meergeren admitted that it was, indeed, seventeenth century canvas—perhaps the only authentic item in the entire fabrication. A creation called *Resurrection of Lazarus,* by a minor seventeenth century artist, had originally been painted on that canvas. The forger had carefully removed much of the original artist's work, but had slyly left in certain portions which were used as the base for the forged paintings. Because many of the original pigments were left intact, when experts scanned the painting they were led to believe that it was, in fact, authentic.

Now, new X-rays and chemical tests were made. The results revealed what art experts had already been told: that the canvas originally bore a painting by a minor artist; that the painting had been partially removed, and then covered with a Vermeer-styled creation.

By now, tearful art lovers had to admit that the beautiful *Emmausgangers* was a forgery. Museums in the Netherlands and other parts of the world re-examined their newly acquired Vermeer works; they learned that they, too, had been duped.

Van Meergeren had seized his one chance for glory. True, he had never expected to be found out. But he had, at least, fooled the experts. Furthermore, he had already collected some three million dollars by passing off his forgeries as authentic works of art. He had, admittedly, sold a Vermeer to the Dutch businessman who had put it in his attic for reasons best known to himself. The lawyer who ventured forth to the late Dutch businessman's home in Paris had discovered it by sheer accident.

Cries of outrage were heard. Museums demanded refunds of their monies. But van Meergeren was penniless. He had had to split the monies with those who had purchased his paintings. He could not make any refunds. Legally, he declared bankruptcy. But he was still charged with criminal acts of fraud and collaboration with the Nazis. He was confined to his home in Amsterdam as preparations for his trial were under way.

In various interviews (that he granted for a small financial consideration), van Meergeren later told just why he had concocted the hoax. He spoke with the bitterness of a creative person whose talent has gone unrecognized and unheralded. "For years, I painted and painted. But the museums and art collectors said that my work was little more than 'dime store' pictures. They said I should use them for picture postcards. Imagine that! I was told I had no artistic ability. I was told to

become a commercial artist—to draw sketches, to sell tooth-
paste or face cream! It was an insult. I was going to teach the
art world a lesson. I was going to prove, once and for all, that I
Hans van Meergeren, was a great painter! I could do it only
one way . . . to convince the so-called experts that I had great
talent.

"So I conceived the idea that I would copy the style of a
great painter and duplicate it so perfectly that the imperious
rulers of the art world would accept it as genuine. Oh, my
idea is not new. Did you know that Michelangelo did the same
thing to get some money? Nobody would buy his original
works. So he sold them as newly discovered antique sculptures
that he discovered while excavating throughout Italy. Then he
commanded a big price and received it. He was that brilliant
and talented. So, I have done the same thing."

Hans van Meergeren had researched the history of other
such little-known and long-buried stories of hoaxes in the art
world.

"It was just the beginning for me. I found out that Gio-
vanni Bastianini of Florence also created beautiful busts and
statues but sold them as newly discovered works of the ancient
Greek and Roman eras. Did you hear of Alceo Dossena? Well,
he was an Italian sculptor of great talent. But the authorities
laughed at his work, just as they did of mine. They told him
to make little trinkets and souvenirs to be sold in the streets
of Rome or Venice. What a mockery of a man's artistic ability!

"Alceo Dossena plotted his revenge. He studied and mastered the distinctive styles of the Greeks, Etruscans, Romans—
even Gothic and Baroque art. He created complete sets of
authentic sculpture of that period. Then he sold them to the
leading museums and royal families throughout the world as
authentic, ancient sculpture that he found while on archaeologi-
cal expeditions throughout the Middle East and Southern
Europe. He fooled the experts. Now he convinced them that
he did have talent and ability. He had the last laugh. No, it
was not a laugh. He must have felt what I did: *satisfaction!*"

Hans van Meergeren was an embittered man.

What of van Meergeren's own paintings? Investigators looked
carefully through his studio. There was little doubt: he did
have ability. His canvases were largely dark-colored portraits

of a singular theme—tortuous agony of mind and body. It was noted that an original van Meergeren usually portrayed wide eyed people, those with horror in their tormented souls, those who endured the agonies of an untold horror. The Nazis had purchased many of van Meergeren's own works. But this minor recognition and acceptance was not enough; van Meergeren wanted and needed more widespread recognition. However, the truth was that while van Meergeren was brilliant as a forger, he was poor as an original artist. He lacked style. Only when copying the style of a great artist did a real talent appear.

"My paintings—that is, the copies—were admired by people the world over. Yes. I feel a bit sad," he later said, "that they were admiring Vermeer and not myself, but I am grateful that I had fooled the experts and convinced them, if anonymously, that I was a worthwhile artist and not a picture postcard sketch artist."

Van Meergeren meticulously collected all newspaper and magazine stories about the "Vermeer" discoveries. A set of scrapbooks served as consolation to the embittered artist.

Bit by bit, his life story was revealed. A native born Dutchman, Hans had had an unhappy childhood. For one thing, he was diminutive in size, resembling a dwarf. As he matured, his short stature made him the butt of jokes by schoolmates. Though lonely, he continued to withdraw and shun outside companionship for fear of being ridiculed.

Hans was quick to learn, and the record showed him to have been a good student of architecture at the Institute of Technology at Delft. (This was the birthplace of Vermeer.) Since he could not develop any physical appeal, he developed his mind and became quite a scholar. After earning various degrees, van Meergeren focused his interest on art and was soon named a professor of art history at the Delft Institute.

He created many watercolors, drawings and oils, and while they received some acclaim at minor art shows, when he created what he considered his "masterpiece," it was ignored at exhibitions and went unsold.

Van Meergeren might have lived out his life in bitter frustration had he not chanced to overhear another artist at an exhibition, boast how he had forged a Rembrandt. He laughingly told of selling it for a very high price, and then disappearing. He heard that the Rembrandt forgery was detected and the art world was stunned. But this other artist laughed and said, "Now they are convinced I am a great artist." It gave van Meergeren an idea.

Why not do the same? Either that, or die in obscurity. True, if his hoax was successful, he would never receive the recognition for which he yearned. But, even so, he would enjoy unheralded glory, and would feel secure in the knowledge that his *ability* had been recognized.

Why did he select Vermeer? In his own words, "He was a great, although lesser-known artist. Little mention of Vermeer is in the books. Unlike other artists whose works are catalogued, Vermeer can have many 'lost' paintings newly discovered. Also, unlike Da Vinci or Rembrandt, the experts are not that familiar with Vermeer. It is easy to fool them with a Vermeer."

Van Meergeren was a meticulous worker. He studied every available Vermeer; he researched the arts and techniques of the 1600s as related to Vermeer in Delft; he worked with the materials used by Vermeer, paying high prices for authentic paints. Hans knew that a "discovered" Vermeer would be subjected to laboratory tests—infrared, X-rays and quartz lamps. Everything had to be executed flawlessly.

Van Meergeren described how he went about his work:

"To begin with, I did not use any living models. They might talk. I painted from my imagination. Then, I baked the picture so it would look aged. When the painting was perfect, I brought it to an art attorney. I told him that I was the agent for a famous European family who wanted to remain completely anonymous because they had fallen upon financial disaster and did not want to risk the social scandal of having to sell off treasured family heirlooms.

"I told the art attorney I was appointed agent for the sale of a few Vermeers and that all payments should be made to me. It was simple. That is how they were sold and how I received my payments."

Indeed, he had received millions of dollars. But he lived simply. His money was deposited in a numbered Swiss bank account; even the Nazis could not touch it.

But when van Meergeren's hoax was discovered, the legal

battle that followed was as complicated as the forger's scheming mind. It was like trying to unravel a Gordian knot. How could he be charged with selling Dutch art treasures when, indeed, they were forgeries and not treasures at all?

Collaboration with the Nazis? All he did, he maintained, was sell a few pictures . . . just as so many Dutch had sold food and clothing and trinkets to the Nazis. No Dutchman could refuse to sell anything to a Nazi who walked into a shop. Van Meergeren's position was no different. He had a few paintings and had sold them for a price! Was that a crime?

The leading Dutch experts were stumped.

Return the money? But the charges of collaboration with the Nazis were dropped and the Dutch courts ruled that he had not committed any such crime. So he could not refund the money when no crime was committed!

Baffled, all the Dutch court could do was charge van Meergeren with "deception" and sentence him to a few months in prison.

No doubt, van Meergeren chuckled and laughed throughout his confinement. He was still laughing when he was released. He purchased a vast estate in the country and acquired a beautiful young wife. He divided his time between his much-liveried country estate and his home in the Riviera. He made frequent business trips to Switzerland to reap the rewards of financial success from his art hoax. His funds were unlimited; he could live like a gentleman. Indeed, he could live in the manner of a wealthy artist—which he was!

In the early 1950s, Hans van Meergeren contracted influenza and died. The little man was said to have been smiling as he lay in state. His ego had been satisfied.

20

WILLIAM HAMILTON HARKINS

The Brilliant Check Forger

IT WAS A CRISP, cool October morning in 1926 and the residents of Boston were just beginning their daily routines. There were few customers in the Commercial Bank of Boston and as one of the bank tellers was counting a roll of bills, a shadow fell across her counter. She looked up. There stood a tall, slim, elegantly dressed young man; he had the look of the typical businessman.

"Good morning," he flashed a smile. "May I have the cash for this check, if you please?" He was very polite, very reserved.

The bank teller looked at the check that had been pushed her way. "Payable to Andrew Ryan, M.D." The check, in the amount of $5,000 had been written out entirely by hand. The teller turned it over and noted that it had been approved by B. J. Ryan, the assistant cashier for the Commercial Bank of Boston.

B. J. Ryan—who was working at his desk a few dozen feet away had okayed the check, marking it: "Okay for cash. My Uncle Andrew." B. J.'s initials were included.

Although the teller's initial instinct was to show the check to B. J. Ryan, she noticed that he was now talking to another customer. They appeared to be involved in a heated discussion over some certificates. The teller decided not to disturb him.

She looked into her cash drawer. "Oh, will you excuse me, sir? I have no large bills here. Will you go to this teller, please?" She pushed the check to the teller in the next booth. "Please take care of this for Dr. Ryan. He's B. J.'s relative."

The other teller glanced at the face of the check, then the endorsement and remarked politely, "Surely. How would you like the cash, sir?"

"In one hundred dollar bills, if you please."

The teller stamped the back of the check, and automatically counted out a sheaf of one hundred dollar bills. He recounted them several times, then pushed the small pile toward the customer.

"Thank you," the tall man smiled as he quietly took the money, put it in his wallet, pocketed it and quietly walked out of the Commercial Bank of Boston.

He was never seen again. Neither was the $5,000.

The check had been a forgery. There was no Andrew Ryan, M.D. The bank cashier, B. J. Ryan, disclaimed any relationship to the "doctor" and said under oath that he had never endorsed any such check.

Bank officials were outraged: they had been swindled. Bank customers, upon hearing about the episode, protested. Should such carelessness continue, the bank could lose a fortune. The teller who had neglected verifying the approval was quickly dismissed. Immediately, the William J. Burns International Detective Agency—the official check fraud and forgery investigation service for the American Bankers Association—was called into the case.

The agency's manager advised the bank: "You have been the victim of an impostor. His name is William Hamilton Harkins, one of the best in the lone wolf, bank swindling business. Our files show that for some 30 years, we have been on his trail. Yes, we have caught Harkins some 12 or 15 times. He has been arrested. But through good lawyers, he has managed to avoid conviction and sentencing."

The Burns Agency manager, well acquainted with the career of Harkins. continued: "Harkins is more than just a forger and hoaxer. He is a theatrical impostor. He looks at you with a professional's countenance, exuding an aura of confidence. He acts as if he were on the stage. Every physical movement is so precise, so exact, he would give you the impression that they are natural.

"He forges checks and presents them with so much self-assuredness that he is able to fool some of the best bank tellers. But underneath it all, William Hamilton Harkins is a hoaxer with a heart of ice and nerves to match. Be grateful he did not hoax you out of $25,000 or even $100,000, as has happened before."

After a six-month absence, during which time Harkins obviously enjoyed the fruits of his labors, word spread that the impostor was again making the rounds of various banks. Bank officials were told to be on the alert, to check and double-check all suspicious or doubtful persons who presented checks for cashing.

But Harkins was not one to be easily caught. He, himself, had been a bank clerk in his youth—and an exemplary one at that. He knew the in's and out's of bank procedure.

Harkins was not only quick with figures, he was a genius with a pen, too. He devoted himself to perfecting the art of forgery, and when he forged someone's handwriting to a check, the country's leading graphologists were unable to identify it as a positive forgery. Added to all this, he had an excellent memory.

He would often boast: "I may forget a face, but I never forget a signature. Just give me one look at a signature and I can forge it perfectly within a matter of moments. I have a 'signature memory' in my brain."

Harkins was the proud possessor of other gifts as well. He had a glib tongue and was a master at legal maneuvering. Although he had been apprehended repeatedly, he had never been placed on the witness stand. By calling technicalities to the attention of his lawyer, he was able to avoid direct cross-examination by the court.

Harkins never hesitated to submit himself to a lie detector or truth-serum test; he always emerged victorious. When faced with impending confinement, he would pretend to be emotionally unstable, and thereby avoid incarceration.

There were several occasions when Harkins was apprehended, arraigned and actually imprisoned while waiting for the case to come to court. Here, too, his unmitigated gall was evident. He would manage to find a change of clothes, assume a disguise, and successfully escape from prison.

Harkins was so adept at imposture that more often than not he could convince a judge or an arresting officer that he had been the *victim* of the crime, not the criminal. And, usually out of sympathy, the arrest would not be made, or, if made, the charges would soon be dropped.

William Hamilton Harkins loved the good life, the free and easy life: he frequented fancy restaurants, wore fine clothes and entertained interesting women. To maintain his lifestyle, he required a great deal of money. Unable to earn enough by legitimate means, he resorted to forgery, thievery and hoaxing.

One of Harkin's great weaknesses was gambling on horses; he thrived on it. But, while generally lucky at gambling, he was not always as fortunate at the track. After a week or two of fun, women and the races, William Hamilton Harkins would find himself penniless and back in the business of trying to dupe a bank.

Because an alarming number of fraudulent checks were being passed, many banks in the United States instituted a new policy. It was said to be "fool-proof." Before a bank would cash a check, the check had to be approved by a bank officer. The new system did discourage many small-time thieves—but not Harkins. Harkins developed a simple plan to overcome the obstacle.

Whenever he wanted to cash a forged check in a particular bank, he would buy several cashier's checks. Affixed to these were the initials or signature of the bank officer to whom the tellers would turn for approval when a check was submitted for cashing. Harkins quickly mastered the technique of copying the signature or initials. He would then write phony checks and affix either the initials or signature of the bank officer. No questions asked, the tellers willingly cashed the checks. This simple scheme netted him tens of thousands of dollars in a short period of time.

It has been pointed out that any new law that might have served as a barrier to most check forgers served only as an incentive for Harkins to continue his activities. On one occasion, he entered a bank in a leading New York hotel, filled out a form for a $13.95 bank check, received the check, then went over to a bank officer and calmly and confidently said: "Pardon me, sir. I just purchased this bank check but realize now I won't be needing it. May I have my money refunded? If there is any service charge, I'll be glad to pay it."

The bank officer smiled unctuously. "Quite all right, sir.

There is no charge. I'll initial my approval. Take it to any teller's window and receive your cash."

"Thank you."

Harkins did not cash the initialed bank check. Instead, he requested another check in the amount of $75.00. He left the bank with the two checks, returned to his hotel, and painstakingly changed the figures on the $75.00 check to read $7,500. He was an expert: with use of the proper pen, the right amount of pressure and the identical color of ink, Harkins was able to forge the numbers perfectly.

The very next day, he returned to the bank with the two checks in his possession. One was the small $13.95 check which had previously been initialed for cashing; the second was the forged $7,500 check which had yet to be initialed.

Harkins approached a teller's window and presented the uninitialed $7,500 check for cashing. The teller looked at it, then politely said, "Oh, sir, I'm so sorry, but you will have to get this check initialed before I can cash it."

"Yes, yes," Harkins smiled, "how stupid of me. I should have known that. I'm so sorry to have taken up your time. Whom shall I ask?"

"The gentleman seated just around the corner, sir. He will accommodate you."

Moments later, Harkins went to the same bank officer who had previously initialed his $13.95 check. Harkins now displayed both the initialed $13.95 check and the uninitialed $7,500 check.

"I was in a hurry yesterday," he said, "and didn't cash in this check. You initialed it. See? I wonder if I could cash this check today, together with this other check which I cannot use. My business associate changed his mind about this transaction so I will not be giving him either of these checks."

This simple maneuver instilled a feeling of confidence in the bank officer. He glanced at the initialed $13.95 check, then quickly glanced at the other check and scribbled his initials. Of course. Just go to the teller over there."

"Which one?"

"That one, sir." He stood up and signalled to a teller who nodded. "He'll take good care of you."

Standing before the teller's window, Harkins laid both

checks on the counter and moments later, walked out of the bank with a total of $7,513.95 in his pocket. Since he had paid a total of $88.95 for the checks, he had made a profit of $7,425.00!

It was a simple hoax. When Harkins had his $13.95 check initialed for cashing, he had established good credit rating. When he sought approval of the second check for cashing, the banker assumed that he was dealing with a regular customer of the bank and was not at all hesitant to affix his initials to it as well. Harkins had earned $7,425.00 from the transaction. It was a relatively small amount, but it helped pay some current bills and left him enough to spend on those luxuries he so enjoyed.

William Hamilton Harkins never failed to enjoy the fruits of his hoaxing labors. He hailed a cab right outside the bank, was driven to the race track, and walked directly to the pari-mutuel window. He bet $2,500 on a horse to win. Luck was with him. By the time he left the track, he had close to $10,000 in winnings.

Feeling confident over the success of his most recent "transaction," Harkins decided to use the same ploy at other banks. This he did and, in the end, he had swindled them out of $100,000.

Because many of Harkins' hoaxes were not officially reported to the American Bankers Association, it is difficult to determine exactly how much he swindled. As he once admitted, "Oh, people have claimed that I made about one million dollars by hoaxing banks. No, sir. That is not true. I must have made about five million!"

The question as to what impelled William Hamilton Harkins to embark upon a "career" as an impostor and hoaxer can be answered by examining his childhood. William was born on January 14, 1870 in the State of Washington. His parents came from strong pioneer stock, were of modest means, but saw to it that their child received an ample education.

His Scottish heritage may have influenced his outlook. Harkins recalled his early life in this manner:

> While we were not deprived, we were always making the best use of everything. The slogan, "waste not, want not,"

was imprinted upon my mind. My mother would wear clothes until they wore out. So would I. My father always impressed me with the virtues of thrift. We were churchgoing people, too. My younger brother became a Presbyterian preacher, in the mold of my thrifty father. My older brother was a schoolteacher and he, too, kept extolling the virtues of the frugal life and the rewards of being of modest desires.

I suppose they meant to do the right thing. But frankly, I could not see myself keeping up such a struggle throughout my life. I wanted fun and laughter, women and entertainment. These were taboo in our family. I wanted a life of luxury. This, too, was considered sinful or too worldly in our household. My parents may have believed they were happy, but I think it was more a feeling of resignation.

They believed that the evils of Satan lurked everywhere and that they had to maintain a constant vigil against temptations.

Well, I decided to be tempted and enjoy myself. If I would have to pay the penalty in Hades, I would take my punishment. But for now, I wanted to have the best that life could offer. It took money. I needed lots and lots of money. All the time. Could I ever have earned it by conventional means? I doubt it.

William Hamilton Harkins went to college and graduated in 1893 as a licensed schoolteacher. He was revolted by the idea of spending his entire life drawing a meager teacher's salary and he might have been doomed to such an existence had not something extraordinary happened. It was a strange quirk of fate that led his life in an entirely unexpected direction.

William married another schoolteacher in 1895 and they moved to Washnigton, D. C. There, they put their savings into a small bank. They scrimped and saved in the hope of eventually saving enough money to buy a house of their own. But the bank failed. The young couple lost all of their $20,000 in savings.

Harkins forever maintained that the bank had swindled him, and that he was going to get his money back *with interest.* His was more than just a grudge; it was a burning desire to avenge. He assured his wife that he was not going to let the banking system get away with the swindle; they would get their money back—and much more.

Convinced that such dishonest talk would lead only to problems, she left him in 1898.

Alone, William began to plot. After forging several small checks and cashing them without a hitch, he started to forge larger ones. The lure of "easy money" and the thrill of hoaxing was so great that Harkins could not stop. It became a great adventure.

One of Harkins' schemes demanded that he play the role of a "bereaved relative." He explained it in this way:

> I would pretend to be a grief-stricken son or husband, seeking a suitable memorial for my mother or wife or even brother or sister. While I was in the office of the memorial-maker, I would pretend to be so stricken with grief, that I would fake a faint. The memorial maker would have to go out of the office for some smelling salts. While he was gone, I would open his desk drawer and steal out blank as well as cancelled checks.
>
> You would be surprised how many people keep these in the top drawers of their desks. It's almost a sure thing. When the memorial maker returned with salts or water, I would be recovered and would thank him, saying that I was too shaken and would come back at a future date.

Once both blank and cancelled checks were in his possession, it was simple for Harkins to do the necessary forging. He would write out and cash checks for thousands of dollars, and by the time the bank officials were aware of what had transpired, Harkins was thousands of miles away.

> A little rule I made was not to use the same city too often. If I cashed checks in New York, I would then go to California. Or else, I would do it in Maine, and then

go to Texas. I would go across the country this way, and it would give the impression that there were many forgers, instead of just one.

Oh, I wouldn't cash checks all the time. I would give myself . . . and the banks . . . a little respite, during which time I would have a good time at the horse races, with some women, good hotels, good restaurants.

After all, what's money for, if not enjoyment?

On one occasion in 1922, Harkins cashed $2,000 in a Connecticut bank, walked to the curb, and entered his car. Outcries were heard from the bank. He had hardly begun to start the car, when a bank clerk, a bank officer, and a policeman stopped him, ordered him out of the car and charged him with trying to pass a phony check. This particular bank had just installed an electronic system that was able to detect a forged signature.

William Hamilton Harkins acted the role of the suave gentleman. He insisted that it was an authentic check. The bank official said it was a fraud and accused him of being an impostor. Harkins was taken into custody, pending the arrival of the judge the next morning. He politely agreed to go to prison. Right after breakfast the next morning, he managed to saw his way out of a second-story window, slid down a rope of tied sheets, and vanished. All this . . . in broad daylight!

Three weeks later, in Arizona, the indefatigable Harkins was again working at his craft. By now, however, the entire banking community was alerted. During an attempt to swindle an Arizona bank, Harkins was caught. This time, he was put in a jail from which there could be no escape. Instead, he feigned insanity. He put on such a good show, that he was remanded for treatment at a special mental hospital. He remained there for exactly one day. His preacher-brother used his influence to have him released in his custody with the understanding that psychotherapy would be arranged for him.

But Harkins had no need for therapy. As he later said, "I *enjoy* the good life. I *enjoy* hoaxing the banking experts. I'll bet anything that if they had the chance, they would do the same to the rest of us. So who needs therapy?"

He left his brother's home in a few days, and started on a cross-country hoaxing adventure. As always, he had spent much time with women; as always, he favored the best of hotels; and, sought out the best restaurants. To this extent, Harkins' hoaxing career was a success.

As the years went on, and as he grew older, his ability to forge and to escape when necessary lessened. He had to employ many new devices to stay out of jail. On one occasion, he was given a lie detector test. He talked openly and glibly, saying that he was not the man they sought, that he was honest and God-fearing. The operator of the polygraph machine could make no determination as to guilt or innocence.

On another occasion, Harkins was given a pentathol truth-serum test. But even this proved inconclusive. The investigator assigned to the case later said: "I know that this man Harkins is the hoaxer who has criss-crossed the country. But he is such a magnificent hoaxer, he has such a persuasive way of talking, that even under truth serum, he gives the impression of being honest and sincere."

By now, other states had warrants out for Harkins' arrest. He was extradited to North Dakota in 1929 where he was charged with having posed as a physician, and duping the banks out of some $100,000. He denied the charges.

During the trial, his brother swore that on the day of the alleged crime, June 7, 1928, William was home with him. This was true.

Actually, the bank charged that the crime took place on June 7, 1928, the date that appeared on the check. It occurred to no one that Harkins had predated the check so as to make it appear that he had been at the bank one week earlier. At the trial, in 1929, William did not take the witness stand. He was thus able to avoid interrogation by the prosecution. But his preacher-brother did take the stand. He offered proof that William was a guest at his home on June 7, 1928, the date appearing on the check. William was declared not guilty.

Age eventually began to take its toll on William Hamilton Harkins. In 1930, as he was entering his sixtieth year, Harkins was apprehended in Louisiana. He looked distinguished with his white hair, but the courts would not be fooled. Harkins was convicted and sentenced to prison.

As he was led away, he remarked to newspaper reporters: "It looks like the honeymoon is over. Actually, I have no regrets. I have hurt no one. I have no enemies except the bankers . . . and they are of no concern to me. After all, they bankrupted me once, and almost ruined me. An eye for an eye . . ."

He took his punishment with the dignity characteristic of most impostors. Yet, he was a pitiful sight. His brother had disowned him. All his money was gone. When he entered prison to serve his 10-year sentence, he had exactly $2.87 to his name. He later used this . . . to purchase a very good fountain pen!